Marxism, Socialism, and Democracy in Latin America

Latin American Perspectives Series

Ronald H. Chilcote, Series Editor

† Available in hardcover and paperback.

Marxism, Socialism, and Democracy in Latin America

Richard L. Harris

Routledge
Taylor & Francis Group

LONDON AND NEW YORK

First published 1992 by Westview Press, Inc.

Published 2018 by Routledge
52 Vanderbilt Avenue, New York, NY 10017
2 Park Square, Milton Park, Abingdon, Oxon OX14 4RN

Routledge is an imprint of the Taylor & Francis Group, an informa business

Copyright © 1992 Taylor & Francis

Library of Congress Cataloging-in-Publication Data
Harris, Richard (Richard Legé), 1939–
    Marxism, socialism, and democracy in Latin America / Richard L. Harris.
        p. cm. — (Latin American perspectives series ; no. 8)
    Includes bibliographical references (p.   ) and index.
    ISBN 0-8133-1322-8. — ISBN 0-8133-1321-X (pbk.)
    1. Communism—Latin America.   2. Socialism—Latin America.
I. Title. II. Series.
HX110.5.A6H37   1992
335.4'098—dc20   91-41765
                                                                                        CIP

ISBN 13: 978-0-367-00432-3 (hbk)
ISBN 13: 978-0-367-15419-6 (pbk)

Contents

Tables

Acronyms

AMNLAE	Nicaraguan Women's Association
ANAP	National Association of Small Farmers (Cuba)
APP	Area of People's Property (Nicaragua)
ARENA	National Republican Alliance (El Salvador)
ASI	Socialist Accord (Peru)
CDR	Committees for the Defense of the Revolution (Cuba)
CLS	Committee for Labor Solidarity (Trinidad)
CPSU	Communist Party of the Soviet Union
CTC	Confederation of Cuban Workers
FDR	Democratic Revolutionary Front (El Salvador)
FMC	Federation of Cuban Women
FMLN	Farabundo Martí Front for National Liberation (El Salvador)
FOCEP	Worker Peasant Student Popular Front (Peru)
FSLN	Sandinista Front for National Liberation (Nicaragua)
GDP	gross domestic product
GNP	gross national product
IU	United Left (Peru)
MAPU	Movement for Unified Popular Action (Chile)
MAS	Movement Toward Socialism (Venezuela)
MRTA	Revolutionary Movement Túpac Amaru (Peru)
NEP	New Economic Policy (USSR)
NJM	New Jewel Movement (Grenada)
PCP	Peruvian Communist Party
PRG	People's Revolutionary Government (Grenada)
PUM	Unified Mariateguist Party (Peru)
SDPE	System for Direction and Planning of the Economy (Cuba)
TVP	total value of production
UNIR	Union of the Revolutionary Left (Peru)
UP	Popular Unity (Chile)

1
Introduction

Marxism has penetrated so profoundly into our history that, in some way or other, at times without realizing it, we are all Marxists. Our moral judgements and categories, our ideas of the future, our opinions about the present or about justice, peace and war, everything—including our negations of Marxism—is impregnated with Marxism. It is now part of our intellectual lifeblood and our moral sensibility.

—Octavio Paz

Marxism is an important element in the contemporary social reality of Latin America and the Caribbean. In fact, it has influenced the thinking and social practice of Latin Americans to such an extent that they are often unaware of the many ways in which it is a part of their reality. At a time when the validity of Marxism is being questioned as a result of the collapse of the former self-styled communist regimes of Eastern Europe, it is more relevant than ever before to examine the extent to which Marxist thought and practice continues to be a significant force in the Western Hemisphere.

The continued relevancy of Marxism stems principally from the powerful theoretical and moral basis of this body of thought and practice. These qualities of Marxism have been recognized by many contemporary social scientists and intellectuals. For example, in her recent work on feminist theory, Catharine MacKinnon has stated:

Marxism is the contemporary theoretical tradition that—whatever its limitations—confronts organized social dominance, analyzes it in dynamic rather than static terms, identifies social forces that systematically shape social imperatives, and seeks to explain human freedom both within and against history. It confronts class, which is real. It offers both a critique

1

of the inevitability and inner coherence of social injustice and a theory
of the necessity and possibilities of change. (MacKinnon 1989:ix)

Because of its theoretical power and moral appeal and its preoccupation
with radically transforming social reality rather than merely explaining
it, Marxism has been and continues to be relevant to those who oppose
social injustice and seek to build a more just social order. This is
especially true in the Third World where there is so much injustice,
exploitation, and human suffering.

This book demonstrates the extent to which Marxist thought on the
transition from capitalism to socialism provides an essential framework
for understanding the successes and failures of recent and past attempts
to construct socialist societies in Latin America and the Caribbean. This
demonstration is accomplished by providing a critical overview of the
more important issues in the extensive body of Marxist literature dealing
with the construction of socialist societies and then relating these issues
to contemporary cases in Latin America and the Caribbean where
revolutionary transformations have been and continue to be made by
leftist regimes and political movements. These cases are Cuba (1959–
1991), Chile (1970–1973), Grenada (1979–1983), Nicaragua (1979–1990),
and El Salvador (1980–1991).

These contemporary cases of revolutionary transformation or attempted
transformation are viewed from three vantage points: the perspective
provided by classical Marxist theory on the transition to socialism, the
viewpoints offered by Marxist critics of both the Soviet Union as well
as other existing self-proclaimed socialist regimes, and the various
perspectives found in Marxist and neo-Marxist thought on the problems
and conditions confronted by revolutionary regimes in the underdeveloped
societies of the Third World. These different viewpoints provide a
historical background and a comparative frame of reference for understanding the efforts that have been made in Latin America and the
Caribbean to bring about revolutionary social change and to construct
socialist societies.

The cases that I have chosen to analyze best illustrate the issues of
Marxism, socialism, and democracy that are the focus of this book. I
have chosen not to examine what others might argue are relevant cases
of attempted socialist transformation in the Western Hemisphere, such
as Jamaica under the first Michael Manley government, Guatemala under
the Jacobo Arbenz Guzmán regime, Bolivia during the short-lived government of General Juan José Torres, and Peru during the regime of
General Juan Velasco Alvarado.

I have excluded these possible cases from my analysis because I do
not consider them to provide valid instances of an attempted revolutionary

transformation of the societies involved. At best, they offer examples of popular reformist regimes that attempted to carry out a social democratic or national democratic program. They certainly do not provide contemporary examples of a revolutionary regime with a socialist project. I invite readers who disagree with my choice of cases as well as with the lessons I draw from the analyzed cases to challenge my analysis, as this will no doubt advance the discussion and understanding of the issues.

The focus of this work is primarily on Latin America and the Caribbean, but it discusses the common and recurring questions faced by all revolutionary regimes that have attempted a socialist transformation of an underdeveloped capitalist society. It is one of the ironies of modern history that socialist revolutions have only occurred in underdeveloped capitalist societies. At the beginning of this century, most Marxists assumed, and many others feared, that socialist revolutions would take place in the advanced capitalist societies of Western Europe and North America. They thought that the conditions in these advanced capitalist social formations, with their large and increasingly politicized working classes, were ripe for a socialist revolution. Because of these assumptions, most of the early Marxists did not think that a socialist revolution could succeed in "backward" and underdeveloped capitalist societies—either in Europe or in the rest of the world.

This unforeseen location of revolutionary change has forced those who believe in the continued validity of Marxist theory to reevaluate the elements of this theory that refer to the transition to socialism. As a result, Marxist theory has been revised so that it takes into account the problems of constructing socialism in underdeveloped capitalist societies.

Therefore, in spite of the fact that classical Marxist theory did not address the problems of constructing socialism under contemporary Third World conditions, this book argues that Marxist theory, with certain revisions, can be effectively applied to revolutionary transformations in the Third World. Moreover, it is further contended that the Marxist conception of the transition from capitalism to socialism provides an essential perspective for understanding the difficulties Third World revolutionaries have encountered in their attempts to transform their underdeveloped capitalist countries into developed socialist societies. In other words, I make a case for the contemporary and enduring value of Marxist thought and analysis through applying it to the examination of contemporary cases of socialist transformation. However, my purpose is to demystify Marxism and clarify its basic premises rather than to glorify it or apologize for its deficiencies. I demonstrate how Marxist theory can be used in a flexible, undogmatic manner to analyze, interpret, and critically reflect upon important instances of revolution and socio-political change in the modern world.

I also argue that a critical analysis of the successes and failures of revolutionary movements in the Soviet Union, China, Cuba, and Vietnam demonstrates that the construction of socialism in underdeveloped capitalist societies cannot be successful if Marxist thought is applied in a dogmatic and inflexible manner. Moreover, I contend that the successful application of Marxism requires the careful adaptation of this body of thought to the particular conditions of each society.

This does not mean, however, that the previous debates among Marxists about the transition to socialism do not offer any insight into contemporary problems and issues of socialist transformation in the Third World. On the contrary, this book contends that an adequate understanding of contemporary efforts at socialist transformation requires an understanding of the past debates among Marxists over such important issues as the nature of the revolutionary state in the transition to socialism, the importance of democracy and mass participation in the transition period, the pace of the transition process, the vanguard role of the revolutionary leaders and militants, the importance of class alliances and class conflict in the transition period, the expropriation of capital, the socialization of agriculture, central planning versus market relations, the role of revolutionary ideology and popular education, the emancipation of women, gender equality, and other important issues. In this book, these past debates are examined from the point of view of what they have to offer in terms of understanding contemporary efforts at revolutionary change and the construction of socialism in Latin America and the Caribbean.

In the pages that follow, I argue that Marxist thought in combination with an adequate understanding of the experiences of other societies that have experienced attempts to construct socialism can be an invaluable theoretical instrument for interpreting contemporary revolutions and recent efforts to construct socialism in Latin America and the Caribbean. However, this book also reveals that recent efforts to build socialist societies in this important region clearly confirm the general proposition that there are no universal models for revolutionaries to follow in constructing socialism. Instead, I conclude that Marxism provides a powerful theoretical framework and an evolving body of revolutionary thought that has been and can be used to develop unique approaches to the revolutionary transformation of contemporary societies.

In addition, two major propositions are developed throughout this book. The first is that Marxism is based on inherently democratic values. The second is that genuine socialism can only be achieved through a profound democratization of all aspects of social life. In this regard, I argue that socialism requires not only the unlimited democratization of politics and government, but that it also requires the unlimited democratization of production and distribution, of work, and of the social division of labor. This includes the democratization of gender, racial, ethnic, cultural, and all other forms of social relations as well as the democratization of education, health care, science, technology, the armed forces, the communications media, art, religion, the use of natural resources, and the relations between nations.

These arguments are not based upon a utopian vision of socialism or a "post-Marxist" attempt to reconstrue Marxism as a discourse on radical democracy. They reflect an honest intellectual effort to clarify the essential and enduring significance of Marxism as well as the democratic essence of socialism, both of which have been distorted throughout most of this century by the anti-Marxist views and anti-communist propaganda prevalent in capitalist societies. They have also been distorted by the sectarianism, dogmatism, and opportunism of leftists and by bureaucratic statist elites in the Soviet Union and elsewhere who have misused Marxist thought and socialist ideals as an ideological justification for political and economic measures that, in many cases, have contradicted the very premises upon which this body of thought and these ideals are based.

The democratic essence and continued relevance of Marxist theory are demonstrated in the closing chapter of this book through a speculative discussion of the prospects for democratic socialism in Latin America and the Caribbean in the 1990s. This discussion centers on a brief examination of the contemporary strategies and political positions of present-day leftist parties and movements in Latin America and the Caribbean. The politics of these social forces are examined to see whether they reflect the lessons of previous attempts at revolutionary transformation and socialist transition in the region. The contemporary relationship between democracy and socialism is analyzed in this context. I also argue that progressive social forces in Latin America and the Caribbean cannot afford to abandon Marxism or the struggle for socialism and that the continued democratization of the societies in this region requires the realization of a democratic socialist project.

The intellectual foundations for my analysis can be traced to those currents of Marxist and revolutionary socialist thought that have historically opposed dogmatic, sectarian, and authoritarian approaches to transforming the prevailing social order and that have offered in their place self-critical, nonsectarian, and democratic alternatives. The research for this book has its origins in earlier work on the Nicaraguan revolution, which I had the good fortune to experience personally and to observe at close range for several years. My interest in understanding this important historical event in the context of other instances of revolutionary transformation in the twentieth century led me to undertake the research upon which this book is based. This work is also influenced by research carried out over the course of three decades on the politics, economics, cultures, social conditions, and history of Latin America and the Caribbean.

2

The Relevance of Early Marxist Thought on the Transition to Socialism

Marx and Engels on the Transition to Socialism

Karl Marx and Friedrich Engels theorized in general terms about the transition between capitalism and communism (Marx and Engels 1972:331). They reasoned that between capitalist and communist society there would be "the period of the revolutionary transformation of the one into the other" (Marx and Engels 1972:331). They also contended that the social order during this period would be "a communist society, not as it has *developed* on its own foundations, but on the contrary, as it has *emerged* from capitalist society" (Marx and Engels 1972:323). They referred to this transitional social order between capitalism and communism as the "inferior stage of communism" and frequently as "socialism."

In the *Manifesto of the Communist Party* Marx and Engels first set forth their general ideas on how the transition to communism would take place. As the following statement indicates, they believed the first step in the transition to communism would be "to win the battle of democracy" and that this would involve the seizure of state power by the proletariat.

The first step in the revolution by the working class is to raise the proletariat to the position of ruling class, to win the battle of democracy. The proletariat will use its political supremacy to wrest, by degrees, all capital from the bourgeoisie, to centralize all instruments of production in the hands of the State, i.e., of the proletariat organized as the ruling class;

and to increase the total of productive forces as rapidly as possible. (Marx and Engels 1972:52)

This basic conception of the first steps involved in the establishment of socialism has influenced revolutionary thought and practice ever since it was first introduced in 1848.

Marx and Engels believed that the victorious proletariat would most likely take similar measures in the various advanced capitalist countries to initiate the process of socialist construction. The following measures, Marx and Engels reasoned, would be "pretty generally applicable" (Marx and Engels 1972:52–53):

1. The abolition of property in land and the application of all rents of land for public purposes;
2. A heavy progressive or graduated tax;
3. The abolition of all rights of inheritance;
4. The confiscation of the property of all emigrants and rebels;
5. The centralization of credit in the hands of the State, by means of a national bank;
6. The centralization of the means of communication and transport in the hands of the State;
7. The extension of factories and instruments of production owned by the State; the bringing into cultivation of waste-lands, and the improvement of the soil generally in accordance with a common plan;
8. Equal liability of all to labor (i.e., work for everyone), and the establishment of industrial armies, especially in agriculture;
9. The combination of agriculture with manufacturing industries; and the gradual abolition of the distinction between town and country by a more equitable distribution of the population over the country;
10. The provision of free education for all children in public schools. The abolition of children's factory labor in its present form. The combination of education with industrial production.

This list reflects the conditions of the most advanced capitalist societies in the mid-nineteenth century and it gives a fairly clear idea of what Marx and Engels thought would be the initial program of a revolutionary proletarian regime after it seized power.

Most of these measures were adopted in some form by the new Soviet state in the first years of the Russian Revolution. They have also been adopted to a greater or lesser extent by most revolutionary regimes with a socialist program since then. For example, during the first five years of the revolutionary regime in Cuba, most of these measures were undertaken by the new government formed by the successful revolutionary movement (see Boorstein 1968; Pierre-Charles 1976; and C. R. Rodriguez, 1978).

Marx and Engels wrote very little about what they thought might happen in the underdeveloped areas of the world after the overthrow of the capitalist order in Europe and North America. However, in 1882, shortly before Marx's death, Engels wrote a letter to Karl Kautsky in which he speculated about what might happen in Europe's Asian and African colonies after a victorious proletarian revolution had taken place in the advanced capitalist societies. Engels thought there might be revolutions in countries such as India, Algeria, and Egypt, but he also made it clear that he did not think it was advisable to try and predict "what social and political phases these countries would have to pass through before they . . . arrived at socialist organization" (Marx and Engels 1972:688). To do so, he argued would be to engage in the fabrication of "idle hypotheses." What this correspondence as well as other evidence reveals is that the founders of Marxism thought it was impossible to predict the future course of human development except in the most general sense, and as a result they were opposed to developing hypotheses or theoretical propositions about the future course of socialist transformations in different parts of the world.

Lenin's Ideas on the Transition to Socialism

Lenin was the first Marxist theorist and political leader to confront the problem of applying Marxist thought to the tasks of constructing socialism in a concrete historical situation. Moreover, he had to do this in an underdeveloped capitalist society, as this was the nature of Russian society at the time of the Soviet revolution.

In essence, what Lenin did in this situation was to take the basic concepts of Marx and Engels and incorporate them into a new conceptualization of the transition to socialism that could be applied to a "backward country" such as Russia (Harnecker 1986:128–129). Lenin based his conceptualization on the premise that the immediate and direct construction of socialism was *not* possible in a backward society, that is, a society where capitalist development was immature. He contended that the underdeveloped nature of the economy and the low cultural development of the masses made it necessary to first develop rapidly the forces of production through relying initially upon a combination of capitalist relations of production and centralized state control of the economy. He referred to this combination of capitalism and state control as "state-monopoly capitalism" and argued that this combination was necessary in order to achieve "a complete material preparation for socialism" in Russia (Lenin 1976:445).

Lenin's views were severely criticized by a Marxist faction within the new revolutionary regime who called themselves the "Left Communists." They claimed that the new Soviet state's reliance upon the expertise of certain capitalists and the use of capitalist methods of organizing production to revive Russia's war-torn economy constituted a "Bolshevik deviation to the right" and the "betrayal of socialism" (Lenin 1976:440). This perspective has since been applied by leftist critics to the entire Soviet experience as well as to other socialist regimes when they have relied upon capitalist relations of production as a temporary expedient or long-term solution to their problems (for example, see Brinton 1975; Castro 1989; and Castaños 1977).

Lenin replied that his leftist critics failed to take into account the fact that Russia's backward economy was dominated by petty-bourgeois producers (that is, small-scale commodity producers); and that, as a result, the development of state capitalism was a necessary step in the transition to socialism.

> Firstly, the "Left Communists" do not understand what kind of transition it is from capitalism to socialism that gives us the right and the grounds to call our country the Socialist Republic of Soviets. Secondly, they reveal their petty-bourgeois mentality precisely by not recognizing the petty-bourgeois element as the principal enemy of socialism in our country. Thirdly, in making a bugbear of "state capitalism," they betray their failure to understand that the Soviet state differs from the bourgeois state economically. . . . The question arises: what elements predominate? Clearly, in a small-peasant country, the petty-bourgeois element predominates and it must predominate, for the great majority of those working the land are petty commodity producers. The shell of our state capitalism (grain monopoly, state-controlled entrepreneurs, and bourgeois co-operators) is pierced now in one place, now in another by profiteers, the chief object of profiteering being grain. It is in this field that the main struggle is being waged. (Lenin 1976:440–441)

Lenin argued that the Left Communists were wrong in claiming that the struggle was between state capitalism and socialism. He criticized them for not seeing that "the petty bourgeoisie plus private capitalism [were] fighting together against both state capitalism and socialism" as both of these social forces opposed state monopoly and state control, whether it was "state capitalism or state socialism" (Lenin 1976:441).

Lenin's idea of a "preliminary transition" or initial stage of preparation before beginning the actual construction of socialism has been adopted by most contemporary socialist regimes in underdeveloped societies.

However, there appears to be considerable variation between regimes in the time allotted for this period of preparation. For example, in Cuba, this period is considered to have taken place during the first four years of the revolutionary regime. Thus, Cuba's President Oswaldo Dorticos stated in January 1963 that "these first four years constitute the stage during which the conditions for the construction of socialism have been created in our country" (quoted in Pierre-Charles 1976:173).

It is important to note here that Lenin's ideas on the transition to socialism were challenged at the time they were first formulated not only by Marxists in the Soviet Union, but by Marxists in Western Europe as well, notably by Karl Kautsky and Rosa Luxemburg (for example, see Luxemburg 1971:365–395; and Stephens 1986:53–69). They differed with Lenin over such important issues as the pace of the transition process, the use of coercion in the process, the nature of the class struggle during this period, whether a dictatorial form of government was necessary, the importance of establishing political democracy in the transition, and the role of the revolutionary party during the transition period.

For example, Kautsky argued that the transition from capitalism to socialism in the more advanced capitalist countries could and should take place in a democratic manner following the electoral victory of a mass-based socialist party. He thought that this parliamentary road to socialism would quickly lead to a revolutionary break with capitalism and the rapid construction of socialism within one or two decades (Stephens 1986:57). Kautsky contended that this could take place with a minimum of coercion and under the direction of a democratic regime committed to a socialist program of reforms.

This idea of a peaceful, parliamentary road to socialism became the perspective of social democratic parties throughout Western Europe and elsewhere in the first part of the twentieth century. In the recent history of Latin America, this approach was, of course, adopted as an important aspect of the strategy of the Popular Unity (Unidad Popular or UP) government of Salvador Allende, whose attempt to bring about a peaceful, democratic transition to socialism in Chile was brought to a tragic end by the military coup in 1973.

Lenin totally disagreed with the idea of a parliamentary road to socialism espoused by Kautsky and other theoreticians. He reminded them that Marx had thought that the proletariat could not seize power by simply assuming control of the old state apparatus, rather that the proletariat would have to smash this apparatus and replace it with a new one (Lenin 1976:345). In his essay, *The Proletarian Revolution and the Renegade Kautsky*, Lenin criticized Kautsky for having forgotten that "every state is a machine for the suppression of one class by another" and for having thrown the class struggle overboard in his conception of the transition to socialism (Lenin 1976:471).

Lenin also theorized that dictatorship and coercion were necessary during the transition from capitalism to socialism because of both the continuing resistance of the bourgeoisie and the external, internal wars which socialist revolutions generate.

> It is not difficult to see that during every transition from capitalism to socialism, dictatorship is necessary for two main reasons. . . . Firstly, capitalism cannot be defeated and eradicated without the ruthless suppression of the resistance of the exploiters, who cannot at once be deprived of their wealth, of their advantages of organization and knowledge, and consequently for a very long period will inevitably try to overthrow the hated rule of the poor; secondly, every great revolution, and a socialist revolution in particular, even if there is no external war, is inconceivable without internal war, i.e., civil war, which is even more devastating than external war. . . . (Lenin 1976:421)

Recent history in Latin America and the Caribbean has shown that the resistance of the bourgeoisie and counterrevolutionary warfare are, indeed, conditions that must be confronted by revolutionary regimes in that part of the world. The decade-long war of attrition to which the revolutionary regime in Nicaragua was subjected is the most recent example of this.

The Cuban, Chilean, Grenadian, and Nicaraguan cases reveal that the U.S. government can be expected to contribute to, if not undertake itself, the overthrow of a revolutionary regime that is established anywhere in the Western Hemisphere. The U.S. government in the past has utilized a variety of overt and covert measures to do this, including:

1. The curtailment of credits from both public and private U.S. sources;
2. The veto of loans and credits from international financial institutions such as the World Bank, the International Monetary Fund, and the Inter-American Development Bank;
3. The imposition of a trade blockade;
4. A disinformation campaign to discredit the new regime;
5. Covert financial and political support of dissident producer associations, unions, and so on;
6. Economic sabotage and support of military attacks on important economic targets by mercenary and/or counterrevolutionary forces (for example, see Conroy 1985b; Mars 1984; Matthews 1986; and U.S. Senate 1976). The support of the Soviet Union, other socialist states, and Third World countries has been critical to the survival

of a revolutionary regime subjected to these measures (Thomas 1974:247).

Returning to the debate between Lenin and Kautsky, we should note that this debate over the parliamentary road to socialism continues to have great relevance for the Left in Latin America and the Caribbean. The demise of the UP regime in Chile appears to provide evidence in support of Lenin's position in this debate. Further support for his position could be derived from the overthrow of Cheddi Jagan's government in Guyana by British troops during the fifties (see Mars 1984:83–110). However, in the case of the Allende regime in Chile, some observers argue convincingly that it was not the choice of a parliamentary democratic road to socialism but the way this strategy was carried out in Chile that was at fault (Bitar 1979).

Rosa Luxemburg's Ideas on Democracy and Dictatorship

Rosa Luxemburg, like Lenin, rejected Kautsky's conception of the parliamentary road to socialism, but she also disagreed with Lenin and Trotsky on the need for an authoritarian party dictatorship during the transition to socialism.

> The basic error of the Lenin-Trotsky theory is that they too, just like Kautsky, oppose dictatorship to democracy. "Dictatorship or democracy" is the way the question is put by Bolsheviks and Kautsky alike. The latter naturally decides in favor of "democracy," that is, of bourgeois democracy, precisely because he opposes it to the alternative of the socialist revolution. Lenin and Trotsky, on the other hand, decide in favor of dictatorship in contradistinction to democracy, and thereby, in favor of the dictatorship of a handful of persons, that is, in favor of dictatorship on the bourgeois model. They are two opposite poles, both alike, being far removed from a genuine socialist policy. The proletariat, when it seizes power, can never follow the good advice of Kautsky, given on the pretext of the "unripeness of the country," the advice being to renounce the socialist revolution and devote itself to democracy. It cannot follow this advice without betraying itself, the International, and the revolution. It should and must at once undertake socialist measures in the most energetic, unyielding and un-hesitant fashion, in other words, exercise a dictatorship, but a dictatorship of the *class*, not of a party or of a clique—dictatorship of the class, that means in the broadest public form on the basis of the most active, unlimited participation of the mass of the people, of unlimited democracy. (Luxemburg 1970:393)

Luxemburg's basic position, quite similar to that of Marx and Engels, was that the working class needed a mass-based, democratic party that would overthrow the existing capitalist order through mobilizing the masses in a revolutionary general strike. She criticized Lenin and the Bolsheviks for their dictatorial methods and "ultra-centralism," which she felt would end up delivering power to the intellectuals and confining the working class "in the strait jacket of bureaucratic centralism" (quoted in Friedland 1982:90). In view of the type of regimes that subsequently emerged in the Soviet Union and later in Eastern Europe and China, Luxemburg's predictions about bureaucratic centralism now appear to be quite prophetic.

Luxemburg argued that, following the overthrow of the capitalist state, "unlimited democracy" and the "unlimited participation of the mass of the people" along with civil liberties and popular democratic forms of organization would have to be instituted in order to ensure that the working class remained in control of the process of constructing socialism. She made it clear that the goal of a socialist revolution was not to eliminate democracy, rather it was to replace the limited formal democracy of bourgeois capitalist society with the unlimited democracy that only socialism could make possible because it would bring to an end the social inequalities and hierarchical class structure of capitalist society. This view is stated clearly in the following passage taken from a pamphlet on the Russian Revolution that she wrote while in prison in Germany.

> We have always distinguished the social kernel from the political form of *bourgeois* democracy; we have always revealed the hard kernel of social inequality and lack of freedom hidden under the sweet shell of formal equality and freedom—not in order to reject the latter but to spur the working class into not being satisfied with the shell, but rather, by conquering political power, to create a socialist democracy to replace bourgeois democracy—not to eliminate democracy altogether. (Luxemburg 1971:393)

This distinction between bourgeois democracy and socialist democracy is an important element in the classical Marxist position on democracy and socialism.

In her criticism of the Bolsheviks, Luxemburg contended that freedom only for the supporters of the government and the members of the revolutionary party amounted to no freedom at all. She stated forcefully the case for unrestricted freedom of the press, the right to assembly, general elections, and so on, during the transition to socialism.

> Without general elections, without unrestricted freedom of the press and assembly, without a free struggle of opinion, life dies out in every public

institution, becomes a mere semblance of life, in which only the bureaucracy remains as the active element. Public life gradually falls asleep, a few dozen party leaders of inexhaustible energy and boundless experience direct and rule. Among them, in reality only a dozen outstanding heads do the leading and the elite of the working class is invited from time to time to meetings where they are to applaud the speeches of the leaders, and to approve proposed resolutions unanimously—at bottom then, a clique affair—a dictatorship, to be sure, not the dictatorship of the proletariat, however, but only the dictatorship of a handful of politicians, that is a dictatorship in the bourgeois sense, in the sense of the rule of the Jacobins. . . . (Luxemburg 1971:391)

This quote clarifies not only the classical Marxist conception of socialist democracy, but also the distinction made by early Marxists between bourgeois forms of dictatorship and the class dictatorship of the working class in a socialist society.

Luxemburg's conception of the transition to socialism involves the immediate establishment of socialist democracy and not a dictatorship of the revolutionary party.

But socialist democracy is not something which begins only in the promised land after the foundations of socialist economy are created; it does not come as some sort of Christmas present for the worthy people who, in the interim, have loyally supported a handful of socialist dictators. Socialist democracy begins simultaneously with the beginnings of the destruction of class rule and of the construction of socialism. It begins at the very moment of the seizure of power by the socialist party. It is the same thing as the dictatorship of the proletariat. Yes, dictatorship! But this dictatorship consists in the *manner of applying democracy*, not in its *elimination*, in energetic, resolute attacks upon the well-entrenched rights and economic relationships of bourgeois society, without which a socialist transformation cannot be accomplished. But this dictatorship must be the work of the *class*, and not a little leading minority in the name of the class—that is, it must proceed step by step out of the active participation of the masses; it must be under their direct influence; subjected to the control of complete public activity; it must arise out of the growing political training of the people. (Luxemburg 1971:393–394)

As this quote reveals, Luxemburg's conception of the transition to socialism rested upon the fundamental notion that the construction of socialism must be a mass-based, democratic process of revolutionary social transformation. Unfortunately, this democratic approach to the construction of socialism has never been followed in any of the countries where socialist regimes have been established, but this does not mean it will never be followed.

Conclusion

It is important to recognize that the differences between Lenin, Luxemburg, and Kautsky were to a considerable degree the product of the different sociopolitical contexts in which they operated (Stephens 1986:62). Lenin's perspective was obviously influenced by the objective realities of carrying out a revolution in a worn-torn, largely agrarian, and autocratic society, whereas Kautsky was influenced by the fact that Germany, at the time of his writings, had become a major industrial power with the largest, legal, working-class party in Europe. Luxemburg, on the other hand, was an activist in the revolutionary movements of Germany, Poland, and Russia. As a result, she was exposed to the varying conditions and various currents of leftist thought and practice in these three societies, which had an important influence on her thinking and helps to explain her distinctive perspective.

These three perspectives, with local modifications, can be recognized in the thought and practice of socialist movements and parties in Latin America and the Caribbean. Generally speaking, during most of the last fifty to sixty years Lenin's perspective has been dominant, but in recent decades leftists throughout the region have begun to adopt perspectives similar to those of Kautsky and/or Luxemburg.

3
The Lack of a General
Theory of the Transition
to Socialism

Why There Cannot Be a General Theory
of the Transition to Socialism

In the last three to four decades, many Marxists have concluded that there cannot be a general theory of the transition to socialism—that is, a theory applying to all societies that undertake a socialist course of development. For example, Marta Harnecker, a Chilean Marxist scholar who has lived many years in Cuba, writes: "Because the historical transition depends upon the concrete form of the class struggle in each country, no general theory of transition can exist" (Harnecker 1986:128). She further contends that "each transition is materially different, therefore, conceptually different." As a result, Harnecker claims that it is up to the revolutionary vanguard in each country to elaborate a strategy for that country's transition that is based upon a careful analysis of the characteristics of the country's class struggle.

The importance of taking into account the particularities of each country in the construction of socialism is stressed by Carlos Rafael Rodriguez, one of the leaders of the Cuban Communist Party, in his lengthy essay entitled *Cuba in the Transition to Socialism, 1959–1963*. He states: "Ignorance of what is particular leads to grave errors in strategy and tactics" (Rodriguez 1978:14). His definition of the transition to socialism is perhaps one of the most concise to be found in the contemporary Marxist literature on the subject.

The period of transition consists of the phase that goes from the defeat of the social and political forces that represent capitalism—and imperialist domination in colonial and neo-colonial countries—until the moment that the social regime of the country in which the revolution has taken place can be characterized as completely socialist, having established, in a definitive and permanent manner, socialist forms of property and relations of production, and having commenced the process of the construction of communism. (Rodriguez 1978:13)

In sum, Rodriguez's definition of the transition period commences with the overthrow of the capitalist state and extends to the completion of socialism.

The problems involved in applying Marxist thought to the conditions prevailing in revolutionary societies today have been addressed at length by the French Marxist scholar Charles Bettelheim, particularly in his book *The Transition to Socialist Economy* (1978). In this important study, he argues that the application of Marxism to concrete situations should not be confused with the practice of applying abstract models to a specific social reality, so common in the bourgeois social sciences, because this approach always fails to account for important "accidental conditions" or "external factors" that fall outside the model (Bettelheim 1978:148). According to Bettelheim, the use of "purest" conceptions and abstract models in the analysis of complex, concrete conditions leads to either "ultra-leftism" or to "opportunism."

Instead, Bettelheim explains that Marxism considers "every reality as a structured whole which has to be analyzed as such," that is, the analysis of a particular transitional society must take into account the totality of concrete, historical conditions existing in that society.

The Transition to Socialism in the Third World

Bettelheim uses Marxist theory and analysis to demonstrate that there are different forms of societal transition in existence today in the Third World and that one should not be confused by the label "socialist" in cases where no transition to socialism is involved. According to him, only societies undergoing a "radical form of transition" from the capitalist mode of production to the "socialist mode of production" are engaged in a genuine transition to socialism. He contends that this kind of transition requires "the passing of state power to the working class, or a coalition of formerly exploited classes within which the working class plays a dominant role" (Bettelheim 1978:21). Without this preliminary condition, the transition to socialism is not possible.

According to Bettelheim, a genuine transition to socialism also requires certain political and ideological conditions and a conjuncture of internal and international contradictions that enable a society to do without the further development of capitalism and to "pass directly to the building of socialism" (Bettelheim 1978). As examples of genuine socialist transitions, he cited China, Cuba, and Vietnam. However, if Bettelheim's conception is applied to Chile during the regime of Salvador Allende or Jamaica under the first government of Michael Manley, neither of these cases would qualify as instances of socialist transition. In both situations, state power did not pass into the hands of the working class or a coalition of exploited classes, and in neither of these cases was there a conjuncture of internal and international contradictions that would have enabled these societies to do without further capitalist development and pass directly to the construction of socialism.

The case of revolutionary Nicaragua (1979–1990) is somewhat more problematic in terms of this conception of transitional regimes. It can be debated that state power in 1979 passed into the hands of a revolutionary vanguard that represented the exploited classes, but it cannot be argued that a conjuncture of internal and international contradictions existed in which Nicaraguan society could have passed directly to the building of socialism. As will be contended subsequently, the Nicaraguan revolution was a popular revolutionary struggle for national liberation, but not a socialist revolution.

Bettelheim has warned against confusing societies that are engaged in a genuine socialist transition with Third World countries that are involved in what he refers to as a more limited "postcolonial transition" (Bettelheim 1978:12–13). In the latter case, the previous structures of domination are not abolished but merely modified or there is an unstable situation of "momentary equilibrium between the social classes confronting each other" (Bettelheim 1978:22). Quite often, the postcolonial regimes in these countries use terms such as "Islamic socialism," "Buddhist socialism," or "African socialism" to describe their ideologies (for example, see Babu 1981). These labels, as the Yugoslav Marxist scholar Branko Horvat noted, are frequently little more than "a proxy" for ideological notions based upon nationalism and a commitment to rapid economic growth (Horvat 1982:963).

In societies where a limited, postcolonial transition has taken place, Bettelheim contends that it is essential to undertake an analysis that goes beyond the ideological claims of the regime in power to include a critical examination of the exact nature of the transformations that have taken place in their class structure and relations of production (Bettelheim 1978:13). He argues that this kind of analysis reveals that most of these societies are not undergoing a socialist transition, rather they are undergoing what he refers to as "the last stage" of the capitalist mode of production (Bettelheim 1978:82).

Samir Amin holds a somewhat similar perspective on this question. He contends (1980, 1981, and 1985) that national liberation struggles in the Third World can serve as the "primary force" for a socialist transition, but that more often than not they produce a postcolonial regime based upon either some form of neocolonial capitalism or a pseudosocialist "state mode of production" (Amin 1980:189–202). According to Amin, the struggle for national liberation gives rise to a socialist transition only if it involves "an uninterrupted revolution by stages," if it is led by the peasant and worker masses, and if it results in a classless socialist society (Amin 1980:252). A strict application of these criteria, especially the last two, could lead to the conclusion that so far none of the national liberation struggles in the Third World have given rise to a genuine socialist transition.

Amin claims that "the specific contribution of Maoism to Marxism-Leninism is precisely in having developed the theory of the contradictions of the transition" (Amin 1980:208). According to Amin, Mao Tse Tung identified the forces that tend to undermine the transition to socialism and cause either a restoration of capitalism or the emergence of what Amin refers to as the "state mode of production." These forces are: (1) the continued existence of commodity relations, (2) the reliance upon a basically capitalist infrastructure of technical organization, and (3) the continuation of an essentially capitalist division of labor during the transition period. Depending upon the nature of the class struggle during the transition period and whether or not these forces are held in check as a result of this struggle, Amin contends that an attempted transition to socialism results in either a classless society or the development of a new class structure (Amin 1980:210).

Counterpoised to this perspective is the Soviet conception developed during the Brezhnev period of "the noncapitalist way," which was based upon the fundamental assumption that a direct transition to socialism is not possible in most contemporary underdeveloped societies. Therefore, this view assumes that these societies must go through a stage of "noncapitalist development" before they begin the transition to socialism (Brutents 1983; Liss 1984:279; and Thomas 1978). According to this perspective, the noncapitalist path of development involves the nationalization of the holdings of the large bourgeoisie and feudal landlords, restriction of the activity of foreign capital, state control of the commanding heights of the economy, the development of state planning, the strengthening of the government apparatus with cadres loyal to the people, the pursuit of an anti-imperialist foreign policy, and so on (Brezhnev 1981:7).

During the Brezhnev period, the Soviets assigned the designation "socialist orientation" to the Third World states that they considered to be involved in a noncapitalist path of development. Some of the states to which they gave this designation were: Afghanistan, Algeria, Angola, Burma, Ethiopia, Mozambique, South Yemen, and Syria. Grenada was also included during the period of the People's Revolutionary Government under Maurice Bishop (Pryor 1986:238–239). The Soviets have tended to reserve the designation "socialist states" for countries that have eliminated most forms of private property and that have institutionalized centralized economic planning as well as a government with a Marxist-Leninist party firmly in power. Countries given this designation at one time or another include: Bulgaria, China, Cuba, Czechoslovakia, the German Democratic Republic, Hungary, Laos, Poland, North Korea, Rumania, Vietnam, and Yugoslavia.

In the case of Nicaragua, the Soviets appear to have been reluctant to use either of these designations, preferring instead to characterize the country as being "on the road of democracy and social progress" (Edelman 1987:39). This reluctance seems to have been due to the heterodox nature of the Sandinista revolution, the country's geopolitical position, and Soviet concern about the possibility that Nicaragua's revolutionary process could be rolled back by the United States (Edelman 1985:40–41). Nevertheless, Soviet military and economic assistance was crucial to the survival of Nicaragua's revolutionary regime in the face of U.S. aggression (Edelman 1987:27). This assistance cost the Soviet Union very little compared to the extensive amount of assistance it has provided Cuba over the last three decades, and it was a good political investment due to the fact that Washington obtained very little support in Latin America or elsewhere for its efforts to overthrow the Sandinistas.

Although the Sandinista revolutionary regime did not undertake the construction of socialism in Nicaragua, the revolutionary process inspired a great deal of interest in the transition to socialism among leftist circles. One prominent leftist intellectual in Nicaragua, Orlando Núñez Soto, produced the following list of steps that he contended a revolutionary project would have to undertake in order to make a transition to socialism:

- Collectivization of the means of production and exchange;
- Democratization and proletarianization not only of the working class but also of society as a whole (including political power and daily life);
- Planned growth and development of the economy;
- Hegemony of the strategic interests of the working class and the government of society through science and creative labor;
- Decommoditization of production and consumption;

- Decommoditization of culture and love; reaffirmation of values of cooperation and solidarity;
- Workers' administration of and social control over the distribution of the surplus;
- Direct participation of all sectors of society—women, youth, children, the elderly, ethnic groups, artists, professionals, and so on—in the resolution of their own problems. (Núñez Soto 1986:233–234)

He stressed the importance of taking these steps in order to affect the "collective consciousness" of the population as well as to establish the basis for the socialist transformation of society.

A General Framework for Conceptualizing the Transition to Socialism

Having reviewed these different conceptions of the transition to socialism, we can see that there is no generally accepted theory. Moreover, the arguments of contemporary Marxists such as Harnecker and Bettelheim appear to be quite convincing that a universal or general theory of the transition to socialism does not exist and that it is not possible or appropriate to formulate such a theory.

This conclusion does not, however, mean that it is impossible to make generalizations about this important subject. Because there is a considerable body of thought and experience having to do with the transition to socialism, generalizations can be made and tested for their validity against the historical record. Table 3.1 provides a general framework for conceptualizing the transition to socialism that is based largely upon what Marta Harnecker calls the "general principles" of socialism that can be derived from Marxist thought and practice (Harnecker 1986:120–121).

These principles represent a set of basic generalizations about the fundamental nature of the transition to socialism. They can be applied to the analysis of contemporary instances of revolutionary transformation and attempted socialist transformations in Latin America and elsewhere. Moreover, they provide a basic conceptual framework for assessing the progress of any society that claims to be involved in a process of socialist transformation. In the following pages, this framework will be applied to the historical record of attempted transitions to socialism and to revolutionary transformations that have had socialist aspirations.

TABLE 3.1   The Transition to Socialism: A General Framework

The precondition for initiating the construction of socialism is a revolution at the political level, involving:

a. The seizure of political power by a revolutionary block of popular forces in which the working class is a central element;
b. The destruction of the existing, procapitalist state apparatus;
c. The establishment of a revolutionary regime that functions as a genuine democracy for the popular classes and as a dictatorship for those who seek to overthrow the new revolutionary regime.

There must also be a revolution in the relations of production, involving:

d. The elimination of large forms of private property in industry, commerce, and agriculture;
e. The guarantee of work for everyone who is able to work;
f. Economic planning that ensures the harmonious development of the productive forces and the satisfaction of all basic needs;
g. Pay according to the type of work performed and the progressive elimination of any other source of income;
h. Workers' control of production and the establishment of a new division of labor based upon free association and cooperation.

And there must be an ideological/cultural revolution, involving:

i. A continuing struggle against the remnants of bourgeois ideology, including sexism, racism, classism, and so forth;
j. Universal popular education and technological training for the working population;
k. The development of a new, socialist consciousness based upon social equality, social cooperation, and social justice.

4

The Transitional State: Democracy or Dictatorship or Both?

Marx's Ideas on the Dictatorship of the Proletariat and the Paris Commune

In his *Critique of the Gotha Program*, Marx asserted that "the revolutionary dictatorship of the proletariat" would be the form taken by the state during the transition between capitalism and communism (Marx and Engels 1972:331). He was reluctant to give a blueprint for the exact form of this state, but in his 1871 address on the civil war in France presented to the First International (that is, The International Working Men's Association, which Marx and Engels helped found), Marx praised the Paris Commune as the harbinger of the form of "working-class government" that would likely be created by the proletariat once it had seized power and smashed the bourgeois state. The main characteristics of the Paris Commune that Marx praised were:

1. The abolition of the standing army and its replacement by the armed populace, organized into militia;
2. The disestablishment and disendowment of all churches as proprietary bodies;
3. Direct election of all public servants, including administrative personnel, magistrates, and judges;
4. Universal suffrage;
5. The combination of legislative and executive functions in the hands of the communal council, whose members were elected on a ward basis for short and revocable terms of office;

6. The immediate recall of elected delegates to the communal council by the citizenry when dissatisfied with their actions;
7. Local self-government within a federation of urban and rural communes;
8. Workingmen's wages for all public servants;
9. Free education, divorced of religious teachings, for all. (Marx and Engels 1972:274–313)

These characteristics reveal that Marx saw in the commune a radical form of popular democracy that would provide the political means for the working class to govern society in their interests.

Moreover, it is important to recognize that Marx and Engels were opposed to the identification of socialism with state control. For example, in a note appended to his critique of the Erfurt Program (1891), Engels stated:

What goes by the name of "state socialism" is a system that substitutes the state for the individual entrepreneur and thereby assembles in one hand the power of economic exploitation and the power of political oppression. (quoted in Sanchez Vasquez 1985:271)

Thus, Engels regarded "state socialism" as a false form of socialism, and warned against equating statization with socialism. It should be noted that this definition of state socialism can be applied to the contemporary Soviet Union and all the existing socialist societies.

Dictatorship for the Old Ruling Class and Democracy for the People

Based upon Marx and Engels's writings, most Marxist writings at the beginning of the century agreed that the dictatorship of the proletariat would be a regime that would be dictatorial toward the old ruling class and its allies but genuinely democratic toward the formerly exploited classes (Sweezy 1980:116). We have seen already that this position was taken by Rosa Luxemburg and it was shared by Lenin prior to the establishment of the Soviet state, as evidenced in his work *The State and Revolution*.

Democracy for the vast majority of the people, and suppression by force, i.e., exclusion from democracy, of the exploiters and oppressors of the people—this is the change democracy undergoes during the *transition* from capitalism to communism. (Lenin 1976:327)

This perspective is still shared by many Marxists today. Orlando Núñez Soto has written that the revolutionary state in a transitional society must be "a combined form of dictatorship and democracy: intransigent towards those who oppose or endanger the proletarian project, but democratic in implementing that project" (Núñez Soto 1986:247).

The Soviet Case

However, this "dictatorship and democracy" conception of the transitional state was not realized in the Russian Revolution. The new Soviet state that emerged was far more authoritarian and centralized than anything imagined by the early Marxists. Existing conditions such as the backwardness of the economy, the civil war, foreign intervention, the unfamiliarity of the masses with democracy, and the general state of economic chaos forced the new regime to take exceptional measures (Harnecker 1986:116). According to Leon Trotsky and his followers, these objective conditions, particularly the underdeveloped nature of the forces of production, made it impossible to establish a genuine workers' democracy in Russia and gave rise to a deformed bureaucratic regime that blocked the transition process to socialism (Mandel 1978; Trotsky 1972).

Many contemporary Marxists reject the Trotskyist thesis that the Soviet Union was stalled in the transition process by the bureaucratic deformation of the Soviet state. Instead, they argue that a new type of statist society developed in the Soviet Union, unlike anything foreseen by Marx, Engels, and Lenin (see Amin 1980:207–210; Bartra 1982:140–142; Sanchez Vazquez 1985:273–275; Sweezy 1980:137–138; and Horvat 1982:43–56).

For example, Branko Horvat has argued that the Soviet Union and other so-called socialist societies did not undergo a transition to socialism, rather they developed into a new kind of statist society, with a self-reproducing centralized, authoritarian state that "has swallowed the entire society" (Horvat 1982:48). He calls this type of society "etatist" (that is, statist) and contends that the form of state it possesses is incompatible with socialism because in the transition to socialism "political domination must be eliminated just as any other form of domination" (Horvat 1982:56).

Horvat claims that statist systems such as the Soviet Union tend to be viewed by their critics as either capitalist or socialist rather than as a distinct system by itself.

Once it had been realized that the new society had failed to achieve the socialist goal, it was natural for socialists to refuse to consider it socialist. Since in the inherited deterministic scheme only two systems were known, if a society was not socialist it could only be capitalist. And because of the dominant position of the state, the system was termed state capitalism. Many radicals all over the world—Soviet dissidents included—share this view. The socialist revolution only appeared to be successful. In fact, Stalin and his associates, assuming dictatorial power, carried out a bloody counterrevolution, and so the system degenerated into state capitalism. The fundamental characteristic of the system is that the state owns all capital, and employs workers and extracts surplus value in the same way as private capitalists. (Horvat, 1982:46–47)

However, Horvat rejects this line of reasoning because it mistakenly assumes that a class society dominated by an all-powerful state represents state capitalism. He claims that it is possible to find historical examples of societies where the state owned the means of production but where the society was not capitalist. Moreover, he argues that "capitalism—private or state—implies "the existence of capitalists" and that it is "difficult to identify capitalists in etatist societies" (Horvat 1982:47).

As for those who equate statism with socialism or at least the first phase of the latter, Horvat objects to this perspective because it is founded on a series of misconceptions about the nature of the state in the first stage of socialist transformation.

The second variant is more sophisticated. It starts from the observation that capitalism cannot be transformed into socialism overnight. There will be a transition period, initiated either by a parliamentary victory or by a victorious revolution, in which the state will nationalize all the means of production and carry out the necessary institutional changes. This is state socialism, the initial phase of socialist development. This conception, plausible as it is, is open to the following objections: (1) state ownership is not a necessary transitional stage between capitalism and socialism; (2) complete state monopoly of economic and political power is not a precondition for transition; (3) if state socialism is a transitional period, it will be short, with a clear tendency present for the role of the state to be reduced to its proper dimensions and for typically socialist institutions to be developed. In contemporary etatist societies, this is not the case. What might have been a transitional, state socialist, period crystallized into a well-established system that shows no tendency toward basic structural changes. (Horvat 1982:47)

Horvat argues that the Soviet Union is not a state socialist society because state socialism only exists as a brief first stage in the transition to socialism. Moreover, he maintains that as statism "crystallized" into an established system in the Soviet Union and "shows no tendency toward change," the system cannot be considered state socialism.

According to Horvat, Marx provided the basic criteria for distinguishing social systems in the first volume of his classic work *Capital*. These criteria concern the mode whereby the surplus labor of the producers is extracted.

> The essential difference between the various economic forms of society, between, for instance, a society based on slave-labor and one based on wage-labor, lies only in the mode in which this surplus labor is in each case extracted from the actual producer, the laborer. (Marx 1967:217, cited in Horvat 1982:48)

Horvat argues that if this criteria is applied to etatist or statist societies such as the Soviet Union, then it is clear that they are not capitalist; in capitalist societies surplus labor is extracted by the capitalists. But they are not socialist either; in socialist societies the surplus labor is controlled by the associated producers themselves. However, in etatist societies, according to Horvat, the political elite in charge of the state extracts and controls the surplus labor of the producers because "the state not only insures the reproduction of production relations but also, and first of all, the reproduction of relations of domination and hierarchy" (Horvat 1982:48).

Similar to Horvat's views on this question are those of Adolfo Sanchez Vazquez, a well-known Mexican Marxist scholar, who reasoned that the Soviet Union could not be considered socialist.

> We can hardly regard as socialist a society in which state ownership predominates and in which the state, through the bureaucracy, monopolizes or totalizes social life. . . . We are dealing here with a new centralized and hierarchized society in which a new class—the bureaucracy—unites economic and political power in its own hands and subjects every sphere and institution of social existence to the logic of its double domination. (Sanchez Vazquez 1985:274-275)

He attributed the consolidation of bureaucratic statism in the Soviet Union to Stalinism and contended that other courses of development existed in the first years of the revolution.

According to Roger Bartra, another prominent Mexican Marxist, one of the main causes of the contemporary crisis of Marxism has been the failure of Marxists to explain the existence of the kind of authoritarian statist society that developed in the Soviet Union (Bartra 1982:124). Like many other contemporary Marxists, he has concluded that a genuine transition to socialism cannot take place in the USSR or anywhere else unless there is a thoroughgoing democratization of political and social life. Recent developments in the Soviet Union suggest that the democratization of the Soviet political system may now be taking place, but it does not appear to be compatible with the development of a democratic socialist society.

Some contemporary neo-Marxists explain that the development of socialism in Russia was unlikely in 1917 because the working class was such a small minority of the population and the vast majority consisted of peasants with a petty bourgeois mentality (for example, see Stephens 1986:63–64). Moreover, these explanations often contend that the development of socialism in Russia was also precluded by "the elitist authoritarianism" inherent in Lenin's thought and in the Bolshevik Party, which is faulted for substituting the dictatorship of the party for the dictatorship of the proletariat.

Critical Views of Latin American Marxists on Statism

Among the Latin American Left today there appears to be widespread acceptance of the belief that authoritarian statism is incompatible with the construction of socialism. For example, the Brazilian leftist scholar Theotonio dos Santos observes that the necessity of building socialism in accordance with democratic socialist ideals is widely accepted now among the Left in Latin America (dos Santos 1985:181). Furthermore, he is optimistic that the experience accumulated through past efforts to construct socialism has enhanced the possibility that future socialist revolutions will be increasingly democratic (dos Santos 1985:189).

Chilean Marxist Pedro Vuskovic, who was an important member of Allende's cabinet, contends that the recent Latin American experience suggests that any future socialist project will need to contain as one of its key components "a conception of socialist transformation that involves the growing democratization of society" (Vuskovic 1985:293). Another member of Allende's cabinet, Sergio Bitar, who has written an insightful, critical analysis of the Chilean attempt to make a peaceful transition to socialism, has concluded that "it is absolutely necessary to affirm and demonstrate that democracy is inherent in socialism" (Bitar 1979:322).

Bitar maintains that the Popular Unity government under Allende failed to convince the Chilean people of its commitment to democracy. Therefore, the open debate within the Popular Unity coalition on the need for a "dictatorship of the proletariat" and the "seizure of total power" made it possible for the opposition to convince many people in Chile that the Popular Unity's commitment to democracy was only a tactical expedient that would be subsequently replaced by "totalitarian" forms of government (Bitar 1979:322).

Regarding the Caribbean Left, it is important to note that Gordon K. Lewis, a prominent leftist intellectual, has written that the most urgent lesson to be learned from the destruction of the Grenadian revolution is that "socialism must go hand in hand with democracy" (Lewis 1987:175).

> Grenada has shown us that there are certain principles involving "democracy" that are, as it were, immutable. . . . These principles apply as much to nongovernmental bodies as they do to governmental institutions. No progressive party, in particular, should follow the road of the New Jewel Movement which ultimately led to secrecy, intrigue and murder. (Lewis 1987:175)

Lewis has argued that the tragic failure of the short-lived revolution in Grenada has shown that if democracy is worthy of the name, it must be based on public policy decisions made by bodies accountable to public opinion, on decisions that are arrived at by discussion rather than coercion, on a government that can be changed peaceably through popular elections, and on an informed electorate that has free access to information and different viewpoints so that they are able to make free choices on public policy issues (Lewis 1987:175–176). According to Lewis, the Grenadian revolution was destroyed largely because these principles were not followed by the New Jewel Movement and the People's Revolutionary Government formed by this movement.

Michael Lowy, a well-known Marxist in both Latin America and Western Europe, also has claimed that "the tragic example of Grenada demonstrates the terrible consequences of the absence of socialist democracy" in societies that attempt to make a transition to socialism (Lowy 1986:267). He reasons that the absence of democratic structures within the revolutionary regime in Grenada made it possible for "a small, sectarian, bureaucratic and authoritarian faction" to gain control of the state apparatus and murder Maurice Bishop, who was recognized by the people of Grenada as the leader of the revolution. As a result, the regime lost its popular support and the pretext for U.S. intervention was created. According to Lowy, this tragic example "demonstrates that socialist democracy is not a luxury or a concession to the petty bourgeoisie," rather that "the survival of the revolution in its confrontation with imperialism" may depend upon it (Lowy 1986:268).

Like many contemporary Latin American Marxists, Lowy is concerned with the problem of establishing popular democracy in the transition to socialism. This concern has led him to examine the lessons to be learned about this problem, not only in Grenada but in revolutionary regimes throughout the Third World. His analysis is based upon the following basic premise:

> Democracy is not a problem of "political form" or institutional "super-structure": it is the very content of socialism as a social formation in which workers and peasants, young people, women, that is, the people, effectively exercise power and democratically determine the purpose of production, the distribution of the means of production, and the allocation of the product. (Lowy 1986:264)

This conception is quite similar to that of Rosa Luxemburg, whom he credits with having set forth in the clearest fashion the central role of democracy in the transition process.

As a result of his examination of the democratizing efforts of existing revolutionary regimes in the Third World, Lowy concludes that effective democratic participation has been limited primarily to the local level in the revolutionary states of the Third World (Lowy 1986:267). He further concludes that the absence of effective democratic participation within the revolutionary party and in the political process as a whole gives rise to the bureaucratization of the revolutionary state. In its worst form this results in "a social layer of bureaucrats" with interests different from those of the working class and the rest of the masses, the concentration of power in the hands of a single individual, repression of all forms of political opposition, and a bureaucratic regime over which the people exercise no control whatsoever.

Thus, it seems that many Marxists and Latin American leftists hold the view that the democratization of the state and the empowerment of the general citizenry is absolutely necessary in order to avoid the bureaucratization of the revolutionary state and to prevent the subversion of the transition from capitalism to socialism.

The Risks of Democracy and Dictatorship

Nicaragua provides an enlightening case study of what can happen when a revolutionary regime attempts to legitimate its continued existence on the basis of the institutionalization of representative democratic institutions and national elections. Under pressures from foreign opponents as well as supporters, and in an effort to enhance its legitimacy, the Sandinista regime established representative democratic institutions (a popularly elected president and vice-president as well as a national legislature) and held national elections on two occasions—November 1984 and February 1990. In the first elections, the bourgeois right-wing opposition boycotted the elections, but in the 1990 national elections they united with other political factions, including the Nicaraguan communist and socialist parties, to oppose the Sandinistas. The coalition succeeded in electing their presidential candidate and denying the Sandinistas control of the national assembly.

The reasons for the outcome of the 1990 elections will be the source of much debate for some time to come, but what the outcome of these elections demonstrates is that a revolutionary regime with socialist aspirations risks the loss of control over the state and the derailment of its revolutionary project if it holds parliamentary elections in which the bourgeoisie and its allies are free to contest the revolutionary leadership. The defeat of the Sandinistas at the hands of their bourgeois opponents in national elections that the Sandinistas themselves administered may be regarded by some as a testament to their integrity and democratic credentials, but it also lends credence to what Lenin and the Bolsheviks emphasized: the need for a dictatorship of the proletariat during the transition to socialism.

Lenin argued that a special type of dictatorship is necessary in the transition period. This dictatorship of the proletariat over the bourgeoisie is necessary because the class struggle between these two classes and their allies continues even after the bourgeoisie has been overthrown and the proletariat and its allies have seized political power.

> If we compare all the basic forces or classes and their interrelations, as modified by the dictatorship of the proletariat, we shall realize how utterly nonsensical and theoretically stupid is the common petty-bourgeois idea shared by all representatives of the Second International, that the transition to socialism is possible "by means of democracy" in general. The fundamental source of this error lies in the prejudice inherited from the bourgeoisie that "democracy" is something absolute and above classes. As a matter of fact, democracy itself passes into an entirely new phase under the dictatorship of the proletariat, and the class struggle rises to a higher level, dominating over each and every form. (Lenin 1976:504–505)

Lenin believed that in the transition to socialism bourgeois democracy had to be transformed along the lines of the Paris Commune, that is, a form of workers' self-government would have to be established in place of bourgeois forms of representative democracy. The fact that this type of democratic transformation did not take place in the Soviet Union does not, in itself, negate the validity of his thinking, and that of many other Marxists, on this subject. According to Lenin, "democracy for the vast majority of the people, and suppression by force, i.e., exclusion from democracy, of the exploiters and oppressors of the people—this is the change democracy [must undergo] during the *transition* from capitalism to communism" (Lenin 1976:327). Only under these conditions did Lenin and his supporters believe that the less politicized sectors of the exploited classes and the petty bourgeoisie could be weaned from bourgeois habits of thought and practice. In other words, they believed strongly that the restoration of bourgeois domination during the transition period is a very real possibility unless determined efforts are taken to prevent this from happening.

As mentioned in Chapter 2, Mao Tse Tung argued that a society undergoing the transition to socialism faces certain fundamental contradictions, and he attempted to elaborate a theory about the nature of these contradictions, and how they could be overcome. According to Mao, one of the most fundamental contradictions of the transitional period is the continued existence of classes and class struggle. What follows is one of Mao's best statements on this question:

> Socialist society covers a fairly long historical period. In the historical period of socialism, there are still classes, class contradictions, and class struggle; there is the struggle between the socialist road and the capitalist road, and there is the danger of capitalist restoration. We must recognize the protracted and complex nature of this struggle. We must heighten our vigilance. We must conduct socialist education. We must correctly understand and handle class contradictions and class struggle, distinguish the contradictions between ourselves and the enemy from those contradictions that are among the people, and handle them correctly. Otherwise a socialist country like ours will turn into its opposite and degenerate, and a capitalist restoration will take place. (quoted in Chan, Rosen, and Unger 1985:34)

In view of the course of development that China has followed in recent years, Mao's statement on this question seems quite prophetic, but our concern here is with the continuing class struggle that takes place in the transitional society. From a Marxist perspective, because of the continued existence of classes and the continuance of the class struggle during the period of socialist transition, there is a continuing need for the state. The socialist state must mediate the class struggle, prevent the restoration of capitalist society, and facilitate the development of a classless society.

Mao and many other Marxists have justified the use of dictatorial methods by the socialist state on the grounds that these methods are necessary in order to prevent the reactionary classes and class elements that continue to exist in the transition period from restoring capitalism.

> Our state is a people's democratic dictatorship led by the working class and based on the worker-peasant alliance. What is this dictatorship for? Its first function is to suppress the reactionary classes and elements and

those exploiters in our country who resist the socialist revolution, to suppress those who try to wreck our socialist construction, or in other words, to resolve the internal contradictions between ourselves and the enemy. For instance, to arrest, try and sentence certain counter-revolutionaries, and to deprive the landlords and bureaucrat-capitalists of their right to vote and their freedom of speech for a specified period of time— all this comes within the scope of our dictatorship. (Mao 1971:435–436)

Mao was quite explicit about the need for dictatorial methods to suppress the reactionary forces within Chinese society, but he also stressed that "democracy operates within the ranks of the people" and that a "socialist democracy is democracy in the broadest sense."

Our socialist democracy is democracy in the broadest sense such as is not to be found in any capitalist country. Our dictatorship is the people's democratic dictatorship led by the working class and based on the worker-peasant alliance. That is to say, democracy operates within the ranks of the people, while the working class, uniting with others enjoying civil rights, and in the first place with the peasantry, enforces dictatorship over the reactionary classes and elements of all those who resist socialist transformation and oppose socialist construction. By civil rights we mean, politically, the rights of freedom and democracy. (Mao 1971:436–437)

Of course, the problem is where to draw the line between the use of dictatorial methods and people's democracy, between those who resist socialist transformation and those who seek to exercise their civil rights.

The recent political history of the People's Republic of China makes it clear that there has been little opportunity for the exercise of democracy within the ranks of the people. Moreover, as Samir Amin has noted, "the continued existence of the state during the transition testifies to the continued existence of classes," and here we are not just "dealing with the vestiges of the old classes but above all with the new, rising class—whether we call it a bourgeoisie or something else" (Amin 1980:209). As a result, Amin contends that "the contradiction of the socialist transition thus lies in the alternatives of a classless society or a new class society, either of which can emerge during the transition" (Amin 1980:210).

The Problem of Bureaucratism

In relationship to the restoration of capitalist relations and the emergence of a new class during the transition period, Marxists have also been concerned about the problem of bureaucratism. To be sure, the spread of bureaucracy (bureaucratization) is a feature of all contemporary social formations, in capitalist as well as in the existing socialist societies (for example, see Horvat 1982:174–190; Michels 1962; Rizzi 1980; Weber 1966:329–341). However, Marxists have continuously sought to eliminate bureaucracy in the transition to socialism.

Lenin addressed the question of eliminating bureaucracy in the transition to socialism before the Bolshevik Revolution. This is evidenced in his treatise on *The State and Revolution*, where he argued that the gradual abolition of bureaucracy would be one of the most important tasks in the transition to socialism.

> Abolishing the bureaucracy at once, everywhere and completely, is out of the question. It is utopia. But to smash the old bureaucratic machine and replace it with a new one that will make possible the gradual abolition of all bureaucracy—this is not a utopia, it is the experience of the Commune, the direct and immediate task of the revolutionary proletariat. . . . This is our proletarian task, this is what we can and must start with in accomplishing the proletarian revolution. Such a beginning . . . will of itself lead to the gradual "withering away" of all bureaucracy. . . . (Lenin 1976:298)

During the period he served as the main leader and theoretician of the Soviet regime, Lenin became increasingly concerned about the bureaucratization of the Soviet state apparatus. In his essay *Better Fewer, But Better* written shortly before his death in 1923, he referred to the Soviet state bureaucracy as "deplorable" and "wretched" (Lenin 1976:700).

The bureaucratic nature of the Soviet system has been debated among Marxists since the 1920s. For example, Nikolai Bukharin, one of the leading Bolshevik theorists, was concerned in the 1920s about the emergence of a new bureaucratic class of "technological mental laborers" who were taking charge of the state and economy. He warned that during the transition period there would "inevitably develop a tendency to degeneration via the excretion of a leading stratum [of bureaucrats] in the form of a class-germ" (cited in Bellis 1979:72–73). It appears that what Bukharin feared, in fact, took place.

There are many factors that contemporary Marxist critics consider responsible for the bureaucratic degeneration of the Soviet state, among which the following appear to be the most important:

- The ban on factions within the party initiated at the Tenth Party Congress in 1921;
- The adoption in practice of a single-party regime in the same year;
- The elimination of trade union autonomy;
- The decimation of the proletariat in the Civil War;

- The reliance upon capitalist technology and organizational forms in the mistaken belief that they were "neutral";
- The introduction of a centralized "one-man management" system in the factories;
- The suppression of the soviets as effective organs of local self-government;
- The introduction of the doctrine of *partiinost* or "party-mindedness" involving unconditional submission to the ideas of the party leadership;
- The establishment of the top-down *nomenklatura* system of party control over all appointments;
- The merging of the party with the state administration;
- The depoliticization of the working class;
- The forced collectivization (statization) of agriculture;
- The establishment of a formalized system of privileges for top party and administrative officials;
- The physical elimination of most of the original Bolshevik leadership during the Stalinist purges (Bellis 1979:77–95).

Regardless of the causes, it is clear that the bureaucratization of Soviet society has produced considerable differentiation among the Soviet population in terms of income, privileges, and status (Horvat 1982:70–83). This differentiation has given rise to a new structure of social inequality and an elaborate array of privileges and special services enjoyed by those at the top of the bureaucratic pyramid (Bellis 1979:70–74). These privileges and the social stratification that now characterize Soviet society are in sharp contradiction to the classless and egalitarian nature of socialism envisaged by the founders of Marxism and by the early Bolsheviks.

Remedies for combating the bureaucratization of the state and the emergence of a bureaucratic elite in the transition to socialism have been proposed and, in some cases, tried by a long line of Marxists. Lenin himself advocated a number of measures based upon the experience of the Paris Commune.

The workers, after winning state power, will smash the old bureaucratic apparatus. . . . they will replace it by a new one, consisting of the very same workers and other employees, against whose transformation into bureaucrats the measures will at once be taken which were specified in detail by Marx and Engels: (1) not only election, but also recall at any time; (2) pay not to exceed that of a workman; (3) immediate introduction of control and supervision by *all*, so that *all* may become "bureaucrats"

for a time and that, therefore, *nobody* may be able to become a "bureaucrat."
(cited in Bellis 1979:35)

What Lenin envisaged was the conversion of the state bureaucracy into
a simplified system of administration and accounting in which the general
citizenry would take turns performing the necessary tasks. During the
first years of the Soviet regime, the Bolsheviks considered the local
soviets (councils) to be the appropriate revolutionary democratic structure
for involving the general citizenry in the direct administration of public
affairs. However, in practice, the soviets proved to be ineffective and
they were replaced by a centralized system of party control and state
administration that was developed during the early twenties and consolidated during the Stalinist period (see Narkiewicz 1970).

Contemporary Marxists argue that the bureaucratic degeneration of
transitional regimes can be prevented only through the effective deconcentration and decentralization of state power within a federative
socialist democracy. According to Horvat, this requires the separation of
state power between different functional branches of government, free
elections, civil liberties, a free press, the protection of citizens from
administrative abuses through the creation of ombudsmen, the establishment of self-management in work organizations and self-government
at the community level (Horvat 1982:283-327). The deconcentration and
decentralization of state power can be accomplished, according to Horvat,
only if decisions are taken in a democratic manner at the lowest level
possible and if a federative state structure is established for deciding
issues and coordinating matters that affect wider numbers of people
than those within a specific locale or workplace.

It is ironic that the problems associated with bureaucratic degeneration
have been denounced at one time or another by most contemporary
bureaucratic transitional regimes. China offers perhaps the best example
of this. During the Cultural Revolution, Mao and the young Red Guards
attacked the party and state bureaucrats as enemies of the socialist
revolution, and they sought to eliminate "bureaucratism" (that is, not
only the defects and ills associated with bureaucratic practices but also
the emergence of a bureaucratic stratum) from all aspects of Chinese
society. As a result of this antibureaucratic campaign, many party and
state bureaucrats were removed from their positions and sent to work
in the countryside as simple farmworkers (Friedland 1982:199-200).
However, this campaign appears to have succeeded only in disrupting
the functioning of the state and the economy rather than stamping out
bureaucratism. Today, the Chinese regime continues to complain of
bureaucratism, but tends to characterize this problem as merely a result
of organizational deficiencies or corrupt individuals rather than a more

fundamental contradiction in the social system. Dissident leftist intellectuals in China such as Li Zhengtian, Chen Yiyang, and Wang Xizhe, who are famous for their 1974 wall poster "On Socialist Democracy and the Legal System," claimed that China's ruling "bureaucratic bourgeoisie" use frequent attacks on bureaucratism to cover up their own complicity in the bureaucratic degeneration of the Chinese system and also at times to eliminate those among the party cadres who criticize them for abusing their positions of authority (Chan, Rosen, and Unger 1985).

The struggle against bureaucratism has also been a continuing theme in revolutionary Cuba. Writing about the problem of bureaucratism during the early years of the revolutionary regime in Cuba, Comandante Che Guevara argued that this problem was "not the offspring of socialist society"; rather he contended that it was based on "a lack of revolutionary consciousness or, at any rate, on acquiescence in things that are wrong" (Guevara 1987:197). The Cubans have attempted to combat this problem by increasing popular participation in the formulation and implementation of policy. The creation during the seventies of elected organs of People's Power at the local level was aimed at curbing bureaucratism and democratizing the state apparatus (Harnecker 1979:159–193).

Although Cuba does not have a full-fledged decentralized government, the basic outlines of its system of People's Power (Poder Popular) resemble those of the Paris Commune. This system of locally elected bodies has provided for a limited degree of decentralization and self-government at the local level. However, it does not extend to national and foreign policy issues, and national officials are not directly elected by the people. The system is also characterized by the absence of opposing political parties and the open manifestation of different political tendencies. Thus, the people are not presented with a choice between alternative policy proposals on major issues of national importance. This situation leads even sympathetic Marxist observers such as Michael Lowy to conclude that "the masses do not yet have the power of *decision* between alternative economic or political policies" at the national level in Cuba (Lowy 1986:270). According to Lowy, further democratization and debureaucratization of the Cuban state are limited by "the one-party system and the party's monolithic internal structure."

In place of effective democratic participation in the political process, revolutionary regimes have frequently relied upon various forms of "popular mobilization" to mobilize support among the population for the implementation of state policies. But, as one critical leftist writer on this subject has observed, "unless there is increased participation in the determination of policy . . . mobilization degenerates into simple manipulation techniques" that give the people a false sense of participation in the political process and allow the bureaucratic agencies of the state to make policy over their heads (Friedland 1982:127). This kind of false popular participation can do little to combat the bureaucratic and authoritarian tendencies that can emerge in the transition to socialism.

The Role of the Revolutionary Vanguard

Related to the problem of bureaucratization is the nature of the revolutionary vanguard and its relationship to the popular masses in the construction of socialism. Over the years, the role of the revolutionary vanguard has been the subject of intense debate among Marxists (for example, see Rossanda et al., 1976). I will only highlight the main issues in this debate as they relate to the transition to socialism in Latin America and the Caribbean.

First, it is important to recall what Marx and Engels wrote about the political organization of the proletariat. Their conception of this question serves as a historical frame of reference for viewing subsequent developments in Marxist thought. Basic to their conception was the idea that the political organization of the working class would largely arise out of the struggles between the members of this class and the bourgeoisie.

In the *Manifesto of the Communist Party,* Marx and Engels provided a clear statement of what they thought the relationship of the vanguard should be to the working class.

> The Communists do not form a separate party opposed to other working-class parties. . . . They do not set up any sectarian principles of their own, by which to shape and mould the proletarian movement. . . . The Communists are on the one hand, practically, the most advanced and resolute section of the working class parties of every country, that section which pushes forward all others; on the other hand, theoretically, they have over the great mass of the proletariat the advantage of clearly understanding the line of march, the conditions, and the ultimate general results of the proletarian movement. (Marx and Engels 1972:46)

What this quote makes clear is that Marx and Engels considered their party to be an integral part of the larger working-class movement and thought it should be distinguished by its nonsectarianism, internationalism, and superior theoretical overview of this movement.

Based upon the ideas of Marx and Engels regarding the nature of the communist party and its relationship to the working class, early Marxist parties in Western Europe sought to work within the larger working-class movement and provide it with a revolutionary vision. After the demise of the First International organized by Marx and Engels, these parties developed into *mass parties* at the national level, open to the entire working class and often surrounded by an interlocking network of associated unions, cooperatives, and voluntary associations (Friedland 1982:64). For the most part, these were the forerunners of the contemporary social democratic parties of Western Europe.

In the context of the repressive political climate created by the czarist police-state in prerevolutionary Russia, Lenin and the Bolsheviks developed a different type of political organization, called a *vanguard party*. This type of party is characterized by strict internal centralization, secrecy, and a restricted, highly disciplined membership of professional revolutionaries (Connor 1968:62; Friedland 1982:64; Lenin 1976:535). Until recently, this model of a vanguard party was adopted by the official communist parties in Latin America. However, the Cuban, Nicaraguan, and Grenadian revolutions are evidence that at least during the insurrectionary stage this type of party is not a necessary condition for a successful revolutionary strategy.

For example, during the insurrectionary period and for two years after the seizure of power, the Cuban revolution was led by a rural-based, armed guerrilla force—the July 26th Movement—and not by a revolutionary political party with a proletarian ideology. It was not until two years after the formation of the revolutionary regime that the Popular Socialist Party, Cuba's official Marxist-Leninist party, joined with the July 26th Movement to form, under the leadership of Fidel Castro, what is today known as the Communist Party of Cuba (Harnecker 1979:xviii).

In El Salvador, the popular revolutionary movement also does not conform to the traditional Leninist model of a vanguard party. The Farabundo Martí Front for National Liberation (Frente Farabundo Martí de Liberación Nacional or FMLN) is composed of five loosely unified armed revolutionary groups that have distinctly different political origins; and on the civilian side, the Democratic Revolutionary Front (Frente Democratico Revolucionario or FDR) is composed of a wide spectrum of leftist political organizations (Leiken 1987:187–200). The Communist Party of El Salvador plays an important role in both the FMLN and the FDR, but it is not the controlling element in either the military or the civilian wings of the Salvadoran revolutionary movement.

In Latin America today it appears that most official communist parties as well as most leftist organizations realize that they cannot be the exclusive vanguard of the popular forces in their country (Bollinger 1985:62–63). By the beginning of the 1980s, both the Nicaraguan and Salvadoran revolutionary movements provided important examples of unity between different vanguard elements representing different political tendencies. They also revealed that armed vanguard organizations can successfully combine with mass-based popular organizations.

As a result of the recent experience of the Central American revolutions, current concepts among the Left of the relationship between the vanguard and the masses have departed significantly from the traditional Leninist formula. Current strategy involves the formation of a multiclass political movement encompassing a series of mass organizations that represent the proletariat, peasantry, semiproletarianized masses, and important sectors of the petty bourgeoisie. Depending upon the conditions in each country, these unarmed popular organizations may or may not be supported by armed guerrilla forces.

The revolutionary vanguard in these movements consists of political activists who provide the leadership and the entire movement by unifying the various popular forces in a common revolutionary project. They guide the struggle against the existing order to a successful conclusion and afterwards direct the construction of the new society in accordance with the revolutionary project (Núñez Soto 1986:246–247). They are responsible for mediating between revolutionary theory and practice and for shaping the ideological orientation of the revolutionary process. In this conception there is no dichotomy between the vanguard and mass organizations, which are both essential components of the popular "block" or movement that carries out the revolutionary project.

Grenada's revolutionary experience also appears to have contributed to contemporary leftist thinking about the nature of the revolutionary vanguard and its relationship to the masses in the transition to socialism. The split within the New Jewel Movement, the isolation of the vanguard from the masses, and the secrecy that cloaked many of the revolutionary government's decisions have been criticized for contributing to the demise of the People's Revolutionary Government. According to Gordon Lewis:

> The Caribbean left must learn from all of this. It must decline to accept the Leninist concept of party structure, which in its ultracentralism neglects the problem of accountability to the larger working-class movement, for in that structure the party becomes a law unto itself. (Lewis 1987:174)

Lewis believes that the Caribbean Left has learned from the mistakes of Grenada and that it is reevaluating its basic ideas about party organization, respect for basic civil rights, popular participation, and so on. And, according to Guyana's prominent leftist scholar and activist Clive Thomas, "after Grenada no social project carried out in the name of the masses of the Caribbean peoples . . . will receive widespread support . . . if it does not clearly embrace political democracy as its norm of political conduct" (quoted in Lewis 1987:197).

This theme is repeated in leftist circles throughout Latin America today. Clearly, the experience of Grenada as well as that of the existing socialist societies in Eastern Europe and Asia have forced the Latin American Left to embrace democracy. However, as the Nicaraguan case reveals, the adoption of bourgeois representative forms of political democracy is *not* the solution to bureaucratism and the separation of the revolutionary vanguard from the masses. Rather, new direct forms of self-government and effective means of popular participation must be developed and institutionalized during the transition to socialism.

In a system of government based upon indirect representative institutions and basic political liberties, which is typical of bourgeois democracy, the individual's roles as producer and citizen are separated, and bourgeois hegemony (the predominance of capitalist values and social relations) is preserved due to the fact that the individual has almost no means for effective participation in the control of the various aspects of society. However, in a political and economic system based upon forms of direct democracy as well as representative institutions and on social and economic rights as well as basic political liberties, which are the forms of self-government and self-management required in a genuine socialist society, the individual's roles as producer and citizen are combined, and bourgeois hegemony is eliminated by the individual's effective participation in the direction of all aspects of society (Weffort 1989:12).

5
The Stages
of Transition

Lenin on the Stages of Transition

In Lenin's essay on the *Two Tactics of Social Democracy in the Democratic Revolution* (79–109) and his thesis on *The Socialist Revolution and the Right of Nations to Self-Determination* (Lenin 1976:157–168), one can find the basic premises of the revolutionary strategy that he developed for the transition to socialism in underdeveloped societies. In these writings Lenin set forth his thesis that the more immature or backward the society in terms of its readiness for a socialist revolution, the more necessary it was for the revolutionary vanguard to play a directive role in raising the political consciousness of the masses and mobilizing them to take revolutionary action. He also characterized the international order as one divided into a small number of imperialist "oppressor nations" and a large number of "oppressed nations" whose revolutionary struggles for self-determination, he argued, the international communist movement should support.

In underdeveloped and backward capitalist societies, Lenin called for a two-stage revolutionary strategy and the formation, under the aegis of the revolutionary vanguard, of an alliance between the proletariat and the peasantry.

> The proletariat must carry the democratic revolution to completion, allying to itself the mass of the peasantry in order to crush the autocracy's resistance by force and paralyze the bourgeoisie's instability. The proletariat must accomplish the socialist revolution, allying to itself the mass of the semi-proletarian elements of the population, so as to crush the bourgeoisie's resistance by force and paralyze the instability of the peasantry and the

petty bourgeoisie. Such are the tasks of the proletariat, so narrowly presented by the new-Iskra group in all their arguments and resolutions on the sweep of the revolution. (Lenin 1976:117)

This alliance was needed in order to force to completion the bourgeois revolution that the backward and weak capitalist class was incapable of completing on its own. Once this revolution was completed, Lenin argued, the worker-peasant alliance would fall apart as significant sections of the peasantry defected to the bourgeoisie. At this point, the proletariat would have to ally with the poorer, semiproletarianized strata of the peasantry in order to press ahead and make a socialist revolution.

In his thesis on *The Socialist Revolution and the Right of Nations to Self-Determination*, Lenin argued that the revolutionary struggle of the proletariat to overthrow the capitalist order and establish socialism was bound up with the liberation of the oppressed nations and their right to self-determination. For example, in the opening paragraph of this thesis, Lenin states:

Victorious socialism must necessarily establish a full democracy and, consequently, not only introduce full equality of nations but also realize the right of the oppressed nations to self-determination, i.e., the right to free political separation. Socialist parties which do not show by all their activity, both now, during the revolution, and after its victory, that they would liberate the enslaved nations and build up relations with them on the basis of free union—and free union is a false phrase without the right to secede—these parties would be betraying socialism. (Lenin 1976:157)

As this quote indicates, Lenin connected the revolutionary struggle for socialism with the liberation and self-determination of the oppressed nations. At the Second Congress of the Communist Third International in 1920, Lenin's theses on this subject were adopted as the position of the international communist movement. In his report to the congress's Commission on the National and Colonial Questions, Lenin further elaborated the strategy for socialist revolution in the oppressed, backward nations. He argued that—with the assistance of the Soviet Union, the proletariat in the advanced countries, and the international communist movement—these countries could advance directly to socialism without having to first undergo capitalist development.

If the victorious revolutionary proletariat conducts systematic propaganda among them, and the Soviet governments come to their aid with all the means at their disposal—in that event it will be mistaken to assume that the backward peoples must inevitably go through the capitalist stage of development. Not only should we create independent contingents of fighters and party organizations in the colonies and the backward countries . . . but the Communist International should advance the proposition, with the appropriate theoretical grounding, that with the aid of the proletariat of the advanced countries, the backward countries can go over to the Soviet system, and through certain stages of development, to communism, without having to pass through the capitalist stage. (Lenin 1976:605)

Thus, Lenin and the Communist Third International took up the cause of the national liberation of the oppressed peoples of Africa, Asia, and Latin America and advanced the position that under the right conditions these countries could establish socialism without first undergoing the full development of capitalism.

It is important to note that the young Ho Chi Minh, who was destined to become the leader of the Vietnamese revolutionary struggle for national liberation, was so impressed by Lenin's theses on the national and colonial questions that he adopted Marxism-Leninism and decided that only through revolutionary socialism could his country and other colonial societies gain their liberation from Western imperialism (Harrison 1989:39). This was also true for many other Third World leaders who struggled against Western imperialism during the period from the 1920s to the 1970s.

Trotsky subsequently rejected Lenin's and Stalin's conception of a two-stage revolutionary process and the idea that socialism could be constructed in one country (Liss 1984:25). He argued that a "permanent revolution" was necessary and that the revolutionary process would have to extend to other countries and become international in order for it to survive. Some contemporary leftists in Latin America hold to this idea of a permanent, international revolution and oppose the contention that the revolutionary process in any given country must first pass through a national bourgeois revolution before advancing to a socialist revolution.

Another variant of the stages approach is that of the Maoists. For example, the Maoist leadership of the Communist Party of Peru—Shining Path (*Partida Comunista del Perú—Sendero Luminoso*) has been waging an armed struggle against both the Peruvian government and the other leftist parties in Peru since the early 1980s; it adheres to the Maoist thesis that a "new democratic revolution" is a necessary preliminary stage of the proletarian socialist revolution in "semifeudal" and "semi-colonial" Third World countries such as Peru (Vergara 1988). The leadership bases its views on what Mao said about the development in China and other semicolonial societies of a new democratic revolution:

This new kind of revolution is developing in China as well as in all other colonial and semi-colonial countries and we call it the new democratic revolution. This new democratic revolution is part of the world proletarian-socialist revolution; it resolutely opposes imperialism, i.e., international capitalism. Politically, it means the joint *revolutionary-democratic* dictatorship of several revolutionary classes over the imperialists and reactionary traitors, and opposition to the transformation of Chinese society under bourgeois dictatorship. . . . Hence, while clearing the way for capitalism, this democratic revolution of a new type creates the precondition for socialism. (quoted in Schram 1970:230)

Sendero Luminoso's strategy is to carry out a "new democratic revolution" against Peru's semicolonial regime, establish a so-called revolutionary democratic dictatorship, and prepare the way as quickly as possible for the next stage in the revolutionary process, which is a proletarian socialist revolution.

Latin American Views on Stages of Transition

In Latin America, only the Cuban experience conforms in general to Lenin's idea of a two-stage revolution, that is, a national democratic stage followed by a socialist stage. In fact, the Cubans use these concepts to describe the history of the revolutionary struggle in their country. For example, Cuba's vice president, Carlos Rafael Rodriguez, wrote the following about the transition to socialism in Cuba:

If one takes into account the reasons behind the nationalization decisions adopted by the Cuban revolutionary state and examines these reasons in the light of the previously defined character of the Cuban revolution as revolutionary democratic and anti-imperialist (national liberation), we have to admit immediately that in spite of the profound depth and extent of the rationalizations carried out in August 1960 they did not exceed the bourgeois democratic limits of the revolution, even though . . . they constituted a decisive approximation and major preparatory step in the direction of the socialist revolution. (Rodriguez 1978:124)

As Rodriguez reveals, the Cuban revolution initially was *not* a socialist revolution, even though it quickly took this direction.

In Chile, the communists in the UP coalition held the Leninist view that the Chilean revolution would have to go through first a "national democratic" and then a "socialist" stage of development (Griffith-Jones 1981:125–126). The victory of the UP in the presidential elections of 1970 constituted for them the beginning of the national democratic revolution. However, other elements within the UP coalition considered this two-stage strategy unrealistic. They argued that the revolutionary process would rapidly evolve into a struggle for power with the bourgeois opposition, and that the outcome of this struggle could only be socialism or counterrevolution. Thus, a portion of the membership of the Socialist Party, the Movement for Unified Popular Action (Movimento Acción Popular Unificado or (MAPU), and various minor groups within the UP coalition advocated that the Allende government follow a strategy of rapid institutional change and proposed a plebiscite to dissolve the Congress and elect a new People's Assembly (Bitar 1979; Mistral 1974:67–69). President Allende and most of the leadership of the Socialist Party, the Communist Party, and the Radical Party held fast to the view that the popular forces were not prepared for a major confrontation with the bourgeoisie and the armed forces. As a result, they chose to follow a gradualist strategy that sought to postpone a major confrontation with the bourgeoisie until the UP government had consolidated its gains (Griffith-Jones 1981:126; Bitar 1979:319–321).

The Nicaraguan experience is unique in several respects. First, Nicaragua's small official Marxist-Leninist Party—the Nicaraguan Socialist Party—played an insignificant role in the revolutionary process, joined the opposition to the Sandinista regime in the mid-1980s (Ruchwarger 1987:43–44), and was part of the bourgeois-led electoral coalition that defeated the Sandinistas in the February 1990 elections. Second, the Sandinista revolutionary regime did not describe itself as socialist or Marxist-Leninist, but rather as anti-imperialist, popular, and democratic (see Harris and Vilas 1985:1–4, 227–230; and Vilas 1986:264–269).

The Sandinista Front for National Liberation (Frente Sandinista de Liberación Nacional or FSLN) evolved from a guerrilla movement into a political party that combined Leninist, electoral, and mass party characteristics. It adhered to its own home-grown ideology of *Sandinismo,* an eclectic mixture of revolutionary nationalism, Marxism, liberation theology, and classical liberalism (Ruchwarger 1987:74).

The Sandinistas believed that the conditions prevailing in their country precluded an immediate transition to socialism and necessitated a prolonged period of preparation. This is revealed in the following statement made by Comandante Jaime Wheelock, Nicaragua's minister of agricultural development and agrarian reform:

Now, for a series of reasons, many of them political, and others having to do with hunger and desperation, certain peoples have made a revolution in the worst conditions of social development. . . . This is our case. Even though we have socialist principles, we cannot effect the transformation of our society by socializing all the means of production. This would not lead to socialism, rather the contrary, it could lead to the destruction and disarticulation of our society. What we seek is the articulation of a project in which the most strategic and most developed sectors of the economy constitute a spearhead, and the organization of a social project in which associational forms of labor will predominate, although in a rudimentary form. (Wheelock 1983:101–102)

According to the Sandinistas, it was not feasible to undertake a sweeping socialization of their underdeveloped economy. Therefore, the Sandinistas were committed for the foreseeable future to developing a "mixed economy" based on both private and state capitalism (Harris and Vilas 1985:227–230; Vilas 1986:263–269). Although they never advanced a clear position on Nicaragua's transition to socialism, it can be argued that the Sandinista regime represented the first or national democratic stage of a revolutionary process that had the potential to follow a two-stage route to socialism.

In El Salvador, the revolutionary movement considered itself throughout the 1980s to be engaged in a national democratic revolutionary struggle based upon an alliance of the popular classes. At least until 1989, the leadership of this movement saw the revolutionary process in their country as involving both a democratic, anti-imperialist revolution and a socialist revolution. In the words of Salvadoran Communist Party leader Shafik Handal:

It is not possible to move to socialism except through democratic, anti-imperialist revolution, but it is equally not possible to consummate the democratic, anti-imperialist revolution without going towards socialism. Between the two there is an essential and insoluble nexus; they are facets of one single revolution and not two revolutions. (cited in Vilas 1986:37)

This implies a two-stage or phased revolutionary process involving first the mobilization of the masses in a national democratic and anti-imperialist struggle, followed by a period of struggle in which the people learn that the democratic and anti-imperialist objectives of their revolution can only be secured through the construction of socialism (Bollinger 1985:61). Influenced by the changes taking place in Eastern Europe and the peace agreements made by the Sandinistas with the other Central American states, leaders of the Salvadoran revolutionary movement indicated in subsequent statements that they had revised their original perspective on the nature of the revolutionary process in their country.

For example, the statement made by Comandante Joaquín Villalobos (1989) reveals the extent to which the Salvadoran revolutionary movement had distanced itself from orthodox Marxism-Leninism principles.

A one-party system—given the make-up of Salvadoran society—does not correspond to Salvadoran reality; nor should the unity of the revolutionary forces in a single party be confused with a one-party society.

Thus, the Cuban revolution is the only historical case in Latin America that has fit Lenin's two-stage pattern. Neither the Nicaraguan nor Grenadian revolutions moved from a national democratic to a socialist phase, and the Chilean attempt at a peaceful transition to socialism was aborted before it could prove whether a transition to socialism could take place through the kind of parliamentary route advocated by its leaders.

In recent years, certain leftist circles have begun to criticize the evolutionary nature of the stages approach to socialism. For example, in Chile, the Communist Party's reevaluation of its role in the Popular Unity regime and the party's move to the left in the early 1980s gave rise to a critique of "evolutionary" conceptions of the transition to socialism (called *evolucionismo*) and a rejection of the idea that there are certain universal stages of transition. According to one account of this nature:

> In our case, the history of an evolutionary and anti-dialectical conception belonging to an economistic Marxism has left us with the scars of many vain efforts: the useless search for the "national bourgeoisie," the democratic stage of the revolution conceived as a phase of development of the productive forces in the transition to a new order, the defense of the revolutionary order with "the battle for production," our chronic lack of comprehension of the departures of the Cuban revolution from the stereotype. (Palacios 1989:30)

Current conceptions of the construction of socialism tend to view it as a continuing process of liberation and democratization. In this view, it is an open-ended process that has no predetermined stages.

Conclusion

In place of conceptualizing the transition to socialism as a finite period consisting of distinct and immutable stages, today there appears to be a tendency among some leftist circles to place the emphasis on the ruptures and qualitative changes that can take place in the unfolding of an open-ended process of continuing socialist transformation. These leftists argue that theory and strategy need to be adapted to the ruptures and qualitative changes in the on-going process of building a socialist society in a way that responds to changing subjective factors, such as the mood and will of the masses as well as the material forces of change (Gautier 1989).

6

The Expropriation of Capital

Early Conceptions of the Expropriation of Capital

In the *Manifesto of the Communist Party*, Marx and Engels predicted that once the proletariat gained political power, they would use it "to wrest, by degrees, all capital from the bourgeoisie, to centralize all instruments of production in the hands of the State," and to "increase the total of productive forces as rapidly as possible" (Marx and Engels 1972:52). It is important to emphasize that their writings and statements show that they did not foresee the immediate abolition of all forms of capitalist property, rather they believed the working class would have to expropriate the capital of the bourgeoisie "by degrees." Moreover, the expropriation of capital was conceived by Marx and Engels to be only one of the major tasks of the transition period, in which all the conditions responsible for the existence of capitalist relations of production would have to be eliminated.

As Paul Bellis notes in his excellent work on *Marxism and the U.S.S.R.*, expropriation or "nationalization" has to be seen as part of a more comprehensive strategy aimed at eliminating all the material conditions upon which the power of the capitalist class is based:

The nationalization of the means of production was only one of the tasks posited for the working class during the transition period, as is clear from Marx's exposition of the concept of proletarian dictatorship in *The Class Struggles in France*, in which [the transition period] is depicted as the suppression of all the conditions of existence of capitalist social relations of production. Inseparable from this conception, as Marx made clear in his account of the [Paris] Commune, would be the elimination of bureaucracy and thereby the restoration to the social body proper of "all the forces hitherto absorbed by the State parasite feeding upon, and clogging the free movement of Society." (Bellis 1979:20)

As we shall see later, expropriation is a necessary condition for but does not guarantee the elimination of capitalist relations of production. In order to avoid serious economic dislocations in Russia following the Bolshevik seizure of power, Lenin initially opposed full-scale expropriation of the property of the large capitalists and proposed the coexistence of certain forms of large capitalist property with incipient forms of socialist property (Lange 1971:41; C. R. Rodriguez 1978:113). However, the bourgeoisie proved to be uncooperative. Unable to maintain control over their workers, they sought to sabotage the economic policies of the new regime. As a result, the regime was forced to seize their property within a short period of time. This caused serious economic dislocations because the regime lacked sufficient cadres with organizational expertise to administer the large number of expropriated enterprises. Lenin lamented the lack of sufficient cadres and argued that this factor prevented the new regime from accelerating the expropriation of the bourgeoisie (Lenin 1976:438–453).

The Bolsheviks were the first Marxists to theorize that an important factor limiting the scope and pace of the expropriation process is the availability of politically trustworthy personnel capable of taking over the management and operation of the expropriated enterprises and agricultural estates. This factor has been considered an important limitation on the scope and pace of socialization in every revolutionary regime since the Russian Revolution, as, for example, in Cuba during the first years of the revolutionary regime (Bettelheim 1978:78; C. R. Rodriguez 1978:128–129). In Chile, it was also an important factor affecting the Popular Unity government's ability to manage and plan the nationalized sector of industry (Griffith-Jones 1981:162). In Nicaragua, it was one of the main reasons given by the Sandinistas for their limited nationalization of the economy (Harris and Vilas 1985:132–142; Wheelock 1983:100–103).

A situation similar to that confronted by the Soviet regime forced the Cuban regime to expropriate the property of the country's large producers. The extent of U.S. ownership in the Cuban economy was so great and the hostility of the large capitalists so implacable that the new revolutionary regime was unable to initiate any meaningful reforms without incurring the opposition of the bourgeoisie and U.S. capital, backed by the U.S. government (Boorstein 1968:32–34). Thus, the revolutionary regime had to nationalize important sectors of the economy to break the U.S. stranglehold over Cuban economic life and overcome

TABLE 6.1 Nationalization of Economic Sectors in Cuba, 1961–1968 (in percentages)

Sector	1961	1963	1968
Agriculture	37	70	70
Industry	85	95	100
Construction	80	98	100
Transportation	92	95	100
Retail trade	52	75	100
Wholesale trade	100	100	100
Foreign trade	100	100	100
Banking	100	100	100
Education	100	100	100

Source: Gonzalo Rodríguez, *El Proceso de Industrialización de la Economía Cubana* (Havana: Editorial de Ciencias Sociales, 1980), 168.

the determined opposition of the local bourgeoisie. In fact, the U.S. reaction to the revolutionary regime's initial reforms was so great that the regime was forced to take even more radical measures to offset the efforts of the U.S. government and the bourgeoisie to destabilize the regime. As a result, within two years (see Table 6.1) most of the industrial sector had been nationalized, the best agricultural lands (about 40 percent of the arable land) were also nationalized, along with the banks, railroads, telecommunications, utilities, airlines, ports, major retail outlets, big hotels, and export/import firms (C. R. Rodriguez 1978:116–123).

The original intent of the revolutionary government was to follow a mixed economy strategy of economic development involving a combination of state and private capital, but the hostile reaction of both the Cuban bourgeoisie and U.S. interests in Cuba to the government's initial economic reforms forced the regime to accelerate the scope of its control over the economy to the point of an across-the-board nationalization (statization) of the major means of production (C. R. Rodriguez 1978:116–122). The Cuban case, therefore, like the Soviet experience, tends to support the argument of those Marxists who have contended that a rapid, as opposed to gradual, socialization of the economy is necessary in a society undergoing the transition to socialism.

In the late 1930s, the well-known leftist economist Oskar Lange wrote an important essay, "On the Economic Theory of Socialism," in which he argued that the very existence of a government bent on introducing socialism is a constant threat to private enterprise, and that no amount of government supervision can "cope effectively with the passive resistance and sabotage of the owners and managers" of the private enterprises who see themselves threatened with expropriation.

The opinion is almost generally accepted that the process of socialization must be as gradual as possible in order to avoid grave economic disturbance.

. . . Unfortunately, the economist cannot share this theory of economic gradualism. An economic system based on private enterprise and private property of the means of production can work only as long as the security of private property and of income derived from property and from enterprise is maintained. The very existence of a government bent on introducing socialism is a constant threat to this security . . . for the owners threatened with expropriation have no inducement to make the necessary investments and improvements and to manage them efficiently. And no government supervision or administrative measures can cope effectively with the passive resistance and sabotage of the owners and managers. (Lange 1971:39–40)

Therefore, Lange contended that a government genuinely committed to introducing socialism has "to carry out its socialization program at one stroke, or to give it up altogether."

A socialist government really intent upon socialism has to decide to carry out its socialization program at one stroke, or to give it up altogether. The very coming into power of such a government must cause a financial panic and economic collapse. Therefore, the socialist government must either guarantee the immunity of private property and private enterprise in order to enable the capitalist economy to function normally, in doing which it gives up its socialist aims, or it must go through resolutely with its socialization program at maximum speed. Any hesitation, any vacillation and indecision would provoke the inevitable economic catastrophe. Socialism is not an economic policy for the timid. (Lange 1971:39–41)

According to Lange, unless a socialist regime rapidly expropriates the large producers, the mere threat posed by the regime to the capitalists will paralyze business, provoke a financial panic, and lead to an economic collapse.

However, Lange also argued that a new socialist government should go out of its way to assure the small entrepreneurs and small producers that its socialization program is not directed against them or private property as such, but only against "private property which creates social privileges to the detriment of the great majority of the population" (Lange 1971:41). These kinds of assurances are particularly important in the case of societies with a large number of small producers. In the absence of such assurances, the regime will find it impossible to gain the small producers' support and to prevent them from joining the large capitalists in opposition to the new regime.

The success of a rapid socialization program, according to Lange, depends upon the socialist government mobilizing a mass movement against the large capitalists, whose properties it expropriates because the capitalists are responsible for economic instability, conspiring with imperialism, and for using the means of production purely for their own gain.

To be successful, the socialist government must put itself at the head of a great mass movement against monopoly and restrictionism, against imperialism and the concentration of economic control by a few, against social and economic instability and insecurity. Only under the impetus of such a mass movement, embracing the majority of the population, will it be able to carry out speedily a bold program of socialization. In the absence of such a mass movement, there is little a socialist government in office can achieve. For, as we have seen, if socialization cannot be achieved by a great and bold stroke, the government has to give up its socialist aims altogether. (Lange 1971:41–42)

The Latin American Experience

The Latin American experience in this regard strongly supports Lange's arguments. In the case of Cuba, a bold program of expropriation with mass support succeeded in eliminating the power of the bourgeoisie, whereas in Chile and Nicaragua the failure to follow such a course of action appears to have been one of the reasons a successful transition to socialism did not occur in these countries.

Contemporary Marxist theorists such as Ernest Mandel have also argued against gradual socialization and "mixed economy" strategies of transition. For example, Mandel rejects the claims of those (e.g., Nove 1983:193–195) who theorize that the nationalization of a few key sectors can be combined with the retention of private property in the rest of the economy in order to minimize the disruption of production and reduce the costs of planning, administration, and economic management (Mandel 1968:649). According to Mandel, where such strategies have been attempted, either the extent of nationalization has been so slight that the economy is not really "mixed" or the nationalization is significant and it provokes the flight of capital out of the remaining sectors.

The experience of the UP government in Chile bears directly on this question. The UP program called for the expropriation of Chile's large agricultural estates, banks, mines, telecommunications, and the larger enterprises in its relatively important manufacturing sector (Bitar 1979:18). However, the expropriation process in Chile was carried out too slowly and ambiguously. These defects in the process gave the owners of enterprises threatened with expropriation and those who feared expropriation time to reduce their investments, to allow their equipment to deteriorate, and to sell off their assets (Bitar 1979:272). Moreover, due to the government's failure to define clearly the scope of its expropriation policy clearly, many of the medium and small producers feared that they would be expropriated as well (Griffith-Jones 1981:125) As a result, these producers were susceptible to the propaganda of the bourgeoisie and tended to engage in the same type of disruptive economic behavior as the larger capitalists.

This situation was aggravated by the government's wage and pricing policies (that is, redistribution policies). Because of these policies, demand increased rapidly beyond the capacity of existing production, creating an uncontrollable inflation. The government was unable to obtain the surpluses in production that were expected to come from expropriation, and the functioning of the economy was disrupted. These conditions, along with others (including the actions of the U.S. government to destabilize the economy), prevented the government from winning the support of "the middle sectors" for its program of a democratic transition to socialism. They also provided the right-wing opposition and the armed forces with a pretext for overthrowing the Allende regime (Bitar 1979:299–302; Griffith-Jones 1981:12, 19–21).

According to Gabriel Smirnow, an official of the Chilean Socialist Party during the Allende regime, there was little possibility of persuading the medium entrepreneurs to side with the regime's policies because they saw their class interests threatened in the long run by the government's program of democratic socialism.

We may all agree that the whole private sector cannot be "suddenly" replaced by socialized enterprises, but when a social revolutionary process is under way the threatened classes are moved not only by their present interests but especially by their concern to survive as a class. Thus [in Chile] a short or medium-term alliance was not enough for the middle entrepreneurs, and they minimized their differences with the big bourgeoisie in the face of the main contradiction with the workers and the program of "beginning the construction of socialism." This is clearly a problem of the realities of power, since a government in effective possession of the necessary mechanisms and resources will not immediately undertake to socialize the whole economy, but will be in a position to control supply and demand as well as small- and medium-bourgeois investments and savings. That was of course not the case here and the envisioned growth of "production and productivity" under the anticipated favorable conditions did not materialize. (Smirnow 1979:45–46)

Smirnow blames the "conservative" wing of the UP coalition, dominated by the communist party, for refusing to recognize the realities of the situation and for insisting on a strategy aimed at "consolidating" the regime's position rather than accelerating the socialization process.

The line pushed by the Communist Party proposed in essence to "consolidate" the process, that is, to stop at the stage already reached, extending new long-term guarantees to the "middle classes." It consisted of strategic reordering of the tactical program on the economic level, which meant finding formulas of agreement with the middle bourgeoisie's chief spokesman, Christian Democracy. The Communist line was totally victorious at the Popular Unity meeting with President Allende at Lo Curro. . . . From that time—mid-June 1972—until the coup d'etat fifteen months later, this economic line was applied, in a setting of intensified inflation, shortages, and dismemberment of the mechanisms linking production and distribution. Small and medium entrepreneurs not only remained unconvinced that investments should be made to increase production, but along with other big-bourgeois sectors turned many of their assets to speculation, thus heightening the shortages of popular consumer goods and contributing to the inflation that plagued the country. (Smirnow 1979:46–47)

Smirnow views the consolidation strategy followed by the Allende regime as a serious mistake in view of the intensified class polarization and worsening economic conditions that characterized the situation. He writes that "the expropriation of the bourgeoisie, big and medium" was the only realistic course to follow because "the laws of the capitalist market could not be twisted with promises and vows of good behavior" (Smirnow 1979:47).

The experience of the Sandinista regime in Nicaragua provides the most recent example of this problem. The immediate confiscation of the holdings of the former dictator Anastasio Somoza Debayle and his closest followers gave the state control over approximately 40 percent of the country's gross domestic product (GDP) and left the remaining 60 percent in the hands of private producers (Harris and Vilas 1985:43). As of 1982, the state sector or "Area of People's Property" (APP) accounted for 21 percent of the country's GDP in agriculture, 31 percent of the GDP in manufacturing, 100 percent of the GDP in mining, and 38 percent of the GDP in services and commerce. Large private producers accounted for over half of the GDP in both agriculture and manufacturing—the two main sectors of the Nicaraguan economy. In terms of the total value of production (TVP) in 1983 (see Table 6.2), large private producers generated approximately 64 percent of the TVP in the important agroindustry sector in contrast to the state's 28 percent, they generated 37 percent of the TVP in export agriculture compared with the state's 24 percent, and 32 percent of the TVP in manufacturing compared with the state's 31 percent; the remainder of the TVP in these sectors was generated by medium and small private producers.

As these statistics indicate, the Sandinistas did not transform the basic nature of Nicaragua's economic system and the nation remained capitalist

TABLE 6.2   Nicaragua: Distribution of Property by Economic Sector, 1983 (percentage of total value of production)

Sector	APP[a]	Large Private	Medium Private	Small Private
Export agriculture	24.0	37.3	21.7	17.0
Agriculture for internal market	15.7	14.7	8.1	61.5
Livestock	24.7	11.0	30.4	33.9
Agroindustry	28.0	63.9	5.7	2.4
Fishing	71.9	—	—	28.1
Manufacturing	31.3	32.5	22.0	14.2
Mining, energy, and water	99.9	0.0	0.0	0.0
Total all sectors	37.0	25.0	18.0	20.0

[a]Area of People's Property (state sector).

Source: Barricada, November 28, 1983.

despite the revolutionary regime's expansion of the state sector and implementation of what amounted to a relatively moderate agrarian reform program. As Vilas notes:

> The image spread abroad by counter-revolutionary propaganda and by the Reagan administration—and fed by the fear of the large bourgeoisie— of an omnipresent state that is overpowering and strangling private activity, is therefore false. The reality is that the private sector is still the majority in almost all areas of the economy, and that the action of the state occurs mostly indirectly, through the financial system, the fixing of prices, agro-industrial processing, commercialization and labor and salary legislation. (Vilas 1986:155)

Therefore, the Sandinista regime cannot be said to have gained control of "the commanding heights" of the economy. In fact, the state sector created by the confiscation of the Somocistas' properties was no larger than that of countries such as France, Mexico, and Peru (Vilas 1986:154).

As mentioned previously, the Sandinista leadership did not believe that an across-the-board expropriation of the large private producers was either desirable or feasible in Nicaragua. As a result, the extent of expropriation that took place was not sufficient to eliminate the bourgeoisie's ability to maneuver and obstruct the economic strategy of the Sandinistas (Vilas 1986:162). Therefore, the leadership can be criticized for failing to reduce the bourgeoisie's economic power and their ability to obstruct the regime's economic policies. Because of the bourgeoisie's lack of political power following the overthrow of the Somoza dictatorship, it can be argued that the Sandinistas could have carried out an extensive expropriation of large capital and a more radical economic transformation. This criticism of the Sandinista regime was raised in Nicaragua by certain leftist elements soon after the regime came to power (for example, see Conroy 1985a:240–241). However, most leftists outside of Nicaragua never gave it much credence.

Despite guarantees and favorable inducements from the government, most of the large private producers and many of the medium producers not only failed to cooperate with the Sandinista regime's economic policies, they also engaged in many of the same kind of disruptive tactics used by the private sector in Chile. In addition, Washington greatly aggravated the situation by preventing the revolutionary government from obtaining essential loans and credits from international lending sources, by imposing a U.S. trade embargo on Nicaragua, and by subjecting the country to a brutal war of attrition carried out by proxy counterrevolutionary forces armed and directed by the U.S. government (Matthews 1986).

In the face of this combination of circumstances plus the Sandinistas' own errors in matters of economic policy (to be discussed below), production in Nicaragua fell drastically, shortages of all kinds became prevalent, hyperinflation became uncontrollable, the government was forced to reduce expenditures on social services, the state fiscal deficit and the foreign debt increased astronomically, the country's scarce financial and material resources were diverted to the war effort and most development projects were suspended (Harris 1987:8–10; and Stahler-Sholk 1985).

The Sandinistas thought that they had no choice but to follow a strategy for a mixed economy. However, it appears that this strategy suited their own ideology and long-term goals. Vilas observed:

The economic transformations begun after July 19, 1979, were *more anti-oligarchic than anti-capitalist.* The creation of the Area of People's Property (APP) has taken place on properties confiscated from the Somocista regime; its aim is national recovery rather than state planning. The agrarian reform guarantees efficiently managed large property—with criteria that are not excessively rigid—affecting only idle, abandoned or badly exploited lands, or those on which peasant labor is exploited through rent. . . . The agrarian reform is peasant oriented, favoring cooperative forms of production, but accepting the maintenance of individual property, whether small, medium or large. The outrage of the Nicaraguan bourgeoisie, therefore, cannot be explained by the threat that the revolution poses to their basis of accumulation or by the imperative to modernize and continue productivity. The real nature of the bourgeoisie—the presence within it of typically oligarchic elements, its anti-worker attitude, its profound cultural alienation, its ideological backwardness and lack of political expressions that it can call its own, its dependence on the perspectives of the U.S. government—marginalizes it from a process which, in principle, does not challenge its material bases (at least to the extent that they are employed as capital and not as sources of rent). (Vilas 1986:264)

Vilas also observed that it was "the content of the dominant political discourse" as manifested in the Sandinista slogans and revolutionary rhetoric rather than their economic practices that most alarmed the Nicaraguan bourgeoisie (Vilas 1986:265).

In fact, it is by no means clear that the Sandinista leadership was committed to the long-term goal of transforming Nicaragua into a socialist society. Carlos Fonseca, the founder of the FSLN, certainly was a socialist, and many Sandinistas did and still do consider themselves socialists. However, they were always careful to use the term "Sandinista" instead of socialist when referring to their regime and its policies. This was not a subterfuge to hide their true nature, rather it was an indication of their commitment to an eclectic ideology based upon a combination of populist, social democratic, revolutionary nationalist, radical Christian, and socialist ideals. They did not seem to have any clear idea of how their country would become socialist or how long it would take before a transition to socialism could be undertaken. The Sandinistas in general felt that a radical approach to expropriation would plunge the country into economic chaos, give Washington grounds to justify its claims that Nicaragua was "another Cuba," and probably cost the revolutionary regime valuable international support from Latin American and European social democratic governments that refused to go along with Washington's efforts to isolate and overthrow the Sandinistas (Harris and Vilas 1985:228–229).

The mixed economy strategy and the economic policies of the Sandinista regime had disastrous effects, not only on the economy but also on the regime's base of popular support and its revolutionary project. Indeed, the effects of the Sandinistas' economic policies as well as the war weariness of the population appear to have been the major factors that influenced a majority of the electorate to vote against the Sandinistas in the February 1990 national elections.

The Sandinista regime's efforts to win over or at least neutralize the opposition of the bourgeoisie only served to undermine its mixed economy program and contribute to the economic problems of the country. For example, the regime's policy of providing liberal credits and loans for investments undertaken by the large private producers had the effect of transferring capital from the public sector to the private sector and then out of the country. Vilas described how this took place during the early 1980s.

> It should not be surprising that private sector production has increased less than the increase in financial facilities accorded it by the government. Available evidence indicates that the financing handed over was converted into dollars and taken out of the country through the free foreign exchange market—a market lacking any effective regulation before September 1981; productive capital slowly moved toward the sphere of commerce and speculation; the cattle herd was rapidly reduced by indiscriminate slaughter; overpricing of imports and underpricing of exports permitted the illicit flight of earnings and the consequent reduction of the tax base. Many companies did not create depreciation reserves, and a tendency to decapitalization can be seen in many sectors of private enterprise. All this was in the framework of a financial system that advanced all necessary working capital and reduced all operative risks to a minimum. (Vilas 1986:162)

This situation supports Lange's thesis that a revolutionary regime cannot effectively control or supervise the activities of the private sector unless it eliminates the material base of the large producers. In other words, it is not enough to control certain sectors of the economy—such as the financial system, foreign trade, mining, construction, prices, and salaries— if the large producers continue to control their means of production and through this control can determine whether the economic policies of the regime succeed or fail. The control of the large producers over a substantial portion of the means of production gives them an economic power base that they can use to obstruct policies threatening their class interests.

Moreover, because of the contradictions inherent in the Sandinista's attempts to promote a mixed economy based upon a partnership of state and private capital, it appears that the Sandinistas pursued economic policies that not only transferred funds from the state to the private sector, but also undermined their credibility, disrupted the production and distribution of consumer goods, gave rise to an uncontrollable hyperinflation, and drastically reduced first the real income and then the numbers of wage earners. These conditions existed throughout the 1980s and ultimately cost the Sandinista regime the support of a majority of the population in the 1990 national elections (Vilas 1986:267).

By the end of the eighties, the Sandinistas' efforts to accommodate the economic interests of the large producers (particularly the agro-export producers) through the provision of liberal credits as well as favorable foreign exchange and interest rates, combined with their policies of financing the war effort and public services through increasing the money supply, and trying to control inflation through restricting wage and price increases—had created a monumental economic crisis. The dimensions of the crisis were greatly aggravated by the U.S. economic embargo, the Contra attacks on key economic targets, the disruption of the production process in the war zones, natural disasters, and unfavorable conditions in the international market (*Envío* 1989). One indicator of the effects of this crisis on the population is that the purchasing power of working class wages had dropped by the end of 1987 to a mere 6 percent of what it had been in 1981. This drop contributed to low labor productivity and caused wage earners to go over in massive numbers to the informal sector of the economy (Envío 1989:44).

In sum, the Sandinista regime in Nicaragua, like the Popular Unity regime in Chile, can be criticized for failing to carry out a more extensive strategy of expropriation and for pursuing economic policies that inadvertently aided the efforts of the local bourgeoisie and Washington to discredit the regime and undermine popular support for it. Moreover, it can be argued that the errors committed by these regimes can be attributed to the class alliances and class interests they attempted to serve or accommodate. In the Nicaraguan case, the mixed economy strategy followed by the Sandinistas benefited the interests of the urban middle sectors and the large private producers more than the peasantry and the country's small working class (Envío 1989:49).

The nonsocialist nature of the Sandinista project was clear to those who examined it from a Marxist perspective. Thus, Vilas concluded in the mid-1980s:

> The growth of intermediary capital and the state stimulants to productive capital call attention to the issue of the reproduction of capital within the revolutionary process and, in the broadest sense, to the character of the revolution in its current stage. Rather than a *transition to socialism*, the Sandinista revolution is entangled in a difficult *transition to development.* . . . If *socialism* implies a *proletarian* project—in the sense of the broad socialization of the means of production, of orienting the principal part of the accumulation process, and of economic incentives and benefits to the state/worker pole—it seems undeniable that this project still belongs to the possible long-term goals of the revolution. Nicaragua today continues to be an agro-export capitalist society. . . . Its predominant social bases, its political orientation, and the general sense of its development renders the Sandinista revolution currently a *popular, agrarian, and national liberation revolution,* more than a proletarian or socialist one. . . . National unity, which subordinates the resolution of class contradictions in favor of the struggle against imperialism, thus appears as the current project of the Sandinista revolution. (Vilas 1986:268–269)

Viewed from a Marxist perspective, the Sandinista revolutionary regime did not directly confront the class contradictions in Nicaraguan society, rather it sought to subordinate them to an anti-imperialist project of national liberation.

The Grenadian Case

The Grenadian revolution was somewhat similar to the Sandinista revolution in terms of its approach to the expropriation of capital. However, in the case of the People's Revolutionary Government (PRG) in Grenada, no expropriation of any significance took place. The revolutionary leadership, centered in the New Jewel Movement (NJM), pursued a strategy of mixed economic development that seems to have had at least the tacit support of the majority of the island's business community and certainly did not threaten them with expropriation or unacceptable restrictions.

As Jorge Heine has concluded, probably the most appropriate classification of the PRG is the one used by its leaders, who claimed the regime had a "socialist orientation" and was committed to a "noncapitalist path" of development.

> Many of the distinguishing features of the PRG—the nonantagonistic relationship it developed with the private sector, its reluctance to engage in widespread expropriation of landholdings, the determinedly pro-Soviet stance it took in foreign policy matters, the priority given to the island's infrastructural development—all flow from a diagnosis that identified the national-democratic stage of development as the one Grenada was undergoing. (Heine 1990:23)

The leadership of the regime perceived the country to be going through a national democratic stage of development rather than a socialist revolution per se.

In his confidential Line of March speech to the Central Committee of the NJM on September 13, 1982, Maurice Bishop argued that Grenada's revolutionary process was not socialist in nature, rather national democratic and anti-imperialist.

> The present state of the Grenada Revolution is National Democratic, anti-imperialist. . . . I did not say a socialist revolution as some comrades like to keep pretending that we have. Obviously we do not have a socialist revolution, and it is not socialist precisely because of (1) the low level of development of the productive process, and (2) our working class is too small and too politically underdeveloped. (quoted in Heine 1990:314)

There was disagreement within the leadership of the NJM over this interpretation of the regime, and Bernard Coard (who later engineered the overthrow of Bishop) is reported to have secretly threatened to resign from the Central Committee of the party after Bishop's speech (Heine 1990:314).

Although in theory the PRG was committed to a noncapitalist path of development, in practice it attempted to follow a mixed-economy strategy of development that did not threaten the private sector. According to Gordon Lewis:

> The PRG, following the early NJM policy statements, elected to follow a tripartite developmental program based on an enlarged public sector, the private sector, and a new cooperative sector. The local business groups, after all, had been an integral element of the NJM; their reward was a recognized role in the new economic regime. Both government and the local Chamber of Commerce thus worked together, with remarkable harmony when all is considered, especially in the area of tourism, centered around the construction of the planned international airport at Point Salines. The concept of the "popular front" in the anti-Gairy period was thereby carried over into the new system. (Lewis 1987:29)

Of course, there were rightist critics of the NJM regime who accused the regime of using its mixed economy approach as a disguise for a supposedly hidden socialist program. However, there does not appear to be any evidence to support this contention. To the contrary, the regime's leftist critics argued that "the PRG was really a petit-bourgeois reformist government not seriously interested in moving forward to the necessary stage of radical socialism" (see Heine 1990:24; and Lewis 1987:29).

Although Gordon Lewis does not agree with this criticism of the reformist nature of the PRG, his own characterization of the regime tends to support it. For example, he argues that the regime's policies were similar to those of the "moderate social-welfare economies" in Europe.

> Looked at in comparative terms—that is, within the general framework of British, Scandinavian, Eastern European, and Caribbean economies— it would seem to any serious observer that the Grenadian model, as far as it went in four brief years, would have to be placed more in the British-Scandinavian camp than in any other. Its main programs were those of the "moderate" social-welfare economies, where the modern state has increasingly taken over responsibility for all those services vital to the public welfare. . . . Even the Grenadian policy of putting the people to work through mass mobilization institutions was not too different, in

principle, from the U.S. Civilian Conservation Corps of the old Rooseveltian New Deal; and even its military mobilization of the people, "the Revolution armed," was again not too different in principle from the state policy of limited and obligatory armed service for young males as in, to take only one example, Sweden. In this sense, the Grenada model was more "social welfarism" than socialism proper, not unlike the policies of the left-wing Michael Manley government in Jamaica in 1972–80. (Lewis 1987:28–29)

If the policies of the PRG were indeed similar to those of the social welfare programs of the social democratic governments of Western Europe, then it would seem that the PRG can be appropriately characterized as a reformist regime, in spite of its revolutionary appearance.

At any rate, in place of an explicit socialist program aimed at expropriating capital and eliminating capitalist relations of production, the PRG sought to develop Grenada's stagnant economy through expanding public investments, increasing public services, and establishing new state enterprises. As Lewis stated:

> The four years of the revolution were quite simply, a heroic effort in social and economic reconstruction and, at times, transformation. All of the available sources . . . testify to the personal dedication and collective enthusiasm that went into that effort, now only too easily forgotten by all of the counterrevolutionary, reactionary forces only concerned, after October 1983, to vilify and denigrate the revolution. . . . New state agencies were set up to plan and administer, among other things, the thirty state farms inherited from the Gairy regime, new agro-industrial processing plants, and the new fishing and fish-processing industry. The new Grenada Development Bank, with funds being lent at easy terms to small and medium farmers and business-people with the aim of financing any project, was designed to increase production and employment. . . . while the new publicly owned National Commercial Bank established a general policy of lending half its funds to development projects and half to the established commercial sector. (Lewis 1987:27)

The reformist nature of the PRG's economic program as well as the new state financing system that it established managed to receive the financial support of a wide array of foreign donors—including the World Bank and the International Monetary Fund (Lewis 1987:27)!

Although, it is clear that the Grenadian revolution—in contrast to the Cuban revolution, the Nicaraguan revolution, and the UP regime in Chile—did not seek to expropriate on any scale the material base of the country's small capitalist class, the radical populist and anti-imperialist character of this regime were perceived as a threat by the United States government and by important elements of the neocolonial bourgeoisie in the English-speaking Caribbean, particularly in Barbados and Jamaica (Lewis 1987:86–99). This perception helps to explain why the United States invaded Grenada and put an end to the PRG, after the pretext for invasion was provided by a split in the leadership of the New Jewel Movement and the subsequent assassination of Prime Minister Maurice Bishop.

Conclusion

The Cuban revolution stands out as the only case in Latin America and the Caribbean where a rapid and full-scale expropriation of capital has taken place and where the bourgeoisie as a class have been eliminated. Cuba also provides the only case in the region where a revolutionary regime committed to socialism has survived despite the efforts of a counterrevolutionary movement and the U.S. government to overthrow it. The evidence seems quite clear that without a rapid and full-scale expropriation of capital, no socialist regime—and probably no revolutionary regime of any kind—can expect to survive in Latin America and the Caribbean. However, the full-scale expropriation of capital cannot in itself guarantee the survival of such a regime. Clearly, widespread popular support for the regime as well as the military and economic assistance provided by the Soviet Union have been critical factors in the survival of Cuba's socialist regime. This support and assistance is why the changes in the Soviet Union under Gorbachev, particularly the economic reforms and the USSR's changing relations with the West, have created a precarious situation for the Cuban regime. Without the economic assistance that the Soviets have provided Cuba and the military protection that the Soviet Union has provided, Cuba's socialist project is seriously threatened.

In sum, the expropriation of the capital of the large private producers appears to be an absolute necessity for the survival of any revolutionary regime in Latin America and the Caribbean that seriously seeks to bring about major transformations in the existing socioeconomic order. Moreover, it is clearly a necessary condition for the transition to socialism because unless the capital of the bourgeoisie is expropriated, it will block the socialization of the economy and seek to undermine the revolutionary process. The historical evidence indicates that this lesson should be taken into account in any future efforts to bring about revolutionary transformations in the region.

7

The Socialization
of Agriculture

The transformation of scattered private property arising from individual labor into capitalist private property is a process, incomparably more protracted, violent, and difficult, than the transformation of capitalist private property into socialized property. In the former case, we have the expropriation of the mass of the people by a few usurpers; in the latter, we have the expropriation of a few usurpers by the mass of the people.

—Karl Marx

Marx on the Socialization of Agriculture

In the *Manifesto of the Communist Party*, Marx and Engels included a list of measures that they thought would be taken by the victorious proletariat once they had seized power. The first measure was "the abolition of property in land" (Marx and Engels 1972:52). Also included in this list were the establishment of industrial armies in agriculture, the combination of agriculture with manufacturing, and the gradual abolition of the distinctions between town and country through a more equitable distribution of the population. Thus, it is clear that the founders of Marxism believed that the transition to socialism would involve a radical transformation of agriculture (see Harris 1978).

Certain critics of Marxism allege that Marx, and therefore Marxists, view the peasantry as an abomination, an obstacle to the progressive development of human society, and are enemies of the peasantry who are anxious to see them disappear as rapidly as possible. Perhaps the most known of these critics, David Mitrany, supports this criticism by citing selective passages from Marx's writings in which Marx used terms such as "rural idiots" and "potatoes in a sack" to refer to reactionary elements among the peasantry (Mitrany 1951:23–28). A more recent critic, Michael Duggett (1975), claims that Marx was ambivalent in his writings about the peasantry and that the main problem lies in the fact that Marx's main categories cannot adequately explain the nature and conditions of the peasantry as a class. However, a close reading of Marx's works and those of Engels, Lenin, and Mao, reveals that these criticisms are largely unfounded.

In Volumes 1 and 3 of *Capital*, Marx analyzed the conditions of the peasantry in both precapitalist and capitalist societies. He examined the manner in which the peasants are exploited by capital and transformed into wage laborers and capitalist farmers. Nowhere does he provide any basis for the accusation that he is "against the peasants." For example, in discussing the forcible expulsion of the peasantry from their lands and their transformation into an urban proletariat, Marx stated:

> Thus were the agricultural people, first forcibly expropriated from the soil, driven from their homes, turned into vagabonds, and then whipped, branded, and tortured by laws grotesquely terrible, into the discipline necessary for the wage system. (Marx 1967, 1:737)

This and other passages show that Marx viewed with compassion the plight of the peasantry under the destructive forces of capitalist development.

Moreover, it is also clear from a careful reading of his works that Marx's derogatory references regarding the peasantry were directed at the reactionary elements of the peasantry in certain historical situations and *not* the peasantry in general or in all historical conjunctures. Thus, in his analysis of the peasantry under the Bonapartist regime in France, Marx made a clear distinction:

> But let there be no misunderstanding. The Bonapartist dynasty represents not the revolutionary, but the conservative peasant, not the peasant that strikes out beyond the conditions of his social existence, the small holding, but rather the peasant who wants to consolidate this holding, not the country folk who, linked up with the towns, want to overthrow the old order, but on the contrary those who, in stupefied seclusion within the old order, want to see themselves and their small holdings saved by the ghost of the empire. (Marx in Marx and Engels 1972:172–173)

As this excerpt from Marx's essay "The Eighteenth Brumaire of Louis Bonaparte" reveals, Marx was aware that at least certain elements, if not the entire peasantry, could be a revolutionary force against the established order. In fact, he concluded his analysis of the French peasantry with the statement: "The interests of the peasants are no longer in accord with, but in opposition to the interests of the bourgeoisie, to capital. Hence the peasants find their natural ally and leader in the urban proletariat" (Marx and Engels 1972:175).

Lenin developed a much more elaborate analysis of the peasantry in "backward" countries such as Russia, and at the Second Congress of the Communist International, he spoke at length of the peasantry's essential role in the national revolutions of the underdeveloped countries. However, he always conceived of the peasantry as a revolutionary class that would be led by the revolutionary proletariat. And in the more backward countries, he warned that the "hold of small agricultural production . . . would inevitably lend particular strength and tenacity to the deepest of petty bourgeois prejudices, to the national egoism, and national narrowness" (Lenin 1937, 10:145).

Mao went well beyond Lenin's theoretical formulations on the peasantry. For Mao, in the particular conditions of prerevolutionary Chinese society, the peasantry were the "main revolutionary class" and the "motor of the Chinese revolution," under the direction of the proletariat, of course. In his writings, Mao made an important contribution to Marxist theory on the differentiation of the rural masses and the revolutionary potential of the poor peasantry in social formations dominated by imperialism and feudalism (Mao 1971).

Latin American Marxists' Views
on the Agrarian Question

A number of Marxist scholars interested in the peasantry in Latin America have attempted to utilize the theoretical formulations of Marx, Engels, Lenin, and Mao to examine and interpret the conditions of the peasantry within the present Latin American social formations. One of the more notable examples of this effort is the work of Pierre Beaucage, a French-Canadian Marxist scholar who has done considerable research in Mexico. Beaucage argues that the rural capitalists extract surplus value from the peasants by paying them prices that are below the value of their products, selling them commodities at prices above their value, loaning them money at high rates of interest, and renting them land in return for a substantial proportion of the produce that they cultivate on this rented land. Citing Marx on this question, Beaucage concludes:

If we summarize the position of Marx with regard to the economic characteristics of the peasantry as a social class inserted in a capitalist social formation, we can say that we are dealing essentially with an exploited class, but one that is exploited through different mechanisms than the working class. (Beaucage 1975:51)

He asserts that the contradictions between the small peasant producer and capitalists are such that the peasants increasingly fall under the control of commercial and finance capitalists because their small-scale production is incapable of withstanding the pressures of the market and the competition of larger commercial agriculture.

Marxists such as Roger Bartra have argued that the dissolution of the peasantry and the proletarianization of the rural population are quite advanced in countries such as Mexico. In the 1970s he claimed that 60 percent of the economically active population in the rural areas of Mexico constitute a landless, wage-earning rural proletariat and another 33 percent are semiproletarians (Bartra 1974:171). However, others say that even though more than half of the economically active population in agriculture do not own any land, the majority of this group have access to land through their family ties or through sharecropping and tenant farming so even if they are employed as wage earners, they cannot be considered rural proletarians. This position is taken by Gustavo Esteva, who claims that rural wage earners "retain their quality of peasants, in virtue of their ties with the peasant form of existence of their rural communities" (Esteva 1978:709).

Luisa Paré has attempted to reconcile these conflicting perspectives on the proletarianization of the rural population. For example, in reference to Mexico, she states:

> Given that we are dealing with a process, proletarianization extends from pre-proletarian situations . . . to the complete separation of the worker from the means of production and his subsistence from primarily the sale of his labor. Due to the degree of unemployment in Mexico and the dynamic of the process of expulsion of the peasantry from the land as a result of competition, land takeovers, or simply the demographic explosion, the use of the term depeasantization appears to be necessary and useful so as *not* to confuse the lack of land or the impoverishment of the peasantry with effective proletarianization. To speak of proletarianization it is necessary that the salary of the one who sells his labor be the principal base of his reproduction. (Paré 1977:54–55)

According to Paré, the process of proletarianization, as opposed to depeasantization (the separation of the peasantry from exclusive dependence upon the land for their subsistence), has been relatively slow in most of Latin America in comparison to what happened in the countries that are today highly industrialized. As a means of self-defense against unemployment, wage earners maintain their ties with a family unit of production or rural community where, in spite of the fact they do not own any land, they can participate through sharecropping or working with relatives in agricultural production.

Paré contends that capitalist development has maintained noncapitalist forms of production in the countryside while at the same time it has incorporated ever larger numbers of rural inhabitants into wage-earning employment. Consequently, an agricultural proletariat is being created that is heterogeneous in terms of the different categories of wage earners it encompasses and that reflects the slow process of dissolution of the peasantry that characterizes capitalist development in Latin America (Paré 1977:51).

By analyzing the objective conditions behind the subjective identification of the rural population with the peasant form of social existence, Paré is able to provide important insights into the possibilities of mobilizing the different elements of the rural population in a revolutionary socialist direction. She makes it clear, however, that this kind of analysis can only be of real value if the analyst avoids a mechanical application of Marxist theory to the contemporary situation in Latin America.

> It is the responsibility of the revolutionary movement and the proletarian vanguard to distinguish between different strata of the rural population, to reflect on the actual and potential ideological significance of their demand for land, and to find a means of transforming this demand into a revolutionary demand for the expropriation of all the means of production. At the same time it is necessary to avoid the possible trade unionist deviations of agrarian syndicalism, and admit that in eminently peasant societies, it is not possible to erase with the stroke of a pen the millions of rural petty bourgeoisie who are undergoing the process of proletarianization or at least of pauperization, particularly when they have no possibilities of accumulation. (Paré 1977:233)

Paré reminds the Left that the militant involvement of the rural masses in revolutionary movements has almost always been around their demand for land rather than their interests as wage earners, and that land seizures have generally been carried out by land-hungry, rural, day laborers who have been radicalized by their poor working conditions and their inability to survive solely on the basis of wage-earning employment. These facts by themselves are an important argument against stereotypical thinking in which the demand for land is considered as reactionary and petty-bourgeois and the condition of being dependent upon wage-earning employment is assumed to indicate proletarian class consciousness (Paré 1977:232).

For Marxists, the analysis of the agrarian question in Latin America is aimed at contributing to the base of scientific knowledge upon which a correct strategy can be developed to guide the transition to socialism. From a Marxist perspective, correct revolutionary strategy must be based on the scientific analysis of the existing social reality and in particular the actual state of the class struggle. Within this context, it is absolutely essential to determine who are the friends and enemies of the revolution, that is, the classes and class fractions that can be mobilized to struggle against the existing social order (Harnecker 1975:202–215).

Class Differentiation Among the Rural Population

Engels's essay "The Peasant Question in France and Germany" (Marx and Engels 1972:633–650), serves as an early example of Marxist analysis of the agrarian question with a view toward determining (a) which elements of the rural population could be won over to the revolutionary struggle against capitalism and (b) the conditions under which their political support could be gained by the revolutionary proletariat. In this regard, it is important to note that Engels took great pains to distinguish the different elements of the rural population:

> The rural population to which we can address ourselves consists of quite different parts, which vary greatly with the various regions. In the West of Germany, as in France and Belgium, there prevails the small-scale cultivation of small-holding peasants, the majority of whom own and the minority of whom rent their parcels of land. In the Northwest—in Lower Saxony and Schleswig-Holstein—we have a preponderance of big and middle peasants who cannot do without male and female servants and even day laborers. The same is true of Bavaria. In Prussia east of the Elbe and in Mecklenburg, we have the region of the big landed estates and large-scale cultivation with hinds, cotters, and day laborers, and in between small and middle peasants in relatively unimportant and steadily decreasing numbers. (Marx and Engels 1972:634)

Thus, Engels thought it was necessary to take into account the relatively complex class structure of rural Western European society in order to develop a correct strategy for mobilizing the rural masses in support of the revolutionary struggle for socialism.

In answering his own question as to which of the various elements of the rural population could be won over to the revolutionary movement, Engels singled out the small peasants as "the critical case that decides the entire question." The reason for this was his conviction that no revolutionary transformation could be accomplished against the will of the small peasants because they represented such a large proportion of the population and because their past opposition to the revolutionary struggle had been a crucial factor responsible for its setbacks (for example, the French peasantry's support of the reactionary regime of Louis Bonaparte). Engels believed that it was possible to win the support of the small peasants because the development of capitalism was increasingly destroying their means of existence and forcing them into poverty (and ultimately into the proletariat). However, he warned against trying to win their support by promising to preserve their small holdings, arguing instead that they would have to be persuaded that "we can preserve their houses and fields for them only by transforming them into cooperative property operated cooperatively." Engels also proposed that the small peasant should be promised that "we shall do everything possible to make his lot more bearable, to facilitate his transition to the cooperative should he decide to do so, and even to make it possible for him to remain on his small-holding for a protracted length of time to think the matter over . . ." (Marx and Engels 1972:645–646).

As for the other elements of the rural population, Marx and Engels categorized the rural workers or farm laborers as the "natural allies" of the urban proletariat as their conditions of exploitation were so similar to those of the industrial workers. Thus, in referring to the large estates on which these rural workers were employed, Engels stated:

> Only the big landed estates present a perfectly simple case. Here we are confronted by rural proletarians in masses and our task is clear. As soon as our party is in possession of political power it has simply to expropriate the big landed proprietors just like the manufacturers in industry. . . . The big estates thus restored to the community are to be turned over by us to the rural workers who are already cultivating them and are to be organized into cooperatives. (Marx and Engels 1972:649)

And in the case of the middle and big peasants, Engels made it clear that it was the obligation of the workers' party to fight for the interests of the servants and day laborers employed by these more successful peasants. As for the big and middle peasants themselves, Engels didn't leave much hope that they would support the revolutionary movement, except in the case of those middle peasants living among small peasants and faced with succumbing to the competition of large-scale capitalist agriculture (Marx and Engels 1972:647–648).

The Soviet Case

Like Engels, Lenin theorized that it was necessary to carefully analyze the rural population in order to determine which elements could be won over to the revolutionary struggle (Lenin 1937, 1:389–453). On the basis of his study of the particular conditions of Russian society prior to the Bolshevik revolution, he developed the now famous "two-stage" strategy for winning support for the revolutionary struggle from the different elements of the rural population. This strategy consisted of: (a) first struggling with all the peasants (poor, middle, and rich) against the feudal large landowners, and then (b) struggling with the poor peasants against the *kulaks* (rich peasants).

Because of the semifeudal character of much of rural Russia, Lenin reasoned that the principal class antagonism was between all the peasants and the large (feudal) landlords. However, with the liquidation of the large landlords, Lenin made it clear that the antagonism arising from the differentiation within the peasantry would place the poor peasants and proletariat in direct conflict with the *kulaks*. According to Lenin's analysis, an alliance between the proletariat and all the peasants was necessary and appropriate only during the stage of what he referred to as the "bourgeois democratic revolution," but once this revolution was won it would be necessary for the proletariat to lead the poor peasantry in a struggle against both the urban and rural bourgeoisie in order to carry out the proletarian socialist revolution (Lenin 1937, 3:289–301).

Confronted with the immense task of socializing Russia's predominately peasant society, Lenin tried to follow the ideas of Marx and Engels by emphasizing the gradual cooperativization of the peasantry. This is revealed in his essay "On Co-operation," written one year before his death and at the time of the Soviet regime's New Economic Policy (NEP). It is important to note that Lenin thought that the process of cooperativization among the peasantry would "take a whole historical epoch" of at least one to two decades and that it could not be achieved "without universal literacy, without a proper degree of efficiency, without training the population sufficiently to acquire the habit of book-reading," and without a cultural revolution in the countryside (Lenin 1976:692).

However, the Soviet regime apparently had neither the political support nor the organizational capacity to succeed in the voluntary cooperativization of the peasantry under the NEP (MacEwan 1981:41–42; Mandel 1968:549–560). As a result, from 1930 to 1937, the regime resorted to the forced collectivization (that is, statization) of the country's peasant-based agricultural sector. It forced the peasants to join large-scale, state-managed cooperatives (Deere 1986:105–106; Mandel 1968:553–555).

The Chinese Case

The Soviet experience can be contrasted with that of the socialization of agriculture in revolutionary China. According to Mao, without the socialization of agriculture consolidating socialism in China would be impossible (Mao 1971:382). Due to the fact that the Chinese Communist Party came to power after a long revolutionary struggle based in the countryside, the revolutionary regime was able to rely upon its political support among the peasantry and its administrative experience gained in the liberated areas it had governed prior to the seizure of power at the national level. Thus, it was able to mobilize the country's immense peasant population into agricultural cooperatives and then later into more collectivized, multifunctional communes—but at a great social cost to the rural population (Amin 1981:64–71, 102).

By the time Mao died in 1976, it was clear that the collectivization of Chinese agriculture had failed to increase per capita production of the most critical crops, such as grain. In most parts of China, living standards remained at a subsistence level in the countryside. Most critical accounts attribute the failure of collectivization to the "commandism" that characterized the process (for example, see Dean 1989). In other words, because of the highly authoritarian manner in which it was carried out, the rural population was not given sufficient time to make the transition, they were not given adequate preparation for entering into a collectivized production process, and serious errors in production decisions were made by party bureaucrats who failed to consult the actual producers.

Between 1978 and the mid-1980s, the commune system in Chinese agriculture was completely abandoned and Chinese agriculture was partially privatized. This change restored the family farm as the basic unit of production and permitted the peasants to sell their surplus produce in free markets, after meeting the state quotas for certain critical products such as grain (Smith 1989:30). This semiprivatization of agriculture has been an important component of the post-Mao economic reforms introduced by the party leadership. During this period, the collectivization attempt was criticized for having been premature and unfounded. Even leftist critics of the regime argued that the forces of production in the countryside were too underdeveloped and the cultural level of the majority of the rural population still too traditional to sustain this degree of socialization of the relations of production (Chan, Rosen, and Unger 1985:186–187).

Most indications are that the reforms gave rise to dramatic increases in agricultural production. Grain production is said to have increased by one-third between 1978 and 1984, and peasant incomes appear to have doubled on the average for the years 1978–1982 (Smith 1989:31). One of the main reasons for the increase in productivity and incomes is that the peasants are no longer burdened by a large number of cadres that they have to feed.

On the other hand, the state continues to pay the peasants below-market prices for the products that they must sell to the government. In addition, because of the inflation created by the reforms, prices continue to rise for the basic inputs, such as fertilizer, that are needed by the peasants. This situation caused production in the late 1980s to fall sharply and millions of peasants to abandon farming and go in search of jobs in the cities (Smith 1989:32; Chan 1990:4).

Some leftist critics have argued that the regime's dismantling of the communes and privatization of agriculture has resulted in the systematic undermining of the entire socialist system developed since 1949. Moreover, they claim that the rapid liquidation of public assets since the beginning of the 1980s has led to the enrichment, at the expense of the rest of the rural population, of those individuals and families who were in a position to take advantage of the opportunities afforded by the reforms. For example, William Hinton, the author of the classic study on the Chinese village of Fanshen, has written:

> When the time came to distribute collective assets, people with influence and connections—cadres, their relatives, friends and cronies—were able to buy, at massive discounts, the tractors, trucks, wells, pumps, processing equipment, and other productive property that the collectives had accumulated over decades through the hard labor of all members. Not only did the buyers manage to set low prices for these capital assets (often one-third or less of their true value), but they often bought them with easy credit from state banks and then, in the end, often failed to pay what they promised. It is doubtful if, in the history of the world, any privileged group ever acquired more for less. The scale of these transactions and the depth of the injury done to the average coop member boggles the mind. (Hinton 1989:20–21)

Hinton also notes that the privatization reforms in the rural areas resulted in the creation of minuscule land holdings, the overgrazing of grasslands, reckless deforestation, the deterioration of the infrastructure, usurious money-lending, begging, prostitution, widespread official corruption, accelerating inflation, and growing public dissatisfaction.

The Cuban Case

The Cuban case is a contrast to those of China and the Soviet Union. In Cuba, because the agricultural sector contained mostly large sugar plantations and cattle ranches (many of which were owned by U.S. capitalists) and because a very sizable proportion of the rural population served as a wage-earning agricultural proletariat on these large units

TABLE 7.1 Ownership of Cultivable Land in Seven Nations According to Organization of Production (in percentages)

Country	State Farms	Prod. Coops	Service Coops	Peasants and Peasant Holdings	Capitalist Farms
Vietnam (1975)	5	90	—	—	5
Cuba (1983)	80	11	—	—	9
Algeria (1980)	27	14	—	—	59
Ethiopia (1981)	4	—	3	—	93
Mozambique (1982)	4	—	1	—	95
Angola (1980)	12	—	2	—	86
Nicaragua (1983)	24	—	6	16	54

Source: Richard Fagen, Carmen Deere, and José Luis Coraggio (eds.), *Transition and Development: Problems of Third World Socialism* (New York: Monthly Review Press, 1986), 110. Reprinted by permission of the Monthly Review Foundation.

of production, the revolutionary government was able to carry out in only a few years a radical agrarian reform program that ended up placing most of Cuban agriculture under the control of large-scale state farms (see Table 7.1). Approximately 80 percent of the arable land in Cuba is owned by state farms, 11 percent by peasant production cooperatives, and 9 percent by individual peasant families (Deere, 1986:110). As a result, Cuba has the highest percentage of agricultural land under direct state administration of any country in the world (Deere 1986:136).

The Cubans emphasized state farms over other forms of agricultural organization because: (1) there was an absence of widespread popular pressure among the rural population for land redistribution; (2) the landless rural laborers that worked the large estates and sugar plantations were not interested in working them as cooperatives, rather they were interested in improving their incomes and working conditions as wage earners; (3) the revolutionary government wanted to maintain centralized control over the food supply because there was an excess demand over supply; and (4) the revolutionary regime's commitment to social equality made it reluctant to promote cooperatives because it feared there would be too much inequality between them due to local differences in land, material resources, and the skills of their potential members (MacEwan 1981:50–51). Moreover, according to Vice-President Carlos Rafael Rodríguez, the revolutionary leadership believed that direct state control over the majority of agricultural production would serve as "a guarantee" that Cuba's economy would "not be dependent on the will and actions of the individual peasants," as it is in most other socialist countries (Benjamin, Collins, and Scott 1984:93).

The Cuban agrarian reform program expropriated the large farmers' holdings in stages. Initially, the government had wanted to go slow in doing this so that it would not have to take control over more land than it had the organizational resources to administer. However, food shortages and the opposition of the large farmers to the revolutionary regime forced the government to accelerate the expropriation process. As a result, by the end of 1963, the state had control over 63 percent of the cultivated land in the country (Benjamin 1989:96).

It should be noted, however, that during the first years of the revolutionary regime, the government did redistribute land to the country's small sector of peasant farmers. Former sharecroppers, tenant farmers, and squatters were given title to the land that they had cultivated prior to the revolution. This action increased the number of small farmers in the country from about 45,000 to 110,000 (Benjamin 1989:94). Thus, the small farmers benefited from the first stage of the agrarian reform as they were freed from having to pay rent and they were able to increase their income as a result of the new government policies that provided low-interest loans, guaranteed fixed prices for their crops, and gave them access to free health care, education, and special stores with low-priced goods. The government also set up the National Association of Small Farmers (ANAP) and gave this organization the responsibility for coordinating production and allocating credit.

Since that time, the government has bought out a number of small farmers and tried to persuade the rest to voluntarily incorporate themselves into producer cooperatives. To encourage the small farmers to do this, the government offers them preferential access to equipment, credit, reduced taxes, membership in the national social security system, and the provision of construction materials so that they can build new housing, schools, day care facilities, laundries, and so on (Deere 1986:135). It is important to note, however, that Fidel Castro and other Cuban leaders have promised the small farmers that they will never be forced to join a cooperative or give up their farms. Since three decades have now gone by, it appears that the government has followed faithfully the course advocated by Engels, in contrast to the Soviet and Chinese cases.

On the other hand, the small farmers cannot sell their land except to the government and they must sell a fixed quota of what they produce to the government for the prices fixed by the latter. Moreover, farms can only be inherited by the offspring if they agree to operate them. They cannot be sold or transferred without government permission. Thus, private ownership of land is restricted, and these restrictions over time will reduce the size of the private sector in agriculture.

During the early 1980s, as part of the Soviet-style economic reforms that were introduced during this period, the government permitted the development of a free market in which the small private farmers and cooperatives could sell their surplus produce after fulfilling their contracted amounts with the government (Benjamin, Collins, and Scott 1984:98–99). This free market encouraged a number of capitalistic tendencies, including profiteering, pilfering state farms to obtain inputs for market-oriented production, the reemergence of sharecropping and other forms of illegal land use, a deviation away from increasing socialization of production, and increasing income inequality in the countryside. The government was thus prompted to terminate the free market and related reform measures.

The Nicaraguan Agrarian Reform

Revolutionary Nicaragua's experience in the transformation of agriculture was quite different from that of Cuba, the Soviet Union, and China. The new revolutionary regime's immediate confiscation of the land owned by the Somoza family and their associates placed about 20 percent of the country's arable land under the control of the revolutionary state (see Collins 1986:31). For the most part, these confiscated properties were turned into large state farms; a small portion was distributed to rural workers or poor peasants so that it could be farmed collectively in state-organized cooperatives. Approximately 20 percent of all cultivable land came under state ownership during the high point of the agrarian reform program's first and most collectivist phase (1982–1984), and another 11 percent of the land was placed in the hands of government-organized and directed producer cooperatives (Gianotten, de Wit, and Montoya 1987:38). However, *over 60 percent* of the cultivable land in the country remained under private capitalist or peasant ownership; and another 15 percent was owned by individual small farmers in loosely organized service cooperatives (Escoto and Amador 1991:21).

In essence, this first stage of the revolutionary regime's agrarian reform established the state as a major agricultural producer and terminated the predominance of large capital in the Nicaraguan countryside. However, it did *not* eliminate the large capitalist producers. In fact, they retained control over the majority of the country's most important agroexport farms and agroindustries (Collins 1986:39–50; Harris and Vilas 1985:41–46). The new revolutionary regime invited them to participate as partners in the development of the country's new mixed economy and guaranteed that their property rights, profit-making, and access to government credit would be respected by the regime.

Most of the large producers chose not to cooperate with the revolutionary state and to sabotage the regime's economic policies (Collins 1986:44–45; Harris and Vilas 1985:51–53). Originally, the government's agrarian reform program emphasized reactivating agroexport production on the large privately owned estates, concentrating government invest-

TABLE 7.2   Nicaragua: Ownership of Land Distributed Under Agrarian Reform, 1981–1985 (in percentages)

Period	Small-Medium Producers and Cooperatives	State Farms
1981–1982	30	70
1983	35	65
1984	43	57
1985	95	5

Source: Joseph Collins, *Nicaragua: What Difference Could a Revolution Make?* (New York: Grove Press, 1986), 285.

ments in the state sector, and encouraging the small and medium producers to form cooperatives (Collins 1986:155–156). But as U.S.-backed counterrevolutionary attacks and propaganda efforts increased in areas of the country dominated by small and medium producers, the agrarian reform was reoriented toward increased distribution of land to individual peasant producers, without any conditions that they join cooperatives. In this way, the regime attempted to assure many peasants in the war zones that their lands would not, as the counterrevolutionary forces alleged, be taken from them nor would they be forced to form cooperatives or work for state farms (Collins 1986:157).

As Table 7.2 reveals, a good portion of the land distributed in the late 1980s to landless peasants was taken from the state sector through the dismemberment of some of the large state farms (Collins 1986:248). Where state farm lands were not sufficient, the government negotiated with large private producers to purchase their land for cash or to provide them with state-owned land of comparable quality in another part of the country. Thus, the socialization of agriculture was set back, and a process of peasantization and small-scale private production of basic food products was encouraged.

It is important to note that one of the reasons the revolutionary regime in Nicaragua was originally reluctant to distribute land to a significant number of individual peasant producers was the government's fears that this would aggravate the already existing labor shortage in the agroexport sector (Collins 1986:153–154). In other words, it was feared that this would divert a large proportion of the rural labor force into individual, small-scale farming and make it difficult for the large agricultural units to obtain sufficient laborers to harvest the country's agroexports. Serious labor shortages for the agroexport harvests have been a continuing problem in Nicaragua, and in an effort to deal with this problem the revolutionary government raised the wages for many agricultural workers so that they would be comparable with those of the country's small number of skilled industrial workers (Collins 1986:254).

This action was also aimed at narrowing the gap between rural and urban wages and reducing the differences between those who live in the towns and those in the countryside. The problem of labor shortages in agriculture and the contradictions between town and countryside have appeared in other cases of transition. For example, in Cuba, labor shortages in agriculture have been a chronic problem. This problem stems from the gap between urban and rural conditions in Cuba, although the government has pursued policies aimed at balancing the development of these two sectors (MacEwan 1981:214). Mechanization of the harvesting of agroexports as well as the mobilization of voluntary work brigades for the harvests have been the main responses to the labor shortages in Cuban agriculture. These measures were replicated to some degree in revolutionary Nicaragua. Achieving some sort of balance between the urban and rural sectors in terms of labor incentives and policy priorities appears to be the key to resolving this problem (see MacEwan 1981:220–221; and FitzGerald 1986).

The Chilean Agrarian Reform

In Chile in the 1960s the Christian Democratic government of President Eduardo Frei initiated a moderate agrarian reform program aimed at breaking up the large estates and giving land to landless peasants, who would then farm the land in cooperatives. However, thousands of large agricultural estates called *latifundios* remained in the hands of their former owners when the Allende government was elected in 1970 (Smirnow 1979:49). The large landowners retained the equivalent of 80 irrigated hectares (about 200 acres) of their former estates, along with all the equipment, buildings, and animals on these lands. As a result, many of the large landowners were able to use these resources to continue exercising control over all or most of their former lands and members of the rural population who had formerly worked on their estates.

Under Allende, the implementation of the agrarian reform program was accelerated and a large number of land seizures took place as the political consciousness and mobilization of the poor peasantry and the agricultural semiproletariat increased (Smirnow 1979:49). In fact, an intense class struggle developed in the countryside as the poor peasants, farm workers, and share croppers seized the land and the landowners resorted to various forms of resistance, including sabotage, violence, and illegal transfer of produce and equipment out of the country.

By 1972, the large estates had practically disappeared, but the government's program favored the small and middle peasants over the rural proletariat (see Table 7.3). This is clearly revealed in Cristóbal Kay's analysis of the Popular Unity government's agrarian policy (Kay 1978).

TABLE 7.3   Chile: Changes in Land Distribution, 1965–1972[a] (in percentages)

Number of Hectares[b]	Total Farms		Total Area	
	1965	1972	1965	1972
5 or Less	81.4	79.3	9.7	9.7
5–20	11.5	11.3	12.7	13.0
20–40	3.0	3.3	9.5	11.6
40–60	1.3	2.5	7.1	14.5
60–80	0.8	1.6	5.7	12.8
More than 80	2.8	0.1	55.3	2.9
Reformed sector	0.0	1.9	0.0	35.5

[a]Covers only 19 of 25 provinces in the country.
[b]Basic irrigated hectares (1 hectare = 2.47 acres).

Source: Carlos Mistral, Chile: Del Triumfo Popular al Golpe Fascista (Mexico City: Ediciones Era, 1974), 51.

An essential issue that the UP's agrarian policy had to settle was not only how to mobilize peasant groups and which ones were easier to mobilize initially but also which would actively struggle for the seizure of power and for a socialist transformation in the countryside. One of the crucial weaknesses of the UP's agrarian policy was to center its mobilization and land distribution policy on the same peasant groups as the Christian Democrats; in so doing, the UP failed to incorporate those peasant groups that should have been the backbone of a socialist strategy due to their greater revolutionary potential (Kay 1978:128). Kay argues that the UP failed to take into account the massive proletarianization of the peasantry that had taken place in Chile and that it should have relied primarily upon the rural proletariat, instead of the middle and small peasants, to carry out a genuine socialist transformation of Chilean agriculture. Kay's analysis of the Chilean situation supports and is, in turn, supported by the early analyses of Marx and Engels concerning the proletarianization of the rural population and the importance of the rural proletariat as an ally of the urban proletariat in the revolutionary struggle for socialism.

Conclusion

Past experience as well as Marxist theory indicate that the socialization of agriculture under Third World conditions requires a careful analysis of the relations of production and the class structure in the countryside. The capitalist transformation of agriculture in many Third World societies has proceeded slowly, and small-scale peasant agriculture tends to be present. Depending upon the extent to which capitalism has transformed agriculture, there may be a sizable stratum of small peasant producers and/or a semiproletarianized stratum of the rural population with strong ties to peasant subsistence farming. The larger these sectors, the less class basis there is likely to be for the rapid socialization of agriculture. Unless the agricultural sector has been largely commercialized and concentrated in large units of production and the rural population has been largely proletarianized (for example, as in Cuba), the rapid socialization of agriculture in the form of the establishment of collective farms cannot and should not be attempted. Voluntary cooperativization, promoted by material incentives and technical assistance rather than coercive measures, is the appropriate approach to the socialist transformation of peasant-based agriculture.

8
Development of the Forces of Production

Socialism and Underdevelopment

The prevailing Marxist perspective is that unless underdeveloped societies undergoing the transition to socialism rapidly develop their forces of production (both human and material resources), they can only aspire to a "socialism of poverty" (Mandel 1968:610). This perspective is based upon the premise that the forces of production in these societies are so inadequate that they can neither provide the abundance of goods needed to satisfy the basic needs of the population nor make possible the full development of the intellectual and physical abilities of the individual members of the population (Mandel 1968:610–611). Therefore the transition to socialism must involve what has been called "socialist accumulation" (Mandel 1968:611; Castaños 1977:67–76). Generally speaking, this accumulation involves setting aside a substantial proportion of the national income for investment in the expansion and development of the forces of production.

In the Soviet case, accumulation to develop the productive forces resulted in what E. A. Preobrazhensky described as "primitive socialist accumulation" (see Bellis 1979:167). In essence, such accumulation entailed the revolutionary state's extraction of a portion of the surplus product produced by the agricultural population and its use in the expansion of the Soviet Union's industrial sector. This transfer was accomplished through a variety of means including the state's requisitioning of food supplies from the peasantry, the establishment of conditions under which manufactured goods were exchanged for agricultural products at terms unfavorable to the rural population, and the imposition by the state of a tax-in-kind on the agricultural surplus produced by the peasantry (see

Mandel 1968:548–560). In the long run, accumulation under the Soviet regime took place through the forced collectivization of the peasantry and the imposition of a turnover tax that was added to the prices of both the agricultural and manufactured goods consumed by the whole population.

Many contemporary Marxists, such as Ernest Mandel, have criticized the harsh measures used by the Soviet regime to promote accumulation and develop the country's forces of production. Mandel has argued that such measures are not necessary in underdeveloped Third World countries because, among other reasons, the total surplus product in these societies represents a higher proportion of the gross national product than in industrialized countries (Mandel 1968:619).

Mandel claims that a new socialist regime in these societies should be able to increase significantly the accumulation of the surplus product for development purposes by simply expropriating: (1) the share of the agricultural surplus taken previously by the large landlords and spent unproductively on luxuries; (2) the share of the agricultural surplus taken by usurers and traders; (3) the share of the social surplus product exported out of the country by foreign enterprises; and (4) the share of the total surplus product taken by the former state bureaucracy through bribes, corruption, and wastage. However, Mandel does admit that without substantial aid from one or more industrially advanced societies, the difficulties associated with socialist accumulation in an underdeveloped society can lead revolutionary regimes to resort to the same kind of measures that were used in the Soviet Union (Mandel 1968:618).

In the Cuban case the problems of socialist accumulation appear to have been significantly reduced due to the extensive amount of economic assistance provided by the Soviet Union (Castaños 1977:75; MacEwan 1981:221). This factor, added to the fact that Cuba began its transition to socialism with an economic infrastructure superior to that of most Third World societies, has made it possible for the revolutionary regime to develop the country's forces of production without resorting to the kind of primitive socialist accumulation strategy followed in the Soviet Union (Amin 1981:36–37; FitzGerald 1986:47).

Both Mandel and Samir Amin contend that socialist accumulation in the underdeveloped societies should be undertaken in a manner that is based upon the voluntary and willing participation of those involved in producing the surplus product rather than through reliance upon forced collectivization, forced labor schemes, or the extraction of various forms of taxes on consumption. They conclude that such measures are extremely wasteful, politically undesirable, and achieve poor economic results (Amin 1981:36–37; Mandel 1968:620–621). Thus, they advise that the Soviet pattern of accumulation should not be followed by Third World socialist states because this approach involves unnecessarily high social costs and does not produce as favorable results as approaches based upon increasing the basic consumption levels of the general population (Amin 1981:22–28; Mandel 1968:627–632).

Related to the strategy of accumulation followed by the Soviets is what certain Marxist economists have called "the law of priority in the development of the capital goods sector." According to this "law," the amount invested in the production of the capital goods (heavy industry) sector must increase more rapidly than the amount in the consumer goods sector in order to ensure a high rate of economic growth during the transition to socialism (Mandel 1968:627–630). However, many contemporary Marxist economists hold an opposing position based on the thesis that a balanced increase in both of these sectors yields better overall results. This strategy increases productivity by providing the producers with positive incentives in the form of more consumer goods (see Amin 1981:36–37; FitzGerald 1986:49–50; Mandel 1968:627; and Nove 1983:159–160).

FitzGerald argues that small, underdeveloped societies engaged in the construction of socialism must consider their agroexport sector as the priority sector of accumulation, in place of their weak or almost nonexistent capital goods sector (see FitzGerald 1984 and 1986). Because these societies have inherited neocolonial economies that are structurally dependent upon the production of agroexports and foreign trade, this perspective sees the expansion of the net earnings from their agroexport production as the only realistic means to increase the growth of these economies. Through these earnings they can obtain the foreign exchange to purchase both the capital goods and other inputs needed for their development.

This thesis has influenced the economic development strategies of both Cuba and Nicaragua, and it also appears to have influenced the economic strategy of the Popular Unity government in Chile.

Problems with an Agroexport Strategy

One of the problems, however, with an agroexport strategy is that it is susceptible to the same kind of "accumulation bias" evident in the heavy industry or capital goods approach to socialist development (Nuti 1979:248). That is to say, the state planners and administrators tend to overemphasize the production of agroexports at the expense of the production of basic consumer goods.

But this strategy has even more fundamental problems. It is extremely vulnerable to external economic aggression (Stallings 1986:76). This vulnerability is evidenced by the trade and financial blockades that the United States imposed upon Cuba, Chile during the UP government, and more recently upon revolutionary Nicaragua. Clive Thomas, a prominent Guyanese Marxist with considerable experience in Africa as well as the Caribbean, contends that the experience of most small underdeveloped societies clearly indicates that agroexport production in this historical era does not contain enough dynamic potential to transform their economies (Thomas 1974:167). This weakness exists because the international market for most agroexport products has been characterized by instability and declining prices over the last several decades. He also observes that a strategy of development based upon overspecialization in agroexports tends to have harmful effects on rural incomes and reinforces the diversion of key resources away from the production of basic foods for local consumption.

Support for Thomas's argument can be found in both the Cuban and Nicaraguan cases. In Cuba, the reliance upon the production of sugar for export (and agriculture in general) as the center of the country's economic strategy has made the development of the country dependent upon what MacEwan has termed "the vicissitudes of the weather and of international commodity prices" (MacEwan 1981:217). To some degree Cuba's long-term sales agreements with the Soviet Union and other socialist states helped to insulate the country's economy from price fluctuations in the international market for sugar and certain other products, but these arrangements did not keep the development of the economy from being dependent upon what appears to be a weak basis for accumulation, that is, agroexports (MacEwan 1981:217–220). Moreover, the changes that have taken place in the Soviet Union have led to reduced economic ties with Cuba and the Soviet Union has ceased to be a guaranteed market for Cuba's agroexports or a reliable source of cheap inputs for Cuba's industrial enterprises.

Revolutionary Nicaragua's experience appears to provide even greater confirmation of Thomas's argument. The regime's economic strategy emphasized agroexport production as the primary source of accumulation, but the annual earnings from its agroexports steadily declined and they were not sufficient to cover its essential imports or to service its foreign debt, let alone finance developments in other sectors of the economy (Harris and Vilas 1985:56, 75–76). As a result, the country's foreign debt increased at an alarming rate, the government was forced to reduce the country's essential imports and suspend most development projects, and was also forced to reorient the economy increasingly toward the production of basic foods for popular consumption (Collins 1986:250–259).

The fact that small, underdeveloped societies with agroexport economies need foreign sources of economic assistance to ensure both the survival of their revolutionary regimes and the socialist transformation of their economies shows that a socialist development strategy based upon autarkical (self-reliant) disengagement from the world economy does not appear to be feasible for these societies (Nove 1983:186–192; Stallings 1986:54–55). On the other hand, it seems unlikely that a revolutionary regime in any other Third World country will be able to obtain the extensive amount of assistance received by Cuba because the Soviet Union does not appear to be willing or able to provide it (Edelman 1987:24–36; Stallings 1986:55, 76).

The diversification of sources of external assistance as well as internal foreign investment appears to be both more realistic and more desirable; and special arrangements need to be made in advance for servicing loans in such a way that they do not create severe balance-of-payments problems (Stallings 1986:77). However, "foreign-aid socialism," that is, the attempt to construct socialism through extensive dependence upon foreign grants, credits, and concessionary loans, involves high economic and political costs. This fact was demonstrated in revolutionary Grenada and Nicaragua, which were unable to control their foreign expenses to match the inflow of foreign aid or to integrate the various types of assistance into a coherent development strategy (Pryor 1986:62–66; Collins 1986:172–174).

Financial Policy and Prices

An important area of problems associated with the development of the forces of production in underdeveloped countries attempting a transition to socialism is that of finances and prices. For example, the lack of coordination between structural transformations and financial policy appears to have been a major shortcoming of the Allende government in Chile (Bitar 1979:248). One of the most important lessons to be learned from the Chilean case is that the Popular Unity policymakers did not perceive the acute importance of financial policy in the transition to socialism. This appears to have been due to "the implicit belief that structural changes (in particular, changes in property relations) would mechanically ease economic problems in the short-term" (Griffith-Jones 1981:170).

However, in the initial stages of the transition to socialism, the historical evidence indicates that serious financial problems tend to be generated by the economic transformations undertaken by revolutionary regimes. These problems include: accelerating inflation, capital flight, dwindling foreign exchange reserves, difficulties in financing essential imports, currency speculation and devaluation, the emergence of a black market, and so on.

As Griffith-Jones has noted, the role of money and finance during the transition to socialism tends to be discussed at a very abstract level in most of the Marxist literature (Griffith-Jones 1981:3). There is little attention paid to "the concrete issues of how to use monetary and specific financial policies" to achieve the planners' goals in the initial stages of the transition.

In a planned economy, effective financial and pricing policies are needed to control the market links between the state and nonstate sectors of the economy. They are also needed to stabilize the value of money for purposes of planning and controlling the state sector, maintaining a prudent level of foreign exchange reserves for the purchase of essential imports, strengthening the state sector vis-à-vis the private sector, and articulating the transitional economy with the world market (Griffith-Jones 1981:7–8).

Financial and pricing policies affect not only the functioning of the economy but also the level of political support for the revolutionary regime (see Bettelheim 1978:223–234; Bitar 1979:248–302; Griffith-Jones 1981:185–193; and Nove 1983:160–195). High levels of inflation during the initial stages of the transition to socialism disrupt the operation of the market at a time when it cannot be replaced by effective planning mechanisms, and this disruption tends to undermine the political support of the small producers (for example, the peasantry) as well as the so-called middle strata of salaried white collar employees and self-employed professionals. Thus, in Chile, the hyperinflationary effects of the UP government's expansion of the money supply, its inability to control wage increases, ineffective use of price controls, and its continuing budget deficits contributed to the government's loss of support among Chile's middle sectors (Bitar 1979:278–302; Griffith-Jones 1981:162–165).

The Allende government's use of price controls undermined political support for the Popular Unity program among the middle sectors, who blamed these controls for creating shortages, black marketeering, and queuing—all of which impacted adversely upon these sectors (Bitar 1979:278–302; Nove 1983:160–161). Meanwhile, by fixing the wholesale prices for the products produced by the state and nationalized enterprises below their market value, the government inadvertently allowed most of the surplus obtained by the state to be transferred to the private sector!

This incredible development undermined the stability of the Allende government while strengthening its political opponents in the private sector (Griffith-Jones 1981:166–167). A similar situation developed in the Soviet Union during the New Economic Policy period, when private retail traders took advantage of the margin between the retail market prices and the state-regulated wholesale prices for the products produced by the nationalized industries (Griffith-Jones 1981:72).

Commodity Relations

Following the Russian Revolution, Marxists attributed the continuance of commodity relations (that is, money, prices, markets, and so on) in the Soviet Union to the coexistence of state, private, and collective forms of property and the need for exchange between them. More recent explanations suggest that commodity relations are necessary during the transition because "society is still living in a situation of relative shortage of consumer goods" (Mandel 1968:632). Moreover, Bettelheim argues that the requirements of effective planning in even the most advanced socialist societies necessitate a continued reliance upon prices, money, taxation, and some form of market relations (Bettelheim 1978:109–110).

Much has been written by Marxist and non-Marxist economists on the problems of establishing an effective price system and integrating market relations with state planning in transitional economies (for example, see Bettelheim 1978:184–248; Mandel 1968:605–652; and Nove 1983:97–113, 120–125). This is a complex subject, and justice cannot be done to the literature on these questions in this book. Instead, we will focus on only one aspect of this subject—the regulation of commodity production in agriculture—because it is particularly relevant to the Latin American and Caribbean cases discussed in this book.

The difficulties involved in regulating the prices and planning the production of agricultural commodities are evident in the experiences of all the countries that have undertaken the construction of socialism. In fact, the socialization of agriculture has been hindered in every case by what Nicolai Bukharin referred to as the peasantry's "anarchical tendency in commodity production" (Bukharin 1971:92).

Bukharin, like Lenin, believed that the maintenance of the worker-peasant alliance and the survival of the Soviet regime required the continuance of commodity relations (particularly the exchange of products in terms of prices) in agriculture (Bukarin 1982:240–245). In order to ensure sufficient food supplies for the proletariat in the cities and maintain the political support of the peasantry (which was the vast majority of the Soviet population), Lenin and Bukharin reasoned that capitalist commodity relations, controlled by "the proletarian state," would have to be tolerated during the transition to socialism in the Soviet Union.

During the period referred to as War Communism (1918–1921), food supplies for the cities and the army had to be requisitioned from the peasantry, and barter replaced the commercial exchange of goods. However, as this period came to an end, the government introduced a "tax in kind" and a free market for the peasantry's after-tax agricultural surpluses (Lenin 1976:640–641). These and related measures, such as ending the state's monopoly over wholesale and retail trade, were introduced as a part of the regime's New Economic Policy in the 1920s.

This return to commodity relations, and related concessions to the peasantry, succeeded in stimulating agricultural production and the recovery of the economy during the first years of the NEP period (see Mandel 1968:550), but it also had serious negative effects on the socialization process and the country's economic development. It encouraged class differentiation among the peasantry, led to increased food consumption among the peasantry rather than a significant increase in the marketable surplus, permitted the rich peasants (the *kulaks*) to concentrate a large proportion of the agricultural surplus in their hands and hoard it until favorable market conditions developed, undermined the government's control of the economy, and gave rise to violent price fluctuations (Griffith-Jones 1981:48–49; Mandel 1968:550–551).

These conditions provided the context in which the *kulaks* organized a food strike during the winter of 1927–1928, which resulted in the withholding of food supplies from the towns and cities (Mandel 1968:553). This situation, along with the Soviet regime's decision to accelerate the country's industrialization, provoked the forced collectivization of agriculture.

Between 1930 and 1937, some 25 million small agricultural holdings were merged into 240,000 collective farms called *kolkhozy* and 4,000 state farms called *sovkhozy* (Mandel 1968:554). However, the collectivization (statization) of the peasant landholdings did not put an end to commodity relations in Soviet agriculture or in the rest of the economy. Successive reforms aimed at improving the performance of Soviet agriculture resulted in price increases and the relaxation of state controls on the marketing of certain types of agricultural products (Mandel 1968:554–560, 572–584). Under Gorbachev, a number of agricultural reforms were introduced, aimed at increasing the incentives of farmers and removing the bureaucratic top-down organizational structures that have inhibited high levels of productivity in Soviet agriculture. Two of the most innovative reforms are those involving lease contracting for land and reorganization of the *kolkhoz-sovkhoz* structure to permit diverse forms of farming. The lease contracting arrangements are based on market incentive assumptions and involve leasing land and other items to farmers (both individuals and cooperatives). However, price reforms and free markets in agricultural products are to be introduced on a gradual basis after agricultural production has improved and demand is satisfied (Van Atta 1989:70–79).

In the Third World, those countries claiming to be socialist have tended to permit the continuance or have restored commodity relations in the agricultural sector of their economies. In fact, in recent years there has been a tendency to rely increasingly upon the use of market incentives and commodity relations among the small producers in agriculture in order to motivate them to produce a sufficient level of food supplies for the population. Not only does this help maintain political support for the regime among the population of the rural areas, there is considerable evidence that this approach is more efficient than large-scale production by state farms. Moreover, the governments in power have continued to view commodity relations as necessary in most cases in order to provide an adequate supply of food products that can be used to stimulate increased labor productivity and maintain support for the regime among the urban working class as well as other sectors of the urban population (FitzGerald 1984:9–10).

However, the Cuban experience has not followed the general pattern. Because of the revolutionary regime's extensive statization of the agricultural sector and the formation of large state farms out of the former large ranches and plantations, the regime has relied primarily upon state farms and government rationing to provide food supplies to the general population. Nevertheless, there is a small private sector composed of small farmers (which accounts for about 20 percent of the arable land in Cuba) that has continued to produce a substantial proportion of the food crops grown in Cuba.

It is increasingly argued that state farms and rationing are a more costly and less efficient means of providing adequate food supplies than small producer cooperatives and markets controlled by the government (Deere 1986:136, 139; FitzGerald 1984:12). However, Cuba's experience with the creation of free markets to encourage the private farmers and cooperatives to produce more food resulted in a familiar pattern of increased inequality, excessive commercialism, and various forms of speculation, profiteering, and black-marketing. As a result, the Cuban government decided to put an end to this experiment with market measures in 1986. Since then, the government has increased controls on private farmers, cooperatives, and the state farms.

In Nicaragua, the revolutionary government originally attempted to follow a strategy that combined agroexport production on state farms with small producer cooperatives and government regulation of the agricultural commodity markets, but the dislocations cause by the counterrevolutionary war and the political demands of the peasantry forced the regime to reorient its agrarian policies. After 1985, the revolutionary government followed a new course based upon the distribution of land (including state farm land) to individual peasant producers, the promotion of national self-sufficiency in the production of basic food products, and an increased reliance upon market incentives and small producer commodity production (Collins 1986:248–259; *Envío* 1989:51–52).

The reorientation of the government's agricultural policies and its increasing reliance upon small-scale commodity production was in response to the country's grave economic crisis and the government's limited fiscal resources. However, the government appears to have believed that this reliance upon market incentives could be controlled and that it would not undermine the mixed economy strategy of national development. The opening up of the agricultural market for small and medium private producers was viewed by some observers not as a retreat but an advance toward socialism (*Envío* 1989:51). Nevertheless, this economic strategy as well as other aspects of the revolutionary process in Nicaragua tends to support Vilas's conclusion that the Sandinista revolution was "entangled in a difficult *transition to development* rather than a *transition to socialism*" (Vilas 1986:268).

What many leftist advocates of market reforms today do not seem to be aware of is that commodity relations and private production in agriculture have always been considered a retreat from socialism. Lenin was very explicit about that fact when the Soviet regime decided to rely upon free exchange between small commodity producers as part of the New Economic Policy.

> What is free exchange? It is unrestricted trade, and that means turning back towards capitalism. Free exchange and freedom of trade mean circulation of commodities between petty proprietors. All of us who have studied at least the elements of Marxism know that this exchange and freedom of trade inevitably lead to a division of commodity producers into owners of capital and owners of labor-power, a division into capitalists and wage-laborers, i.e., a revival of capitalist wage-slavery, which does not fall from the sky but springs the world over precisely from the agricultural commodity economy. (quoted in Tablada 1989:104–105)

The reliance upon commodity relations and a free market in agricultural goods has produced income inequalities, class differentiation, and fostered capitalist values in every case where this approach has been followed by a revolutionary regime with socialist intentions. The first case was the Soviet Union, and the most recent cases are China, Vietnam, and Cuba (Ngo Vinh Long 1988; Perez-Stable 1987; and Spoor 1988).

The Importance of Planning in a Socialist Economy

Most contemporary Marxist economists recognize that establishing a coherent price system in the transitional economy is absolutely essential because coherent prices are required for both economic planning and the management of state enterprises (Bettelheim 1978:184). However, in contrast to the character of prices in a free-market capitalist economy, the prices for goods and services during the transition to socialism are "administered," "planned" or "regulated" by the state, just as wages and the incomes of most members of the labor force are regulated. This is one of the reasons why the economy of the transition period has generally been thought of as a "regulated" or "planned" economy.

The problem with this type of regulated or administered economy is that, in the absence of popular democratic control over state policymaking, decisions about pricing, resource allocation, investments, incentives, and so forth, become the preserve of a privileged bureaucratic elite. Due to the very nature of this elite, they are incapable of making decisions that take into account the interests and knowledge of the producers. They engage in what has been referred to as "bureaucratic centralism" instead of acting in accordance with Lenin's conception of democratic centralism.

Bureaucratic centralism distorts the planning process and produces erroneous decisions about the economy that are based on inadequate information and inappropriate criteria. The need for democratization of economic decision-making was described by one of Vietnam's top leaders, Truong Chinh:

> Some people have offered the idea that, between centralism and democracy, we should at present accord priority to centralism. That claim is erroneous both in theory and practice. Democratic centralism is a principle that reflects very strict unity. Unless we promote democracy and ensure the right to autonomy of basic units, and the legitimate interests of the worker both in agriculture and industry, both in production and goods circulation, there will be no, or only very few, commodity products, and commodities will not be in normal circulation. In such a situation, can we ensure centralism? If centralism is stressed to the point we lack commodities and goods circulation is stalemated, what is the purpose of centralism? That is the bureaucratic centralism we have been guilty of for a long time, and which the resolution of the Sixth CPV Central Committee Plenum has analyzed, criticized and rejected. (cited in C. White 1989:186)

But it is not enough to criticize the ills of bureaucratic centralism and advocate democratic decisionmaking; the proper structures and processes have to be established to allow for this to take place, and the producers have to be informed and skilled in democratic methods.

According to the classical Marxist perspective, socialism requires a planned economy in order to do away with the anarchy associated with capitalist commodity production and with the class conflict and social equality inherent in capitalist societies. It is clear from the writings of

Marx and Engels that they expected prices, money, wages, the exchange of commodities, and so on, to be dispensed with in the initial stages of the construction of socialist society (Marx and Engels 1972:429, 432).

However, the experience of the existing socialist societies and those in transition to socialism does not conform to this original Marxist perspective. Instead of the social regulation of production based upon a comprehensive plan and the sharing-out (equal distribution) of products, these societies are characterized by the exchange of most products as commodities and a reliance upon prices, money, payments, credit, profits, and differential wages combined with a certain degree of economic planning and the centralized allocation of major resources (Bettelheim 1978:31–33).

Because of the continued existence of various forms of property, the uneven development of the productive forces, and the lack of integration between the different branches of production in existing socialist societies, it is not feasible for the state or any central entity to exercise effective control over all the diverse economic subjects or make all the millions of economic decisions that have to be made in these societies. In fact, as Bettelheim notes: "Even within a single state sector, efficient and therefore socially useful intervention in all decisions by a single social-economic center is still inconceivable" (Bettelheim 1976:71). This situation was first recognized by Lenin and later explained in some detail by Stalin in his treatise *Economic Problems of Socialism in the USSR* (cited in Bettelheim 1978:71, 107–109 passim).

In the existing socialist societies, at least until quite recently, the distribution of labor and material resources between the different spheres of production has taken place through marketlike arrangements that are similar to those in capitalist societies, with the important exception that they are subject to various degrees of state planning and control (Bettelheim 1976:173). In other words, the regulation of the economy through state planning and controls is *partial*.

For example, in the 1970s the Cubans decided to rely more on material incentives, prices, and enterprise profits as part of their new System for Direction and Planning of the Economy (Sistema de Dirección y Planificación de la Economía), which was modeled on the decentralizing economic reforms introduced in the Soviet Union in 1965. According to one Cuban government document explaining the introduction of these economic measures, "the general spread of commodity-money relations, which also include relations between state enterprises, requires . . . categories such as budget, credit, price, cost, profit and also demands that in activities financed by the state budget purchase-and-sale relations be established with the suppliers . . ." (Center for Cuban Studies 1976:17). This approach replaced the earlier system of quantitative targets that were set by the central planning authorities for the country's numerous local units of production.

Under the previous budgetary system there were few incentives for the units of production to minimize their costs. However, under the new system set up in the 1970s, prices, profits, and bonuses were introduced at the enterprise level to induce action in accordance with planned goals and serve as indicators of efficient performance. Resource shortages and bureaucratic resistance undermined the effectiveness of these measures. Moreover, the limited reprivatization of the economy and the distorted manner in which profits, prices, and bonuses were used have been blamed for fostering profiteering, corruption, the growth of a large black market, exorbitant prices, and the use of public resources for private gain.

In Cuba, as in other centrally planned economies such as the Soviet Union and China, major investment decisions are determined by the centralized planning authorities (Mandel 1968:635; MacEwan 1981:184). In the most general sense, these investment decisions are supposed to be aimed at "increasing the socialized productive forces so as to ensure an increasing abundance of goods and services for the citizens . . . and to bring about, as a long term prospect, the withering away of the market economy, classes, social inequality, the state and the division of labor" (Mandel 1968:637). But in a more immediate sense and in the case of each country, major investment decisions as well as other planning decisions are made in relation to the social, economic, and political priorities set down by the central authorities.

In the 1960s, Cuba's investment strategy gave priority to state investments in agriculture and agroindustry. By 1966, agriculture accounted for over 40 percent of the state's total investment portfolio, and most industrial investments were made in the agroindustrial sector of the country's economy (Angotti 1988:533). However, by the 1970s, the main emphasis in investment priorities had shifted from agriculture to industry and the diversification of the economy. In 1975, the country's first five-year plan was introduced. This plan was directed at the accelerated industrialization of the economy. Throughout the late 1970s and early 1980s, investment continued to be oriented toward industry and the diversification of the economy. By 1986, industry accounted for 65 percent of total production and agriculture had declined to 9 percent (Angotti 1988:546). In other words, the regime's investment strategy had succeeded in reorienting the economy away from its traditional overspecialization in agroexport production (although the production of sugar for export still continues to be a critically important feature of the economy) toward a more diversified mix of agroindustry, manufacturing, and services.

Apart from Cuba, there has been little success with comprehensive economic planning in Latin America. During the four and one-half years of the People's Revolutionary Government in Grenada, the government apparently was unable to implement an operational plan for the economy (Pryor 1986:189–190). The UP government in Chile was not even able to plan successfully the nationalized sector or *area social* of the economy, much less engage in effective comprehensive planning (Bitar 1979:15, 82; Nove 1983:183–184).

In the case of revolutionary Nicaragua, a somewhat similar situation to that in Chile under the Allende regime was confronted by the Sandinistas. It was almost impossible for the regime to engage in effective planning, due to the opposition of the large private producers to the regime's economic policies, U.S. efforts to destabilize the economy, the effects of the war on the economy, and the unfavorable international market for its agroexports (Coraggio 1986:151–155; Harris and Vilas 1985:68–69).

In general, most existing socialist societies have found it difficult to achieve an adequate balance between central planning and direction of the economy and the encouragement of local initiative at the level of the individual units of production (Boorstein 1968:259). The pattern that developed in the Soviet Union involved strong centralized control over the local units of production until the 1960s. However, in the fifties, Yugoslavia initiated a more decentralized pattern of center-enterprise relations that was characterized by considerable (some Marxists argue too much) autonomy at the enterprise level (see Bettelheim 1978:54; Horvat 1982:164–165, 302–306).

Market Reforms and Decentralization

Since the 1970s, there has also been a tendency on the part of the central authorities in the Soviet Union, the Eastern European countries, China, Vietnam, and Cuba to devolve more decisions and initiative to the enterprise level (see Boorstein 1968:262; Brus 1975:148–171; and White 1983). The present headlong rush to introduce market reforms in these countries (with the exception of Cuba) entails even greater degrees of enterprise autonomy and, in some cases, the privatization of large sectors of the economy through the sale or lease of state-owned enterprises to private individuals and companies.

The evidence has tended to indicate that when a centralized planning body imposes detailed production targets on individual enterprises, this usually presents them with tasks that they either cannot fulfill or they can too easily fulfill without using their full capacity; and it takes away from them the flexibility they need in order to function effectively.

However, the solution to this problem does not appear to lie in decentralization or a return to the enterprise autonomy of capitalist firms. Greater enterprise autonomy does not resolve the problem; it merely creates new problems. What is needed is for the national planning process and the production relations *within* each enterprise to be brought under the *democratic control* of the producers (Mandel 1968:644).

Yugoslavia's experience with so-called market socialism, decentralization, and worker-managed enterprises reveals the important issues underlying the centralization versus decentralization debate. The key structures in the Yugoslav system are the worker-managed enterprises, which operate as independent, profit-maximizing economic units that are "owned" by their workers. They operate in a market context much like private enterprises elsewhere. This means that those units with the most advantages (favorable access to finance capital, resources, markets, and an appropriate supply of labor) tend to increase their income at the expense of those with the least advantages (Taslim 1984:48–49). In other words, a form of exploitation takes place in which the workers and managers in the more favored enterprises increase their incomes at the expense of those in the less favored enterprises.

This imbalance has also contributed to the lopsided development and unequal distribution of national income between the different regions of the country. Moreover, because the workers and managers of each enterprise seek to maximize their individual incomes through maximizing the net income (profit) of their enterprise and then distributing this income to themselves in the form of wages, these enterprises have largely chosen not to invest in their enterprises or other productive economic activities. In fact, when they do invest, they tend to finance these investments through borrowing at low interest from the state banks rather than by setting aside savings from their earnings. This process has had negative effects on the country's economy by lowering the rate of savings, raising the rate of inflation, and reducing the amount and efficiency of investments.

Furthermore, the profit-oriented, market-determined nature of the Yugoslav system has reproduced bourgeois capitalist ideas and relations while undermining the development of socialism. To quote the conclusions of one of the more insightful studies on this question:

The Yugoslav-Soviet dispute and the subsequent Cominform blockade, real threats of external and internal subversion, the serious drought of 1950 and 1952 and the mismanagement of the economy by the League of Communists—all combined to bring about chaotic economic conditions during 1950–1952. The communist party intellectuals became "disillusioned" and impatient with the existing order of things within a surprisingly short period of time. Abetted and encouraged, no doubt, by the covert bourgeois elements within the party, these intellectuals advocated curtailing the scope of central planning and replacing it by the market mechanism in allocating resources and distributing incomes. The restoration of the market mechanism was accompanied by the establishment of profit-seeking labor-managed enterprises. Such quick rehabilitation of the ubiquitous profit motive to propel the economy forward not only retained and revived the old bourgeois values but also corroded the socialist ideals before they had a chance to spread roots in the society. . . . The integration of the Yugoslav economy with the world market dominated by the capitalist countries came as a natural result of the process. . . . (Taslim 1984:52–53)

As this study indicates, the autonomous enterprises and the reliance upon market relations went hand in hand along with the restoration of bourgeois values and the integration of the Yugoslav economy into the capitalist world market. As a result, the society "has gradually stratified, naturally embracing in its fold the beneficiaries of the new system," which represent what is essentially a new bourgeois ruling stratum veiled by the ideological facade of "workers' self-management" (Taslim 1984:53). In many ways, the transformations taking place in Eastern Europe today appear to be a déjà vu of what has taken place already to some degree in Yugoslavia.

The Nicaraguan Case

Nicaragua demonstrated what can happen in a small Third World country when limited forms of central planning are combined with a mixed economy in which the state sector is not the dominant one and market relations prevail. The Sandinistas tried to institutionalize a system of planning at the enterprise, branch, and sectoral levels in the state sector—the Area of People's Property. An effort was also made to involve the private sector in the planning process. However, this did not progress much beyond consultations and negotiations centered on matters such as the allocation of foreign exchange and short-term financing; they showed no interest at all in the long-range planning of the country's economic development.

The opposition to the revolutionary regime by the large capitalists in the industrial and agroexport sectors was a major obstacle to the institutionalization of indicative, as opposed to mandatory, planning. Moreover, the general economic conditions prevailing in Nicaragua as well as the hostile external environment made it difficult, if not impossible, to formulate and implement any kind of planning. This was clearly stated by Comandante Jaime Wheelock, minister of agricultural development and agrarian reform:

> Every time that we attempt to implement a plan, we have to make an emergency plan, because, apart from the situation of aggression that we suffer, in a certain sense our variables, because we are such a dependent country, are a function of the international market. . . . It is difficult to plan in a dependent country that has open international relations. And it is even more difficult if in addition to economic reasons, such as the international economic crisis, are added political problems and the military aggression which our country suffers. (Wheelock 1983:117–118)

As Wheelock's statements indicate, the extreme external dependency of the country's mixed economy as well as the efforts of the United States government to destabilize the economy and overthrow the regime, undermined all efforts to make and implement plans in the country's mixed economy.

The Sandinista regime's original economic project was aimed at reconstructing the country's economy after the revolutionary insurrection. This project involved:

- A moderate program of redistribution of wealth and income to the popular classes;
- The diversification of the country's dependence upon foreign markets and financing;
- The mobilizaton of the population in the productive process;
- The development of a new mixed economy based upon an expanded and dominant state sector, a reformed private sector, and a new cooperative sector (Harris and Vilas 1985:56–57).

However, the Sandinistas were forced to shelve this original project due to the following factors:

- The country's internal economic difficulties;
- The refusal of most large private producers to return production to prerevolutionary levels or invest in the economy;
- The falling international prices for most of its agroexports;
- The regional political and economic crisis;
- The effects of the U.S. trade embargo;
- The war of attrition waged against the country by the U.S.-backed counterrevolutionary forces (Harris 1987:8–9).

In its place, they were forced to:

- Give priority to national defense;
- Use their investments and meager foreign exchange to maintain agroexport production;
- Discontinue their previous policy of broad subsidies for basic consumer goods;
- Encourage the production of basic foods for internal consumption through allowing their prices to rise;
- Reorient their agrarian reform program in favor of the distribution of large amounts of land to individual peasants without any stipulation that they join cooperatives;
- Limit expenditures on education and other social services;
- Generally place the economy on a wartime survival basis.

In the end, it appears this reformulated economic strategy failed to prevent the erosion of popular support for the regime as the economy deteriorated to unprecedented levels.

Conclusion

Effective forms of centralized planning and the rapid development of the forces of production cannot be attained under the kind of conditions that initially confront revolutionary regimes in the Third World. Unfavorable internal as well as external conditions obstruct the efforts of such regimes. Only after considerable sacrifice, time, and organizational effort can the foundations for effective planning, management, and development of the forces of production be laid. In the meantime, regulated market relations, commodity production, prices, monetary policies, and differential material incentives are "necessary evils" that must be effectively combined with collective forms of production, moral incentives, and increased worker participation in the planning and control of production at the enterprise level.

The continued development of the forces of production under socialist conditions requires the institutionalization of workers' self-management and democratic participation in the planning and direction of production, neither of which can be developed overnight (Horvat 1982:261–262). These important relations of production require extensive preparation and a lengthy learning process in which workers, managers, the general citizenry, state officials, and the political leadership develop the necessary organizational consciousness and skills—including those associated with collaborative forms of problem solving, consensus decisionmaking, and democratic planning.

However, there still is the problem of how best to transform small, agroexport oriented, neocolonial economies that are extremely vulnerable to the international capitalist market into largely self-sufficient, diversified economies capable of satisfying the basic needs and improving the material well-being of their population through the expanded development of their forces of production. The accumulated international experience so far has not provided a clear solution to this problem. Cuba's economy has undergone considerable diversification and the forces of production have been expanded with the extensive assistance of the Soviet Union and the Eastern European states. However, it still remains dependent on the sale of its agroexports in order to obtain critical inputs for its economy that it cannot supply from domestic sources. Thus, its economy remains quite vulnerable to external forces, and its has not achieved the level of self-sufficiency its seeks. It remains to be seen whether Cuba can replace its dependency on Soviet economic assistance and price guarantees for its export with equitable trading relations with other Third World countries and certain capitalist countries in Europe.

Any Latin American or Caribbean country that chooses to undertake the transition to socialism in the future will most likely have to confront the efforts of the United States to undermine its economy and isolate it from international sources of financing and assistance. This probably means that measures must be taken as rapidly as possible to gain control over the major means of production and eliminate the economic power base of the bourgeoisie. Self-sufficiency in food production must be a primary objective of the new regime as well as the mobilization of the full productive capacity of the work force through their incorporation in the management and planning of production. A self-reliant approach to the development of domestic technology and industry, with appropriate foreign technical assistance (from friendly countries in Western Europe, Asia, and/or the Third World) appears to be the most desirable and probably the most successful strategy of socialist development, but this approach has not yet been tested or proven by experience.

9
Moral Stimulation and Material Incentives

The Importance of Incentives in Socialism

Marx and Engels theorized that during the early stage of the transition to communism (the period of socialism), the working class could not be expected to work purely for the good of society and would have to be rewarded unequally. In this long period the distribution of goods and wages would be based upon the principle "from each according to one's ability, to each according to one's work."

Once the higher stage of communism was achieved, and the productive forces were capable of providing an abundance of goods and services for all, the early Marxists believed that the basic principle of distribution would become: "from each according to one's ability, to each according to one's needs." Thus, Marx wrote in *The Critique of the Gotha Program* the following passage:

> In a higher phase of communist society, after the enslaving subordination of the individual to the division of labor, and therewith also the antithesis between mental and manual labor, has vanished; after labor has become not only a means to life but life's prime want; after the productive forces have also increased with the all-around development of the individual, and all the springs of co-operative wealth flow more abundantly—only then can the narrow horizon of bourgeois right be crossed in its entirety and society subscribe on its banners: From each according to his ability, to each according to his needs! (Marx and Engels 1972:320–321)

Because of the low stage of development of the forces of production in Russia, Lenin and the Bolsheviks argued that the transition to socialism would require a long period in which the distribution of goods and services would have to be based, not upon the communist principle, but upon the principle of "to each according to one's work."

In *The State and Revolution*, Lenin's position on this question is elaborated:

> Marx not only scrupulously takes account of the inevitable inequality of men, but he also takes into account the fact that the mere conversion of the means of production into the common property of the whole of society (commonly called "socialism") *does not remove* the defects of distribution and the inequality of "bourgeois right," which *continues to prevail* so long as products are divided "according to the amount of labor performed."
> . . . And so in the first phase of communist society (usually called socialism) "bourgeois right" is *not* abolished in its entirety, but only in part, only in proportion to the economic revolution so far attained, i.e., only in respect of the means of production. (Lenin 1976:331)

Based upon Lenin's and the Bolsheviks' understanding of Marx and the conditions confronting the new Soviet regime, a system of distribution was instituted that involved differential material incentives. However, this approach was regarded only as a necessary expedient during the socialist transition period, and the Bolsheviks held to the view that moral and collective incentives should increasingly be utilized as Soviet society developed in the direction of communism.

Under Stalin it appears necessity was made into a virtue with regard to the differential distribution of material incentives in the Soviet Union. For example, one study indicates that in the years immediately following the revolution, the differentiation of income was approximately 1:1.8 between the lowest and highest paid positions, however, by the 1950s the ratio had increased to 1:40 (Horvat 1982:71). If the various types of nonmonetary privileges received by persons in the highest positions are included in the calculation, the ratio increases to 1:100 (Horvat 1982:546) Moreover, not only is the differentiation in income similar to that in capitalist countries, the basic division between manual and intellectual labor has continued to exist.

The special privileges received by those in the higher positions of Soviet society are, in a sense, more important than money income because they often include access to goods and services that cannot be purchased.

> Since an etatist economy is based on central planning, money plays a less important role and crucial privileges are granted in kind. They are linked directly with position on the bureaucratic ladder and include vacations at exclusive holiday resorts, access to special medical treatment or treatment in a closed system of hospitals, clinics, and dispensaries, residence in

lovely apartments, the use of official cars and of expensive state property (*dacha*), enjoyment of exclusive hunting privileges and other recreational activities. . . . Privileges further include access to a network of exclusive shops that carry imported commodities and other items not generally available. In the Soviet Union this is known as *Kremlevskii paek* (Kremlin ration). (Horvat 1982:73)

These privileges and the differentiation of income found in the Soviet Union as well as the other East European countries have given rise to a system of social stratification that is incompatible with the socialist ideal of a classless society.

Moral Incentives in Maoist China and Cuba

In contrast to the Soviet Union and the East European countries, China under Mao Tse Tung, North Korea, Vietnam, and Cuba offer examples of regimes that have placed a much greater emphasis on moral incentives (that is, symbolic rewards such as peer recognition, prestige, honors, medals, and so on) and relied upon a more egalitarian distribution of income.

The use of moral incentives (often referred to as moral stimulation) in combination with a relatively egalitarian system for the distribution of goods and services has prevented the development in most of these countries of the kind of sharp income differentiation and social stratification that is found in the Soviet Union and Eastern Europe. It can be argued that the greater emphasis on moral incentives is a necessity in these countries because of their poverty and the scarcity of material rewards (Karl 1975:24); however, other factors clearly have been important. Moreover, the recent emphasis on material incentives in China cannot be explained on this basis.

In fact, the current situation in China offers a marked departure from the past emphasis upon moral incentives, particularly during the period of the Great Leap Forward (1958 to 1960) and during the Cultural Revolution (1966 to 1969), when moral incentives were part of the revolutionary regime's efforts to mobilize the population in the pursuit of egalitarian, antimarket and antibureaucratic goals (Bernardo 1971:25–26). During these periods, the regime sought to create a new work ethic that would approximate the kind of communist work ethic mentioned in the writings of Marx, Engels, and Lenin—that is, work done for the good of society without regard to remuneration.

However, under the policies of the current leadership in China, the former emphasis on moral incentives has been eclipsed by the increasing privatization of the economy and the prominence given to material incentives. There is some disagreement among long-time China specialists on the effects of this new emphasis. For example, there are some who claim the new policies have led to an increase in labor productivity, an improved standard of living for the majority of the rural population, and a doubling of the gross national product (GNP) (Deane 1989:7). However, they also admit that there have been disturbing effects as well, including "an infectious selfishness that is shaping social attitudes, a destructive impact on the environment, pervasive corruption, and two-digit inflation that has so far been hardly touched by countermeasures" (Deane 1989:7).

As a result, in place of the emphasis on moral incentives and the communist work ethic that characterized the early decades of the Chinese revolution, today the new work ethic is centered on material incentives and slogans such as "some must get rich first" and "to get rich is glorious" (Hinton 1989:35). This has accompanied the privatization of agriculture and the wholesale dismantling of the collective forms of production that were established in rural China during the Maoist period.

In contrast, Cuba's socialist regime has placed a renewed emphasis on the use of moral incentives as a part of the on-going rectification campaign taking place in that country. The current policy, in fact, seeks to recreate the revolutionary spirit and commitment that characterized the early years of the revolution; and moral incentives are an important part of this renewal.

The exemplary actions and thought of the Cuban revolution's most famous martyr, Che Guevara, are the centerpiece of this effort at revolutionary renewal. In Fidel Castro's October 8, 1987, speech on the twentieth anniversary of Che's death in Bolivia, Fidel referred to the need to rectify the errors that have been committed in Cuba since Che left on his fateful mission to carry the revolution to the rest of Latin America.

What are we rectifying? We're rectifying all those things—and there are many—that strayed from the revolutionary spirit, from revolutionary work, revolutionary virtue, revolutionary effort, revolutionary responsibility; all those things that strayed from the spirit of solidarity among people. We're rectifying all the shoddiness and mediocrity that is precisely the negation of Che's ideas, his revolutionary thought, his style, his spirit, and his example. (quoted in Tablada 1989:20)

The ills that need rectifying, according to Fidel, stem from the regime's having resorted to methods borrowed from capitalism and turned away from its earlier reliance upon moral incentives and communist ethics.

Among the errors criticized by Fidel, the most frequently mentioned are:

- The distribution of food and personal services through private markets;
- The payment of high wages that have no relation to what is being produced;
- The failure to revise outmoded work norms;
- The evaluation of state enterprises in terms of their profitability instead of their efficiency in producing socially useful products;
- Increasing competition and commodity relations between the state enterprises;
- The increasing mechanical application of bonuses, overtime payments, and other material incentives of an individual nature that have contributed to economic and social inequality among the work force and undermined their commitment and concern with quality (Tablada 1989:21–22).

To understand the significance of the present renewal effort and the errors that are now being criticized by Cuba's leaders, we must go back to the first years of the revolutionary regime when Comandante Che Guevara was Cuba's leading theoretician and protagonist of the use of radical measures to bring about the socialist transformation of Cuban society. By the end of 1960, the revolutionary regime in Cuba had nationalized the most important sectors of the economy and paralyzed the market. Che, along with other radical members of the revolutionary leadership such as Raul Castro, Osvaldo Dorticos, and Antonio Núñez Jimenez, theorized that Cuba's small size and relatively well-developed communications system made it possible to introduce central planning and do away with the pricing mechanism of the market. He adopted a radical Marxist perspective and opposed attempts to build socialism by capitalist methods.

The pipe dream that socialism can be achieved with the help of the dull instruments left to us by capitalism (the commodity as the economic cell, profitability, individual material interest as a lever, etc.) can lead into a blind alley. And you wind up there after having traveled a long distance with many crossroads, and it is hard to figure out just where you took the wrong turn. Meanwhile, the economic foundation that had been laid has done its work of undermining the development of consciousness. To build communism it is necessary, simultaneous with the new material foundations, to build the new man. (quoted in Tablada 1989:136)

Che argued that moral incentives should be given primacy over material incentives and that the finances of the state enterprises should be part of the state budget. He was opposed to the Soviet *khozraschet* system in which the state enterprises operate much like capitalist enterprises as independent accounting units responsible for making profits and covering their costs (Bernardo 1971:28). He thought Cuba should rapidly establish a centrally planned economy and make a clean break with capitalist ideas and methods.

Che forcefully advocated the perspective that the transition from capitalism to communism requires linking transformations in the economic structure of society with transformations in the social consciousness of the population. More specifically, he reasoned that in the period of socialist transition the use of capitalist methods corrupts the process; and that it is necessary to create a new communist consciousness in order to bring about the socialist transformation of society.

> A socialist economy without communist moral values does not interest me. We fight poverty, but we also fight alienation. One of the fundamental aims of Marxism is to eliminate . . . individual self-interest and profit from man's psychological motivations. (quoted in Tablada 1989:215)

In other words, Che was acutely aware that the transformation of the motivations and consciousness of men and women are as important as the transformation of the structures of production and distribution. Therefore, he believed that "communism is a phenomenon of consciousness and not solely a phenomenon of production" (quoted in Tablada 1989:216).

Che played a major role in the great debate over alternative models of socialism that took place during the early 1960s in Cuba. Among the various models that were considered by the Cubans was the Yugoslav model of decentralized market socialism, involving a regulated market, commodity relations, profit-making enterprises, decentralized investments, and material incentives (Bernardo 1971:16–17). Che appears to have shared Paul Sweezy's views on this system (Ibid:9), namely that this type of economic system produces individuals with goals and motivations no different from those of capitalism (see Huberman and Sweezy 1964).

In 1965, Che left Cuba under a cloud of secrecy, and shortly afterward the debate over alternative models was settled in favor of a centralized model of socialism in which the primacy of nonmonetary and moral incentives was a distinctive feature. This was the egalitarian variant of administrative (centralized) socialism that Che had advocated, and he left behind many ideas as to how it could be implemented in Cuba, including the use of voluntary work brigades, a form of fraternal competition between workers called "socialist emulation," and a budgetary finance system for the efficient management of the country's state enterprises and the production process in general.

The Cuban model that came into being by the end of the 1960s was based on:

- A narrow range of wage levels;
- The satisfaction of basic necessities through the provision of free services (such as health care and education) as well as the rationing of basic goods at subsidized low prices;
- An emphasis on collective forms of consumption as opposed to private consumption;
- The distribution of certain goods such as refrigerators and televisions on the basis of the decisions of workers' assemblies;
- The establishment of an elaborate system of nonmonetary awards for persons and groups displaying exemplary attitudes and performance (socialist emulation);
- The mobilization of the population to give up freely some of their leisure time to participate in voluntary work projects;
- Public education campaigns aimed at developing communist morals (*conciencia comunista*) in place of the values of egoistic individualism (Karl 1975:39).

Che's views have often been characterized as romantic and idealistic, and his approach has been criticized as giving rise to "voluntarism" (Tablada 1989:174). Critics ask how long can people be expected to substitute moral fervor for improved material consumption, and they question whether the use of moral incentives is anything more than a means for extracting unpaid labor from workers who feel psychologically coerced to give up their leisure time (Bernardo 1971:xvii). It is argued that the "Marxist-Christian" ideal of man not living by bread alone overlooks the fact that in reality there is often a trade-off between material well-being and moral behavior, especially under conditions of scarcity.

However, Che and his supporters knew full well that moral incentives had to be combined with material incentives, and that it was not enough to rely upon the development of a communist work ethic among the working population. In fact, they advocated the establishment of a wage system in which wages would be tied to qualifications and the fulfillment of prescribed work norms. Thus, Che stated:

As for the presence of material interest in an individualized form, we recognize it (although fighting it and attempting to speed up its elimination through education) and apply it in our norms of hourly work plus bonuses, and wage penalties for the nonfulfillment of these norms. (quoted in Tablada 1989:192)

Che developed a wage system based on these principles when he was minister of industries. However, he believed that the wage system during the transition to socialism should not overemphasize material incentives, and he stressed that it should be used in combination with moral incentives to build a communist work ethic.

When we set our work norms for establishing wages, the minimum norm— what must be done by each worker every day—is one's duty to society. What is important is not what must be done to earn a wage. It is instead what must be done to fulfill one's duty to the community, which provides— through wages, and through social services that grow more abundant day by day—the opportunity to live, clothe oneself, to educate one's children, to acquire culture, and to become an ever more rounded human being. (quoted in Tablada 1989:184–185).

For Che, the development of a new consciousness about the social significance of work was critically important, since he saw this new consciousness as a material force in the construction of socialism. He advocated the development of a new ethic of voluntary work. In fact, he originated the system of voluntary work in Cuba that has become one of the hallmarks of Cuban socialism. He was influenced by Lenin's view that voluntary work lays the basis for developing new attitudes about work and for eliminating the self-centeredness inherited from bourgeois culture (Tablada 1989:170). Che saw voluntary work as a "school that creates consciousness" and emphasized that it be well-organized and clearly directed at doing something of real social value so that those who participated felt that what they were doing was useful. For this reason, he was opposed to voluntary work being used to complete unfinished tasks in the workplace or to enable a state enterprise to meet its quotas. Instead, he advocated that voluntary work be used to build schools, day care centers, clinics, and housing for the workers as well as to help harvest the island's important sugar crop (prior to extensive mechanization). He himself participated regularly in weekend voluntary work brigades and studied how to organize and supervise voluntary work projects.

The influence of Che Guevara's ideas on moral incentives is still strong in Cuba, even though it has been a quarter of a century since he left the island. During the late 1970s and early 1980s, voluntary work and the prior emphasis on moral incentives were displaced by an increased emphasis on individual material incentives and administrative methods. However, since the rectification campaign was launched in 1986, Cuba's leaders have revived voluntary work brigades and begun to attack the problems that they believe have been created by the retreat from the ideals and methods introduced in the 1960s (Angotti 1988; Tablada 1989:26–27).

Since 1976 a number of serious problems have developed in Cuba's state enterprises and in the economy in general. Some of these problems, which can be traced to the existing system of incentives, are as follows:

- Widespread absenteeism;
- Lack of labor discipline;
- A blind belief in administrative mechanisms such as the central system for management and planning of the economy (SDPE);
- The distribution of bonuses as a matter of course without regard to performance or quality of output;
- Overly liberal work schedules with abundant time for breaks;
- The fixing of low quotas so that every one can exceed them;
- Misuse and waste of resources;
- Petty corruption of all kinds;
- The accumulation of small fortunes through the sale of houses and the private market in agricultural goods;
- The setting of excessive prices in maintenance, construction, and transportation to cover up for overstaffing, inefficiency, and overspending;
- The payment of high wages and salaries that have no relation to what is being produced;
- The emergence of a layer of administrators and managers that have adopted a petty bourgeois consciousness that has, in turn, undermined the consciousness of many workers;
- A tendency on the part of the managers and workers in certain enterprises to maximize the profitability of their enterprise at the expense of others and society as a whole;
- The development of a bureaucratic mentality on the part of certain administrative and technical employees;
- The continued use of outmoded work norms.

This list of problems reflects in one way or another the Cuban regime's failure to use both material and moral incentives in such a way as to elicit high productivity, commitment to quality, labor discipline, the pursuit of collective goals as opposed to selfish individual interests, efficiency, conservation of resources, honest and professional management, and respect for the consumer/public. It remains to be seen whether the current rectification campaign will be able to overcome these problems through a revival of the combination of moral and material incentives that were advocated by Che and introduced during the late 1960s.

The Nicaraguan Experience

Turning to revolutionary Nicaragua we find a situation that was strikingly different from that in Cuba, although similar problems of labor indiscipline and low productivity existed in both the state and private sectors of the country's mixed economy. The differences stem, for the most part, from the fact that the revolutionary state in Nicaragua had far less control over the production process and the organization of the labor force than in Cuba.

In Nicaragua's war-torn mixed economy, it was not possible for the revolutionary leadership to emphasize moral incentives in the same way as Cuba. The regime was also forced to restrict the use of material incentives due to the economic crisis caused by the war and certain economic policies that contributed to hyperinflation. In fact, because of the continuing economic crisis faced by the country, the regime was repeatedly forced to call upon the working class, the salaried middle sectors, and the small producers to accept the continuing decline in their real income and severe shortages in most wage goods. It has already been mentioned that by the end of 1987, the purchasing power of working class wages had declined to only 6 percent of what it had been in 1980 (*Envió* 1989:44). Moreover, in order to maintain the support of the poor peasantry and increase the supply of basic foods to the urban areas, the government was forced to reverse the direction of its original agrarian reform program and distribute large amounts of land to individual peasants. This reorientation represented a significant turn toward privatization and an increased reliance upon market incentives (Harris 1987:8–10).

In the early years of the revolutionary regime before the full brunt of the war and hyperinflation began to be felt on the economy, the regime did introduce voluntary work and various types of emulation in the state sector as well as in workplaces where the progovernment unions held sway (Vilas 1985). Moreover, the government fostered the establishment of worker participation in the management of the state enterprises. These measures were not undertaken on a scale comparable to that in Cuba, however, because of the economic and political limitations resulting from the country's mixed economy and the regime's attempts to obtain the cooperation of the national bourgeoisie.

In a sense, because of the war and the desperate economic conditions prevailing in the country, the regime was forced to use moral incentives to keep the work force in the state sector at their jobs because the wages that the state paid were totally inadequate to meet their basic needs. Appeals based on patriotism and the defense of the revolution were used to keep people working for wages that had declined in real value to a mere fraction of their previous levels before the country began to suffer the effects of hyperinflation. These moral appeals were coupled with special food rations and/or the access to special stores where a limited number of basic goods could be purchased at reduced prices.

It is not clear if the revolutionary process would have developed in a socialist direction if the country's economic crisis had been overcome and the Sandinistas had remained in power. However, the regime would most probably have followed its original strategy of using increases in the supply of subsidized wage goods (basic consumer goods) as a major form of material incentive. The reasoning behind this strategy was explained by E.V.K. FitzGerald, one of the economic advisers to the Sandinista government, as follows:

> The lesson of the Chilean experience, and to a certain extent in Cuba as well, was that nominal salary increases only served to increase the prices of food to the disadvantage of the popular classes. Therefore, in Nicaragua it was decided that the only way to produce changes in the economy which would improve the distribution of incomes was through increasing the supply of wage goods. (FitzGerald 1984:14)

Not only is this approach more consistent with socialist values, but it offers a realistic means of trying to offset the inflationary pressures caused by increased popular demands for goods in countries recovering from the disruptive effects of wars and popular insurrections. In fact, this approach calls attention to the importance of wage goods as a critical type of material incentive in the transition to socialism. Past experience seems to indicate that an increased supply of wage goods is required to provide the material incentives for increased productivity on the part of all the popular classes (working class, peasantry, middle-class technicians, administrators, and professionals) in the early stages of revolutionary transformation (FitzGerald 1986:37–39).

Conclusion

The use of material incentives in combination with moral incentives is clearly required in the transition to socialism. The Cuban case provides an important body of experience with regard to the use of various forms of moral incentives, not only to increase labor productivity but, more important, to transform the work ethic of the workforce and develop a communist consciousness. Early attempts were made in the Soviet Union and China to use moral incentives, but an increased reliance on material incentives has been the pattern in these countries. This reliance appears to have fostered capitalistic values and practices instead of developing a new socialist work ethic or protocommunist consciousness.

10
Socialist Forms of Organization

Marx and Engels on Socialist Organization

The writings of Marx and Engels did not provide a blueprint for the organization of socialist society. This was not their intention because these authors were opposed to the production of blueprints for the future construction of a social order that they believed would have to be created by the working class once it had seized power from the bourgeoisie and undertaken the tasks involved in the revolutionary transformation of society. However, they did write about what they thought would be the goals and basic nature of the revolutionary social order created by the proletariat. For example, in the *Manifesto of the Communist Party*, Marx and Engels stated:

> When, in the course of development, class distinctions have disappeared, and all production has been concentrated in the hands of a vast association of the whole nation, the public power will lose its political character. Political power, properly so called, is merely the organized power of one class for oppressing another. If the proletariat during its contest with the bourgeoisie is compelled, by the force of circumstances, to organize itself as a class, if by means of a revolution, it makes itself the ruling class, and, as such, sweeps away by force the old conditions of production, then it will, along with these conditions, have swept away the conditions for the existence of class antagonisms and of classes generally, and thereby have abolished its own supremacy as a class. In place of the old bourgeois society, with its classes and class antagonisms, we shall have an association, in which the free development of each is the condition for the free development of all. (Marx and Engels 1972:53)

This passage from the *Manifesto* makes it clear that Marx and Engels thought that in a future communist society, "production would be concentrated in the hands of a vast association of the whole nation" and the state or "public power would lose its political [read: oppressive] character." Moreover, society would be organized as an "association" in which "the free development of each is the condition for the free development of all."

Their choice of the term "association" clearly implied cooperation and voluntary membership, just as their use of the phrase "free development of each" implied individual liberty and equality of opportunity. Therefore, from this famous passage in the *Manifesto*, as well as subsequent writings, one can conclude that Marx and Engels hoped communist society would be organized on the basis of cooperation, voluntary membership, individual liberty, and equality of opportunity. In addition, it seems clear that they hoped the organization of communist society would be free of oppression, class distinctions, and class antagonisms. But they also thought the proletariat might have to "sweep away by force the old conditions of production."

According to Marx and Engels, the Paris Commune of 1871 provided the first opportunity to see how the working class might organize society following a successful seizure of power. However, the commune was more important to them for its potential rather than for what it achieved (Avineri 1971:240–241). Marx's discussion of the Paris Commune in his address on *The Civil War in France* provides a paradigm or model for what he projected might be the organization of a future communist society. Twenty years after the event, Engels went further than Marx and referred to the Paris Commune as an example of what the dictatorship of the proletariat would look like following the overthrow of the capitalist state (Marx and Engels 1972:262).

Paul Bellis, in his work *Marxism and the USSR*, has summarized the five basic structural innovations of the Paris Commune that Marx extolled in *The Civil War in France*.

1. The abolition of the standing army and its replacement by a popular militia as an armed force no longer separate from and opposed to the people.
2. The political functionaries of the Commune consisted of elected and fully recallable *delegates* rather than representatives. The police, judiciary, and other officials were similarly elected by universal suffrage and were *revocable*.
3. The delegated officials received no special material privileges, their incomes being on a par with those of skilled workers.

4. The separation of executive and legislative functions, characteristic of the bourgeois regime, was ended: "The Commune was to be a working, not a parliamentary body, executive and legislative at the same time."
5. The extension of the communal structure was to have created a genuinely unified and coordinated organization at the level of the social formation as a whole. (Bellis 1979:9)

With regard to this last structural innovation, it is perhaps best to quote in full what Marx had to say because it provides the essential outlines of a "bottom-up" federative system of democratic self-government:

In a rough sketch of national organization which the Commune had no time to develop . . . the Commune was to be the political form of even the smallest country hamlet, and . . . in the rural districts the standing army was to be replaced by a national militia, with an extremely short term of service. The rural communes of every district were to administer their common affairs by an assembly of delegates in the central town, and these district assemblies were again to send deputies to the National Delegation in Paris, each delegate to be at any time revocable and bound by the *mandat impératif* (formal instructions) of his constituents. . . . The unity of the nation was not to be broken, but, on the contrary, to be organized by the Communal Constitution and to become a reality by the destruction of the State power which claimed to be the embodiment of that unity independent of, and superior to, the nation itself. . . . While the merely repressive organs of the old governmental power were to be wrested from an authority usurping pre-eminence over society itself, and restored to the responsible agents of society. (Marx and Engels 1972:292)

Marx ingeniously compared this system of participatory and federative democracy with the indirect representative nature of parliamentary democracy and the hiring practices of capitalist employers. Thus, he continued:

Instead of deciding once in three or six years which member of the ruling class was to misrepresent the people in Parliament, universal suffrage was to serve the people, constituted in Communes, as individual suffrage serves every other employer in the search for the workmen and managers in his business. And it is well known that companies, like individuals, in matters of real business generally know how to put the right man in the right place, and, if they for once make a mistake, to redress it promptly. (Marx and Engels 1972:292)

As the passages quoted above indicate, Marx saw the Paris Commune as a genuinely democratic and egalitarian form of government.

In this regard, it is important to note that one of the early acts of the Paris Commune was to order the formation of cooperative societies among the workers of factories that had been closed down. These cooperatives were to operate the factories and be organized into one large union of cooperatives. Marx saw this as evidence that the commune was essentially a working-class government and a means for transforming the relations of production. This is revealed in the following passages from *The Civil War in France*:

> It was a thoroughly expansive political form, while all previous forms of government had been emphatically repressive. Its true secret was this. It was essentially a working class government, the product of the struggle of the producing against the appropriating class, the political form at last discovered under which to work out the economic emancipation of labor. Except on this last condition, the Communal Constitution would have been an impossibility and a delusion. The political rule of the producer cannot coexist with the perpetuation of his social slavery. The Commune was therefore to serve as a lever for uprooting the economical foundations upon which rests the existence of classes, and therefore class rule. . . . The Commune intended to abolish that class property which makes the labor of the many the wealth of the few. It aimed at the expropriation of the expropriators. It wanted to make individual property a truth by transforming the means of production, land and capital, now chiefly the means of enslaving and exploiting labor, into mere instruments of free and associated labor. (Marx and Engels 1972:294)

What Marx saw in the Paris Commune was a form of democratic self-government that would serve as a political agency for "uprooting" the foundations of class society. Unlike representative parliamentary government, he regarded the commune as a form of popular democracy that would enable the proletariat to rule. Moreover, because he regarded it as truly egalitarian, he reasoned that this form of government could not possibly coexist with a social order based on classes and exploitation.

The role that the Paris Commune has played as a paradigm for the political organization of socialist society is of tremendous importance in Marxist thought. In the major works of Marxism and in the various revolutions with socialist ideals that have taken place throughout this century, one can see the influence of this communal paradigm of self-government. The local Soviets in the USSR, the People's Communes in China, the municipal communes in Yugoslavia, and the organs of People's Power (Poder Popular) in revolutionary Cuba—all have their antecedents in the Paris Commune.

People's Power in Cuba

The organizational structure of People's Power in Cuba, instituted nationwide in the late 1970s after a two-year pilot experiment in the Province of Mantanzas, conforms in many respects to the features of the Paris Commune lauded by Marx. On the other hand, it also lacks certain key features of this paradigm.

The introduction of *Poder Popular* represented an important turning point in the institutionalization and democratization of the political system established by the revolution. Prior to this point, there were no elections in Cuba and all government officials were appointed by the political leadership at the pinnacle of the party and the state. Thus, there were no formal means for ensuring the accountability of the leadership to the citizenry and little opportunity for popular participation in the political process, apart from participation in the mass organizations that were constituted by the leadership during the first years following the formation of the new regime. These mass organizations, in fact, continue to be an important channel for political participation. Most Cubans belong to one or more of these organizations, the most important of which are the Committees for the Defense of the Revolution (CDRs) organized at the neighborhood level, the Confederation of Cuban Workers (CTC), the Federation of Cuban Women (FMC), and the National Association of Small Farmers (ANAP) was formed to mobilize support for the regime among the small private farmers.

In 1976, national elections were held to elect delegates to the newly created *Poder Popular* assemblies at the municipal, provincial, and national levels. Over 30,000 candidates contested the 10,725 delegate positions at the municipal level (LeoGrande 1989:195). Voter turnout was 95 percent, the highest in Cuban history, even though voting was not required by law and was secret. A majority of the local vote was required for election to a delegate seat, so runoff elections had to be held in about one-quarter of the districts and these attracted almost the same turnout rate. Since 1976, elections to the municipal assemblies have taken place every two-and-a-half years: 1979, 1981, 1984, 1986, and 1989. All indications are that popular participation in these elections has remained very high, both in the elections themselves and in the local meetings that are held to nominate candidates for the municipal assembly seats.

Although the delegates to the 169 municipal assemblies are directly elected by the citizenry, the members of the 14 provincial assemblies and national assembly are elected by the municipal assemblies. Thus, the people do not directly elect the members of the provincial and national assemblies or the chief executive officers of the provincial and national governments.

According to the new Cuban constitution that took effect in 1976, the legal powers of the municipal assemblies are extensive. They have the authority to make policy on all matters falling within their jurisdiction, to supervise the administration of these policies, and to select and dismiss all administrative officials in the governmental departments under their authority (LeoGrande 1989:194). Unlike the democratic political institutions of capitalist societies, all productive and service organizations that provide goods and services to the population are supposed to be under the management and control of the assemblies (Lowy 1986:269). The municipal assemblies control most of the educational institutions, health care facilities, retail outlets, restaurants, public dining facilities, entertainment facilities, and so on within their boundaries. The national government retains control over all national economic activities, such as the sugar industry, heavy industry, the banks, the fishing industry, and so forth, plus the normal activities of all national governments, including national defense, foreign relations, and trade and monetary policies. The national government also controls the setting of technical and labor norms, such as wages, production standards, health and sanitation regulations.

The municipal electoral districts are divided into neighborhoods, and each neighborhood nominates a candidate for the delegate seat of their electoral district (LeoGrande 1989:194). The nominating takes place in a mass meeting for all the eligible voters and is done by individual voters or groups of voters. The communist party is prohibited from making or endorsing nominations, although a majority of the individuals nominated are members of the party. The nominees are then discussed and voted on by a show of hands, and the person receiving a simple majority becomes the neighborhood's candidate for the delegate seat in their electoral district. This is an important and lively opportunity for popular participation in the political process at the local level.

Another important opportunity comes at the accountability meetings that are held twice a year in which the municipal delegates are required to report (render account) to their constituents on their accomplishments and the affairs of the municipal assembly. These meetings provide an opportunity for the citizenry to ask questions, make complaints, report problems, and make suggestions. They are generally well attended, although the turnout is not as high as in the elections (Lutjens 1992).

These sessions reflect the difference between the delegate's role and that of an elected representative in most bourgeois democratic political systems. The delegate is required by the consititution to serve as an intermediary between the people and the government. Therefore, he or she must periodically report to them and act on their suggestions, complaints, and requests, which are formalized in the People's Power system as *planteamientos*. Failure to perform this role responsibly and effectively can result in delegates being recalled and replaced by their constituents at an accountability session. In 1989, only 45.9 percent of the delegates were reelected to the municipal assemblies and 114 were recalled (Lutjens 1992).

The *planteamientos* are an important part of the responsibilities of the delegates and the municipal assemblies. They are approved by a majority vote of those in attendance at the accountability sessions (LeoGrande 1989:194) and must be presented to the next meeting of the municipal assembly. The performances of the delegates and municipal assemblies are publicly assessed in terms of the number of *planteamientos* that they have successfully resolved within the required six-month limit. Reports must be given at the next accountability session to the citizens who have made these requests for action. The evidence indicates that the rate of resolution of *planteamientos* has generally been quite satisfactory (Lutjens 1992). Thus, they appear to have served two of the main purposes for which the organs of People's Power were originally established: to check bureaucratic tendencies and to provide a channel for the people to resolve problems at the local level (Lowy 1986:270).

However, the People's Power system of representative government in Cuba has significant limitations. These include the general lack of opposing political views and proposals, any competition between different parties and policy proposals, or any popular control over the leadership at the national level. As Michael Lowy notes:

In the absence of political pluralism, of different points of view in discussion, or of different parties that compete in the elections of delegates, the masses do not have the power of *decision* between alternative economic or political policies. The result is that the popular base has very little real control on the provincial and especially the *national* levels of power (the National Assembly, Council of State, and Council of Ministers). The problem is not so much the predominance of party members (or the Communist Youth) in the popular power bodies (75.2 percent in the local assemblies and 96.7 percent in the National Assembly) but rather, the fact that the masses have no possibility to choose from among different proposals presented by various parties or various tendencies within the same party. The one-party system and the party's monolithic internal structure are the principal limitations on socialist democracy in Cuban popular power. (Lowy 1986:270)

Lowy argues that the introduction of "the free organization of all political parties that respect revolutionary legality" would not be "a concession to the bourgeoisie, but rather the condition for the existence of . . . a real confrontation of points of view and the possibility of a real decision by workers on matters essential to the country's economic, social and political life" (Lowy 1986:271).

Lowy, like many contemporary Marxists in Latin America and the Caribbean, contends that the struggle against bourgeois ideology can best be carried out in an open democratic medium.

> Political pluralism implies freedom of expression and freedom of the press. It is undeniable that bourgeois ideology does not disappear after the revolutionary triumph and maintains its influence over sectors of the population. But it is a grave error to believe that it should be fought with administrative or repressive methods. Historical experience demonstrates that repression of bourgeois opinions and ideologies is ineffective. On the contrary, in the long run those methods ultimately reinforce reactionary ideas. . . . Only those who do not have confidence in the superiority of socialist and revolutionary ideas, nor in the proletariat and the workers, fear open ideological confrontation with bourgeois and reactionary ideologies when the proletariat is in power. This confrontation is the sole means by which the working class can ideologically educate itself and free itself from the influence of bourgeois ideas. (Lowy 1986:272)

In other words, Lowy thinks that unrestricted freedom of political expression, political competition, and open ideological debate must be essential features of democratic forms of organization in the transition to socialism. He notes their absence in the Cuban system of People's Power and argues that they would strengthen the system as well as enhance popular participation.

The relationship between the party and the People's Power assemblies imposes a definite limitation on the system. The party controls the nomination of the executive committees of the assemblies and has the right to introduce proposals for the consideration of these bodies (Valdés 1989:172–176). Moreover, the fact that almost all the members of the national and provincial assemblies, and the vast majority of the members of the municipal assemblies, are also members of the party greatly restricts the range of views that are presented and discussed in these bodies, even if the party does not instruct the individual members how to vote (which it is proscribed from doing).

In sum, the Cuban system of *Poder Popular* appears to be an important, but limited form of popular democracy. It has some of the aspects of the Marxist paradigm of the Paris Commune—the direct election of recallable delegates to a local council or assembly that has both legislative and executive authority, the delegated officials receive no special material privileges (they receive the same pay as they receive in their regular occupations), and the municipal asssemblies form the base of a unified and coordinated organization at the national level. However, the police, judiciary, and other officials are not elected by universal suffrage (in contrast with the Paris Commune), and not even the top executive officials are elected. Moreover, the executive function dominates the legislative function at the national level. This domination tends to reduce the national assembly to a largely deliberative body rather than a working body exercising both executive and legislative functions at the same time. Finally, although the popular militia have played an important role in revolutionary Cuba's political history, they have not replaced the standing army.

Forms of Workers' Control

Turning now to other socialist forms of organization in the Marxist tradition, we note that besides the communal form of self-government, the producer cooperative and the workers' council play similar roles as the organizational paradigms for the management of the means of production by the producers. However, the record here, too, is one in which the actual forms have generally diverged from the basic principles of the paradigm.

In the Russian Revolution, the factory committees and the soviets were initially formed as "bottom-up" organizations that could have, and in some cases appeared to have, provided the workers with the means of exercising direct democratic control over their factories and local communities. However, within a short time following the formation of the Bolshevik regime, these organizations were brought under the centralized control of the Bolshevik Party and bureaucratic state apparatus (Bellis 1979:216–218).

The substitution of the dictatorship of the party for the dictatorship of the proletariat, as a result of the decimation of the latter in the Civil War and the central role played by the party in the revolutionary process, prevented the development of effective forms of workers' self-management in the Soviet Union (Bellis 1979:216–218). Moreover, because the Bolsheviks thought workers' control was guaranteed by the new Soviet state, they did not see any reason for the workers to exercise control at the point of production. As a result, they replaced the factory committees with centralized unions and regional economic councils called *sovnarkhozy*. Branko Horvat argues that this course of development eliminated the possibility for workers self-management to develop in the Soviet Union.

On December 1 the Supreme Economic Council was created. It abolished the All-Russian Council of Workers Control and made the control function a component of the overall task of regulating the economy. It coordinated a network of local economic councils [sovnarkhozy]. . . . [The] Bolsheviks were now arguing that there was no need for separate workers' organizations after the conquest of power, as in the time when factory committees exerted workers' control and trade unions organized the struggle against the bourgeoisie. In January 1918, the First All-Russian Congress of Trade Unions decided to transform factory committees into primary trade union organs. This device—killing workers' self-management by unionizing it— would later be used in other countries as well. . . . At the Second Congress of the Comintern many delegates continued to treat factory committees— the organizations of direct producers—as more revolutionary than trade unions, which operated through leadership. Yet the congress approved the amalgamation of the two. In March the Central Council of Petrograd Factory Committees disappeared, absorbed by the sovnarkhozy of the northern industrial region. (Horvat 1982:138–139)

Without any effective organizational means to exercise control over production, the proletariat was deprived of any basis of political power and forced to submit to the domination of a new managerial-bureaucratic hierarchy.

It is worth emphasizing that the Bolsheviks transformed the unions into centralized organizations that were used to mobilize support for state policies and to discipline the work force rather than to defend the interests of the workers and protect their rights. As a result, they used the unions as well as other mass organizations as "transmission belts" for mobilizing support for the party and its policies as well as com-municating directives to the rank and file (Lowy, 1986:272–273). Initially, Lenin pressed for the autonomy of the unions so that they could protect the workers against what he referred to as "a workers state with bureaucratic distortions" (Lowy 1986:273). However, this guideline did not prevent the Bolsheviks from undermining the autonomy and in-dependence of the unions. Later, in 1933, Trotsky argued for the relative independence of the trade unions as an "important corrective in the Soviet state system, which finds itself under pressure from the peasantry and the bureaucracy" (quoted in Bellis 1979:81). But it was already too late; the centralization and bureaucratization of the single-party state had depoliticized the working class and eliminated the autonomy of the unions.

In China and Eastern Europe, unions and other mass organizations have enjoyed little autonomy from the party and the party-state, although this pattern was broken in Poland with the establishment of Solidarity. The cases of Cuba and revolutionary Nicaragua are somewhat different. In Cuba, the unions have experienced both a decline and renewal in their relative autonomy vis-à-vis the state. Since the late 1970s, the unions in Cuba have increasingly played a more important role in the work centers. They oversee the Labor Councils that exist in each workplace, organize the election of council members, train the members to perform their dispute resolution tasks, and make sure the proper conditions exist for the functioning of these councils (Fuller 1987:140). Generally speaking, the Labor Councils investigate the grievances that workers bring against management and they attempt to resolve disputes between workers and managers.

Cuban workers expect the unions to serve as their advocates in disputes with management and to argue on their behalf at formal Labor Council hearings. The unions have played a vital role in this respect, despite formal limitations on the scope of their involvement in labor-management disputes. Thus, one recent study on worker-management conflict in Cuba concludes:

> Unions are a critical factor in the consideration of power in postrevolutionary relationships at the workplace. During the period when unions were the smallest, weakest, and the most dependent on the state administration and the party, the grievance mechanisms, though exemplary in many regards, were least able to remedy the effect of unequal power divisions on those workers who had experienced them in a firsthand and overt fashion. Yet after 1970, as unions became stronger, larger, and more active, they have served to encourage individual producers (who on their own may not have tried or chosen to do so) to challenge their boss's power through the existing grievance resolution mechanisms. And since 1980 when the method for settling disputes over discipline was altered in favor of management, the unions' role in uniting individual Cuban producers into a collective force capable of extending workers' power at the point of production has become critical, not only in situations of overt workplace conflict, but at other times as well. (Fuller 1987:149–150)

What this study indicates is that the unions in Cuba tend to have the confidence of the workers and that at least at the workplace they are an important source of support for workers.

In Nicaragua, the pro-Sandinista unions and mass organizations retained considerable autonomy from the revolutionary regime, although they tended to serve more as support structures than as channels for the representation of their members' interests at the state level. The Sandinista leadership expected the pro-Sandinista mass organizations— the Sandinista trade unions, local Sandinista Defense Committees, the women's organization, the small farmers' union, and the Sandinista youth organization—to act with relative independence. The following declaration of the FSLN National Directorate on this question makes this clear:

Must the mass organizations revert to their own force, expression, and mobilization when their petitions are not heard, when the doors are shut on all sides, without finding an answer anywhere? We believe so. . . . The mass organizations must collect and make their own demands of their members, of their social sectors, and struggle for their materialization through the new mechanisms that the revolution has instituted. But when these roads are closed, when they knock and no one hears, when they are reverted to and are not functional, whether because of bureaucracy, or liberal methods, or because the problems of the masses are not taken into account, etc., our organizations must move to other forms of political persuasion. This means that the mass organizations, framed within the general line of the revolution, have sufficient right, when these organisms are closed, to recur to internal criticism, to public criticism, to the use of all means of communication up to mobilization to demand the necessary measures to guarantee that their claims are heard. (quoted in Vilas 1986:184)

As this declaration makes clear, the Sandinista leadership expected the the mass organizations to defend the interests of their members and bring to light, through public criticism and even mobilization if necessary, bureaucratic obstacles to the realization of these interests. However, as the economic condition of the country became increasingly precarious, the regime prohibited the use of strikes to promote the claims of the unions on the grounds that the country could not afford interruptions in the productive process.

Prior to the institutionalization of an elected representative form of government in Nicaragua in 1984, the mass organizations were directly represented in the Council of State, a psuedolegislative body set up by the revolutionary regime after it took power. The election of the national assembly in 1984 replaced the Council of State and left the mass organizations without any direct representation in the government. A case can be made that the revolutionary regime should have developed a more innovative form of democratic government in which the mass organizations would have been incorporated at all levels—both in the legislative and administrative processes at the national, regional, and local government levels. This would have guaranteed the representation of their members' interests at all levels and in all instances of the governmental system. Michael Lowy suggested something along these lines with regard to the legislature shortly after the national elections in Nicaragua:

An hypothesis that requires consideration is that it perhaps may be necessary to elect a second assembly, constituted of delegates from all the country's mass organizations. This "workers' assembly" would have the task of controlling or complementing the National Assembly's activities. This would permit the mass organizations, representing the most active parts of the working class, to directly influence the country's political and economic policies. (Lowy 1986:276)

Lowy recognized that conventional representative democracy is insufficient as a governmental form of organization for a popular revolutionary society. From a Marxist perspective, he was aware that a socialist transition requires "integrating and overcoming representative democracy" because periodic elections to a national legislature do not provide an adequate means for effective popular participation in the formulation and implementation of state policy (Lowy 1986:276). More direct and *ongoing* forms of popular participation are required at all levels of political and economic decisionmaking to counterbalance the more limited forms of representative democracy.

The Problems of Bourgeois Forms of Organization

The tendency to rely upon bourgeois forms of organization, in the economic sphere as well as the political one, has been present in all socialist revolutions since the Russian Revolution. Lenin and many of the Bolsheviks made the mistake of thinking that capitalist forms of industrial organization and management could be used by the new revolutionary regime to create the conditions for socialism. Thus, Lenin in *The Immediate Tasks of the Soviet Government* argued for the adoption of the latest forms of capitalist industrial organization and, particularly, Frederick Taylor's methods of so-called scientific management:

> The task that the Soviet government must set the people in all its scope is—learn to work. The Taylor system, the last word of capitalism in this respect, like all capitalist progress, is a combination of the refined brutality of bourgeois exploitation and a number of the greatest scientific achievements in the field of analyzing mechanical motions during work, the elimination of superfluous and awkward motions, the elaboration of correct methods of work, the introduction of the best system of accounting and control, etc. The Soviet Republic must at all costs adopt all that is valuable in the achievements of science and technology in this field. The possibility of building socialism depends exactly upon our success in combining Soviet power and the Soviet organization of administration with the up-to-date achievements of capitalism. (Lenin 1976:417)

Lenin went even further than the Taylorists by arguing that *"unquestioning subordination* to a single will is absolutely necessary for the success of processes organized on the pattern of large-scale machine industry" (Lenin 1976:425).

Morever, Lenin saw "absolutely *no* contradiction in principle between Soviet (that is, socialist) democracy and the exercise of dictatorial powers by individuals" in Soviet organizations (Lenin 1976:424). He strongly opposed the demands of the Workers' Opposition for workers' self-management of production under the control of the unions. When Bukharin introduced a resolution for industrial democracy (democratic management of industrial enterprises) in the Central Committee of the party, "Lenin reacted furiously by pointing out that industrial democracy gives rise to a number of utterly false ideas and might be understood to repudiate dictatorship and management by individuals" (Horvat 1982:140). Following the Kronstadt rebellion in 1921, the Workers' Opposition was banned, the trade unions were turned to the task of insuring labor discipline, and any further suggestion of workers' self-management was precluded.

What Lenin and the Bolsheviks failed to realize is that the division of labor, technology, and forms of management characteristic of capitalist forms of organization are antithetical to the emancipation of the workers and the basic principles of socialism. On this subject, they appear to have ignored Marx's writings or at least failed to act upon them. For example, in Volume 1 of *Capital*, Marx wrote the following about the division of labor in capitalist manufacturing organizations:

> By specialization of the instruments of labor, by the formation of detail laborers, and by grouping and combining the latter into a single mechanism, division of labor in manufacture creates a qualitative gradation, and a quantitative proportion in the social process of production; it consequently *creates a definite organization of labor*, and thereby develops at the same time new productive forces in the society. In its specific capitalist form—and under the given conditions, it could take no other form than a capitalistic one—manufacture is but a particular method of begetting surplus-value [profit], or of augmenting at the expense of the laborer the self-expansion of capital—usually called social wealth, "Wealth of Nations," etc. It increases the social productive power of labor, not only for the benefit of the capitalist instead of the laborer, but it does this by crippling the individual laborers. It creates new conditions for the lordship of capital over labor. If, therefore, on the one hand, it presents itself historically as a progress and a necessary phase in the economic development of society, on the other hand, it is a refined and civilized method of exploitation. (Marx 1967:344)

The crippling aspects of the division of labor and use of machine technology in capitalist industrial organizations led Marx to further note:

In handicraft and [simple] manufacture, the workman makes use of a tool, in the factory, the machine makes use of him. There the movements of the instruments of labor proceed from him, here it is the movements of the machine that he must follow. . . . At the same time that factory work exhausts the nervous system to the uttermost, it does away with the many-sided play of the muscles, and confiscates every atom of freedom, both in bodily and intellectual activity. The lightening of the labor, even, becomes a sort of torture, since the machine does not free the laborer from work, but deprives the work of all interest. Every kind of capitalist production, in so far as it is not only a labor process but also a process of creating surplus-value, has this in common, that it is not the workman that employs the instruments of labor, but the instruments of labor that employ the workman. (Marx 1967:398)

Marx also criticized the separation of intellectual from manual labor that characterizes capitalist forms of production. He observed that this artificial separation as well as the technical subordination of the workers gives rise to militaristic forms of discipline and control over the work force.

The separation of the intellectual powers of production from the manual labor, and the conversion of those powers into the might of capital over labor is, as we have already shown, finally completed by modern industry erected on the foundation of machinery. The special skill of each individual insignificant factory operative vanishes as an infinitesimal quantity before the science, the gigantic physical forces, and the mass of labor that are embodied in the factory mechanism and, together with that mechanism, constitute the power of the "master." . . . The technical subordination of the workman to the uniform motion of the instruments of labor, and the peculiar composition of the body of the workpeople, consisting as it does of individuals of both sexes and all ages, give rise to a barrack discipline, which is elaborated into a complete system in the factory, and which fully develops the before mentioned labor of overlooking, thereby dividing the workpeople into operatives and overlookers, into private soldiers and sergeants of an industrial army. (Marx 1967:399)

It is clear from these passages as well as others in Marx's writings that he regarded capitalist forms of industrial organization as exploitive, despotic, and inhumane and, therefore, not compatible with a new social order founded on the interests of the working class.

Although Marx did not provide a blueprint for organizing socialist forms of production, it is clear from his writings that he thought the basic features of capitalist forms of production would have to be replaced by new forms of production that would be based upon democratic decisionmaking and management, the use of technology for the empowerment rather than the subordination of the workers, the integration of intellectual with manual labor, the variation and rotation of work in place of narrow specialization, and the greatest possible development of the abilities of each member of the work force. For example, in Volume 1 of *Capital*, Marx wrote:

Modern industry . . . through its catastrophes imposes the necessity of recognizing, as a fundamental law of production, variation of work, consequently fitness of the laborer for varied work, consequently the greatest possible development of his varied aptitudes. It becomes a question of life and death for society to adapt the mode of production to the normal functioning of this law. Modern Industry, indeed, compels society, under penalty of death, to replace the detail worker of today, crippled by life-long repetition of one and the same trivial operation, and thus reduced to the mere fragment of a man, with the fully developed individual, fit for a variety of labors, ready to face any change of production, and to whom the different social functions he performs, are but so many modes of giving free scope to his own natural and acquired powers. (Marx 1967:458)

Thus, Marx concluded that when the working class came to power, it would have to abolish the capitalist division of labor and introduce "technical instruction, both theoretical and practical" into the schools of the working class.

Marx also believed that the basic work unit or "collective working group" in future forms of productive organization would have to be organized in such a way that it facilitated the "humane development" of its members. Thus, he wrote:

Moreover, it is obvious that the fact of the collective working group being composed of individuals of both sexes and all ages, must necessarily, under suitable conditions, become a source of humane development; although in its spontaneously developed, brutal, capitalistic form, where the laborer exists for the process of production, and not the process of production for the laborer, that fact is a pestiferous source of corruption and slavery. (Marx 1967:460)

In this respect, Marx anticipated the key role that the autonomous work team, as the basic collective work unit, would play in future forms of worker self-managed organizations (for example, see Horvat 1982:240–243).

It also seems possible that Marx thought that the autocratic nature of capitalist forms of organization would have to be replaced by future forms of organization that were managed by representative bodies—

both at the intra- and interorganizational levels. There is a suggestion of this in the following passage from Volume 1 of *Capital*:

The factory code in which capital formulates, like a private legislator, and at his own good will, his autocracy over his workpeople, unaccompanied by that division of responsibility in other matters so much approved of by the bourgeoisie, and unaccompanied by the still more approved representative system, this code is but the capitalistic caricature of that social regulation of the labor process which becomes requisite in cooperation on a great scale, and in the employment in common, of instruments of labor and especially of machinery. (Marx 1967:400)

This passage and others in the *Manifesto of the Communist Party* and *The Civil War in France* suggest that Marx thought the future forms of socialist and communist organization would be governed democratically by representative councils, such as the factory committees and soviets in the early years of the Russian Revolution.

The Soviet and Chinese Cases

By the end of the twenties, the *edinonachalie* or "one-man management system" had become the basic characteristic of Soviet forms of organization. Under this system, the directors of state enterprises were given absolute control over their enterprises and all pretense of worker participation in the management of production was eliminated (Horvat 1982:142). This form of strict hierarchical organization was consistent with the dictatorial nature of the Soviet regime under Stalin and with the "economism" that characterized the regime's approach to transforming Soviet society. In this approach, the transformation of the social relations of production (that is, forms of ownership, management, the division of labor, and so on) was subordinated to the transformation of the forces of production (narrowly conceived as technology, technical expertise, the productive infrastructure, and so on). Thus, the rapid development of the country's material forces of production took precedence over the development of new forms of organization and ownership.

Charles Bettelheim, in referring to the economism of the Soviet regime, has theorized that this is "the form which bourgeois ideology takes within Marxism" (Bettelheim 1976:35). He further claims the Soviet experience makes it obvious that unless the social relations of capitalist production are replaced, the exploitive nature of capitalism will survive and a new bourgeoisie will emerge.

> The Soviet experience confirms that what is hardest is not the overthrow of the former dominant classes: the hardest task is, first, to destroy the former social relations—upon which a system of exploitation can be reconstituted—and then to prevent these relations from being reconstituted on the basis of those elements of the old that still remain present for a long time in the new social relations. (Bettelheim 1976:17)

In analyzing why the Soviet Union has failed to undergo a genuine socialist transformation, Bettelheim observes that it is in part due to the fact that the Soviet system is based upon what are in essence capitalist relations of production.

> There is no question of allowing the Soviet workers to exercise collective control over the utilization of the means of production, over the way current production is used, or over the activity of the party and its members. The factories are run by managers whose relations with "their" workers are relations of command, and who are responsible only to their superiors. Agricultural enterprises are run in practically similar ways. . . . The rules governing the management of Soviet enterprises are to an increasing degree copied from those of the "advanced" capitalist countries, and many Soviet managers go for training to the business schools of the United States and Japan. What was supposed to give rise to increasingly socialist relations has instead produced relations that are essentially capitalist. . . . The producers are still wage earners working to valorize the means of production, with the latter functioning as collective capital managed by a state bourgeoisie. (Bettelheim 1976:44–45)

In commenting upon Bettelheim's analysis, Paul Sweezy has concluded that the Soviet experience elucidates "that classes have their existence in the real relations of production, and it is only through a transformation of these relations that the class structure can be changed" (Sweezy 1980:60).

Although the course of development has been somewhat different in the case of the People's Republic of China, a similar pattern can be found there. Instead of socialist relations of production, what increasingly appear to be capitalist relations of production can be found in the more industrialized sectors of Chinese society, and feudal or precapitalist relations appear to have survived in Chinese agriculture.

During the early years of China's revolutionary regime, factory management committees composed of army officers, factory managers, and representatives of the work force were established, and in the early 1950s the Soviet one-man management system was adopted (Lockett 1983:592–600). Largely powerless elected workers' congresses and official unions were also introduced at the enterprise level. However, criticism of the one-man management system soon developed and it was officially abandoned in 1956. Generally speaking, at this point the factory directors were brought under the control of enterprise-level party committees. During the Great Leap Forward (1958–1960) and the Cultural Revolution (1966–1968), short-lived attempts were made to decentralize decisionmaking and encourage more autonomous implementation of decisions at the lower levels—under overall party control. A limited amount of participation in the management of production at the local level was encouraged during these two periods of mass mobilization, but for a variety of reasons *not* having to do with this limited amount of participation, production levels fell and the economy was seriously disrupted in both cases.

As a result of the mass mobilization efforts undertaken during the Great Leap Forward, the rural Chinese population was organized into People's Communes. These organizations were not only agricultural producers' cooperatives, they were also fairly large territorial units that combined the functions of local government with a wide range of economic, social, and political responsibilities (Aziz 1976:46–47). Each commune was divided into a number of production brigades, which were in turn subdivided into production teams—the latter being the basic organizational unit at the village or small hamlet level. In the more densely populated areas, communes often consisted of between 30 and 35 production brigades and between 300 to 400 production teams. Each team contained between thirty and forty families (100 to 200 members). After undergoing both subdivisions and amalgamations, the total number of People's Communes in China by 1975 was reported to be 50,000 (Aziz 1976:47). Under this system, private land ownership was replaced by communal ownership, and income was based on the amount of work performed instead of the amount of crops produced by each family.

By 1985, due to the regime's new economic reforms, the dismantling of the People's Communes had been completed. They were replaced by 92,000 townships that have primarily governmental responsibilities (*San Francisco Chronicle*, June 5, 1985:14). The Production Brigades were replaced by 820,000 village committees, again with primarily political and administrative, rather than economic, functions. As previously indicated, once again, the family has become the basic unit of production in China.

The reasons for the demise of the People's Communes will undoubtedly be debated for years to come. In terms of their organizational nature, it seems clear that they were not the kind of democratic, self-managed units of production that they were acclaimed to be. They labored under the burden of bureaucratic directives and constraints imposed upon them by the centralized party and administrative structures that formed the upper levels of the organizational pyramid in which they constituted the base. Hinton's observations on the role that bureaucratic "commandism" has played in the organization of agricultural production in China are quite revealing in this regard.

> The commandism that so damaged the cooperative movement was in great measure simply an extension of the bureaucratic centralism of the past, cranked up several notches and reinvigorated by the centralist tradition of the Communist movement. Functionaries in China assume that they have the right to run everything, down to the smallest details of people's lives. This tradition is truly feudal. It is deeply resented down below and that is one of the reasons for the extraordinary attraction that a free market . . . has for ordinary Chinese citizens. For people suffering under feudal restraints, the cash nexus seems to promise a radical liberation where ability and not influence derived from social connections count. The irony built into this commandism question is that the reformers, under the anti-commandist banner, dismantled the rural cooperative economy by command. . . . Just as commandism rushed many unwilling peasants into collectives in the first place, so commandism rushed many unwilling peasants out of them in the second place. (Hinton 1989:18)

As Hinton's observations reveal, the lack of local autonomy and the commandism that characterizes the larger social system in which the People's Communes were a part appear to have been responsible for the poor economic performance of many of the Communes and for their failure to develop into effective forms of socialist organization.

In view of the bureaucratic and centralized nature of the Chinese regime, it seems obvious that the development of genuinely self-governing and self-managed forms of organization at the local level would pose a threat to that regime.

> The political functions which the Maoists assigned to the communes in theory, and the realities of communization, posed a grave challenge to the existing party and state bureaucracies. Had the people's communes actually developed in the manner Maoists originally envisaged, centralized political power in China would have been fundamentally undermined— much in the way in which Marx had attributed to the Paris Commune the potential to restore to the producers those social powers which had been usurped by the state. (Meisner 1977:241)

The potential that the People's Communes offered for the socialization and democratization of rural society was too much of a threat to the party and state bureaucrats who have ruled China since the formation of the revolutionary regime in 1949.

During the Cultural Revolution, in the industrial sector both the unrepresentative official trade unions and the factory party committees appear to have almost disappeared under the waves of criticism directed at the bureaucratic management system (Lockett 1983:601–603). Revolutionary committees (similar in composition to the early factory management committees) and relatively autonomous workers' management teams were chosen by the workers in the factories. Moreover, the existing division of labor was attacked, especially the separation between intellectual and manual labor. Managers and administrative cadres were required to participate in manual labor and limited innovations in the division of labor such as job rotation and job enrichment were introduced in some of the factories. However, in the 1970s, reaction to these developments gained dominance: The factory-level party committees once again took control of the enterprises and the trade unions were revived. The autonomy of the workers' management teams was reduced and they were incorporated, along with the remaining elected workers' congresses, into the official union structure.

Since the introduction of major economic reforms in the 1980s, economism and hesitant moves in the direction of partial democratization appear to have created contradictory influences on the organization and management of the productive structures. However, widespread corruption and profiteering as well as the current emphasis on greater enterprise autonomy, strict enforcement of work quotas, contracting out to individuals, work force reductions, and material incentives appear to have undermined the effects of earlier attempts to transform the division of labor and increase workers' control (Chan 1990).

What both the Soviet and the Chinese experiences reveal is that the transition to socialism cannot succeed unless the social relations of production characteristic of capitalism are effectively eliminated and replaced by genuinely socialist relations of production and democratic forms of organization that prevent the reproduction of class relations and capitalist forms of production. One of the most important contributions of Maoism to Marxist theory is its elaboration of the thesis that "the overthrow of a bourgeois and/or feudal regime does not do away with the old exploiting classes" and that, consequently, a continuing class struggle must take place in the transition period between the revolutionary classes and the remnants of these former exploiting classes as well as new elements that emerge to take their place (Sweezy 1980:92–93).

In the Chinese political discussions, debates, and polemics of the 1950s and 1960s, the meaning of the term "class struggle" gradually shifted. . . . The class enemy, which the workers and their allies were being exhorted to struggle against, started out being the old ruling classes, increasingly became elites (and others as well) still dominated by the ideas, values, etc. of the old ruling classes, and ended up being a "new bourgeoisie" produced (and incessantly reproduced) by the social formation which had emerged from the revolution itself. . . . The notion that the abolition of private property in the means of production ushers in an essentially classless society which, given a sufficient development of the forces of production, will evolve in a harmonious way toward communism—this notion is exploded once and for all. In its place we have a conception of socialism as a class-divided society like all that have preceded it, and one which has the potential to move forward or backward depending on the fortunes of the class struggle. . . . (Sweezy 1980:94–95)

In other words, the elimination of private property by itself does not do away with class exploitation and usher in socialism, since capitalist ideas, relations, and forms of organization remain and must also be eliminated in order to prevent the reproduction of capitalism.

The Need for Democratic Forms of Organization

Only an across-the-board implantation of genuinely democratic forms of organization in the production process can prevent the survival of capitalist social relations and the revival of class exploitation. This fact appears to be increasingly recognized by Marxists who have critically assessed the Soviet and the Chinese experiences. For example, Branko Horvat argues:

A socialist organizational model must be structured so as to eliminate hierarchy, which inevitably generates class stratification. This is achieved by closing the organizational structure in a very specific way: no countervailing power, which generates competing bureaucracies; no party bolt, which gives rise to one single omnipotent bureaucracy; but the combining of management and work by the same people—that is, self-management. (Horvat 1982:189)

According to Horvat, the basic organizational form of socialism is self-management:

The fundamental institution of socialism is self-management. . . . If universal self-management (in both market and non-market sectors) is introduced to either capitalist or etatist [statist] societies, it will gradually resolve the old production relations and eventually the disintegrating system will have to be replaced by something [socialism] more compatible with the institution. By participating in management (and in local government), by fighting for a continuous extension of participation until it reaches self-management, workers can learn in their daily lives how to control their destiny, how to overcome the fragmentation and decomposition of labor, how to achieve meaningful social equality, and how to destroy antiquated hierarchies. They do this without the tutorship of omniscient leaders. They prepare themselves for self-determination. . . . Self-management clearly cannot be established overnight. But neither was the capitalist market. And just as the development of the market, however gradual or irregular, could not be anti-capitalist, the growth of participation from its primitive forms of joint consultation toward full-fledged self-management cannot be anti-socialist, in spite of the attempts to misuse it for the preservation of the status quo. (Horvat 1982:426–427)

Thus, the fundamental organizing principle of socialism is democratic self-management. The introduction of self-management can be viewed as an indispensable step in the transition from capitalism to socialism. Without this form of organization, socialist relations of production cannot be developed and institutionalized.

Horvat has probably written more on self-management than any other Marxist scholar. He writes that the basic organizational unit of self-management is not the enterprise, but the primary work group (Horvat 1982:240–241). In a self-managed enterprise, the primary work group functions as a semi-autonomous work unit within a federated structure of such units. Each self-managed work group/unit has the following characteristics:

1. Participation in decisionmaking is direct on all matters affecting the work unit;
2. The decisionmaking process itself and the decisions reached are transparent;
3. Because of the continuous face-to-face nature of the group, the unjustified and permanent imposition of the will of the majority is unlikely;
4. Because of (1) through (3), the possibilities for the manipulation of opinion are limited.

When decisions must be taken that affect the interests of more than one work group, they are made at the next level of self-management— the workers' council (which is composed of elected delegates from all the work groups in the enterprise). In this democratic organizational structure, there exist certain safeguards against abuses of power. These include institutionalized procedures to defend individuals against the abuses of groups and to defend collective interests against the abuses of individuals (at any level).

As Horvat indicates, self-management cannot be established quickly. It requires the increasing participation of workers in organizational decisionmaking. Generally speaking, Horvat contends that participation passes through three stages of development: (1) joint consultation, (2) codetermination, and (3) self-management. He defines these stages as follows:

> The first stage leaves the capitalist and etatist framework intact, but provides an important psychological attack on the managerial autocracy. The second stage already implies a share in power and represents the beginning of the end. It is important to realize that the first two stages are transitional and consequently unstable. Stability is achieved during the third stage, which is possible only under socialism. Most of the developed countries, both capitalist and etatist, find themselves in the first stage. By 1977, however, nine nations (West Germany, Sweden, Norway, Denmark, Austria, the Netherlands, France, Luxemburg, and Spain) had laws requiring labor representation on the supervisory and management boards of major companies—which is already co-determination. As a rule, this is still minority representation, but strong pressures are exerted toward parity and beyond. (Horvat 1982:166–167)

The institutionalization of self-management represents an organizational revolution involving the abolition within the units of production of the hierarchical structures of decisionmaking and management inherited from capitalism as well as the elimination of the division of labor into strata of intellectual and manual workers.

However, by itself self-management cannot guarantee a successful transition to socialism. At the enterprise level it needs to be linked effectively with democratically constituted national and regional planning bodies to ensure that the decisions made by the workers in each enterprise are conditioned by socially recognized needs and goals (Bettelheim 1978:117–118). Without these linkages, self-management can degenerate into what has been called "workers' capitalism" and obstruct social planning as well as the further socialization of the relations of production. On this point, Bettelheim has warned that "decision-making power must not be *atomized*, if the very foundations for building socialism and planning are not to be destroyed" (Bettelheim 1978:118).

The Yugoslav experience demonstrates both of these propositions. In Yugoslavia, limited forms of self-management at the enterprise level were combined with the economic structures of Yugoslavia's so-called market socialism and its single-party, authoritarian regime. What most of the critical leftist studies on Yugoslavia's market socialism reveal is that under Yugoslav conditions, self-management at the enterprise level did not lead to the increasing socialization and democratization of the society (see Brus 1975:62–95; Comisso 1979; Nove 1983:133–141; Taslim 1984; and Tyson 1980). The type of competitive market relations that characterized Yugoslavia's mixed economy, the weak forms of planning that existed, and the political domination exercised by the ruling party elite deformed and restricted the development of self-management at the enterprise level in that country. For the most part, the participation of the rank-and-file workers in enterprise planning and management was manipulated by the managerial, technical, and party cadres who tended to dominate decisionmaking and the allocation of scarce resources at all levels within the Yugoslav system. Moreover, the rank-and-file workers did not receive the types of education and training they needed to be effective participants in the self-management processes that existed in their enterprises.

Consequently, Yugoslavia's so-called self-management system has given rise to a form of "workers' capitalism" in which the workers try to maximize their earnings at the expense of other considerations, such as the balanced socioeconomic development of the country and the increased socialization of the production process. The evolution of Yugoslavia's system of self-management and market socialism appears to confirm Bettelheim's prediction that this system would obstruct the development of the country's productive forces to an increasing extent and ultimately lead to the reestablishment of unregulated markets and capitalist relations of production (Bettelheim 1978:219–220).

However, it is important that socialists in transitional societies recognize that they do not have to choose between the self-management model of Yugoslavia's market socialism and the bureaucratic model of centralized state management and planning associated with socialism in the Soviet Union, Eastern Europe, and China. This is a false dichotomy; self-management at the point of production and comprehensive planning for the economy as a whole are compatible within a democratic socialist society. Planning in the interests of society, effective workers' control at the point of production, and a democratic state constitute the organizational requisites of socialism.

The Latin American Experience

The Latin American experience confirms some of the lessons that can be derived from the Soviet, Chinese, and Yugoslav experiences in terms of the importance of organizational factors in the transition to socialism. In general, this experience indicates that the reliance on capitalist forms of industrial organization, bureaucracy, and manipulative forms of worker participation undermines the socialization process and reproduces capitalist relations of production. Moreover, the Cuban, Chilean, and Nicaraguan cases reveal that socialist forms of organization are difficult to develop under the kind of economic, social, political, and ideological conditions existing in most Latin American and Caribbean societies.

If one uses the three-stage model of the development of workers' participation offered by Horvat (joint consultation, codetermination, and self-management), then Cuba, Chile, and Nicaragua appear to provide examples of the first two stages. In these countries, organizational arrangements existing at the enterprise level have brought workers and management together to discuss the formulation and implementation of production plans as well as working conditions and related matters (see Harnecker 1979:1–27; Lowy 1986:268–270; and Vilas 1986:189–208). In addition, these cases offer examples of laws or regulations that have required worker representation on the management boards or directive bodies of certain enterprises—the formal basis for what is known in Western Europe as codetermination and in Latin America as *cogestión*. In its most developed form, codetermination means joint management of the enterprise by the workers and the management (Horvat 1982:172–173). Generally speaking, this degree of worker participation does not yet exist in Cuba, did not exist under the Sandinista regime in Nicaragua, and only existed for a short time in certain enterprises during the Allende regime in Chile. Short-lived, partial, and/or isolated instances of workers' self-management (*autogestión*) have been developed in several Latin American countries, for example, Argentina, Bolivia, Chile, Costa Rica, and Peru (see Iturraspe 1986). But the experience in these countries has not been part of an on-going process of socialist transformation.

In Nicaragua, the work force's general lack of organizational skills and low level of education placed a definite limit on worker participation in planning and decisionmaking within the state enterprises under the Sandinista regime (Harris and Vilas 1985:68–69). There was also resistance to workers' participation from many of the enterprise administrators and *tecnicos* who did not know how to function in a participatory organizational process and were not prepared to deal with the problems raised by involving the unions and workers in the management and planning of the enterprises. The form of participation that existed was consultative and was not designed to give the workers control over the production process.

In Chile, workers participation in the state enterprises took the form of codetermination. On the basis of an agreement between the unions and the government, the administrative council of each enterprise was reorganized to include five members and a chairperson appointed by the government and five representatives of the work force elected by secret ballot (Smirnow 1979:41). These joint worker-government councils were empowered to make policy on a wide range of matters, including pay, production, investments, contracts, and so on. And because the government-appointed members of the councils were usually pro-labor representatives from the Popular Unity coalition, their views often coincided with those of the worker representatives on the councils.

Much more significant than the codetermination arrangement established in the state enterprises was the formation of *cordones industriales* (industrial bands) in the last year of the Popular Unity government (Smirnow 1979:82–89). These were completely autonomous workers' organizations that sprang up in the industrial areas around Santiago as the class struggle between the bourgeoisie and the organized working class accelerated qualitatively.

The first *cordón industrial* was formed in June 1972 when the workers of a medium-sized private canning factory in Cerrillos occupied the plant and called on the government to incorporate it into the state sector (Smirnow 1979:83–84). The communist minister of labor refused to recognize the workers' demands and ordered them to leave the plant. In response, the workers joined together with those of other factories and occupied all the plants in the surrounding area. They also closed off the access roads to the industrial area. As a result, they forced the government to incorporate the canning factory into the state sector.

Soon other *cordones industriales* sprang up in other parts of Santiago and in other major cities. They were directed by elected assemblies and managed in a democratic manner. Generally speaking, they were supported by the radical Left parties and regarded with disfavor by the Chilean communist party and the moderate elements within Allende's socialist party. Although many of the *cordones industriales* resisted when the military seized power in September 1973, they were no match for the tanks and planes of the armed forces. This use of power brought to an abrupt end the development of what Smirnow described as "a completely autonomous power vis-à-vis the government and all the institutions of the Chilean capitalist state—a power which developed in a qualitatively new way the consciousness and influence of the working class . . . and which broadened worker participation in the administration of the enterprises" (Smirnow 1979:88–89).

The Cuban Case

In Cuba, the development of socialist forms of organization is embryonic and inhibited by organizational structures and practices similar to those in the Soviet Union and the Eastern European states. However, since the 1970s, the regime has promoted increased popular participation, political democratization at the local level, and increased worker participation in production planning and workplace decisionmaking. Moreover, the struggle against bureaucratism continues to be an important political issue in Cuba and has helped to prevent the development of the kind of bureaucratic elites that have emerged in the USSR, China, and Eastern Europe.

The development of more democratic forms of organization in Cuba has been constrained by the "bad organizational habits" that were introduced in the early years of the revolutionary regime. During the first years of the regime, dramatic organizational changes took place as the private sector was rapidly brought under state ownership. A kind of egalitarian and free-wheeling variant of state socialism emerged that was characterized by considerable disorganization and little central planning (Bernardo 1971:22). Between 1959 and 1963, the state and the newly nationalized (statized) enterprises were characterized by an ad hoc managerial style and improvised organizational arrangements.

The free-wheeling administrative style of this period, which the Cubans called *por la libre*, was adopted by the former guerrilla army officers who assumed the leadership positions in most of the government ministries and new state organizations. Few permanent organizational structures or procedures were established during this early period of the regime, new organizations emerged and disappeared, in many cases individuals with no previous managerial or technical experience assumed important positions, and there was no tightly organized vanguard party to provide centralized coordination of the expanding state apparatus (Boorstein 1968). The commanding figure of Fidel Castro dominated this *por la libre* process by providing audacious leadership and inspiring vision.

Although the new revolutionary society that emerged during the 1960s was characterized by intense popular participation, this participation was largely confined to the implementation of the policies made by Fidel and his lieutenants. Political commandism and bureaucratic centralism developed in this context and led to a host of organizational problems (LeoGrande 1989; Fitzgerald 1989). The failure to reach the goal of harvesting 10 million tons of sugar in 1970, despite the mobilization of much of the country's population to achieve this objective, forced Fidel and the revolutionary leadership to critically reassess the organizational structure of both the country's political system and its economy.

As a result of this reassessment, the leadership decided that a fundamental rectification of the revolutionary process was needed. As one recent account by Frank Fitzgerald indicates, the country's political and administrative structures were reorganized.

As part of this process, between 1970 and 1973 the trade unions, which had virtually "withered away" in the late 1960s, were reconstituted along with other mass organizations. By the time of the first Party Congress in 1975, although the party remained interlocked with, and thereby ultimately in control of, the rest of the administrative apparatus, the organization and role of the party had been formally differentiated from the rest of the system. Soon thereafter, *Organos de Poder Popular* [Organs of People's Power] were created: elected assemblies empowered to administer the state at the municipal, provincial and national levels. In the same period, the revolutionary leadership began introducing a new System for Direction and Planning of the Economy, designed in part to rationalize central economic planning and to create relatively autonomous enterprises, with responsibility for realizing a profit within the limits of centrally controlled prices and credit. (Fitzgerald 1989:285)

As Fitzgerald observes, the early 1970s marked an important turning point in the revolutionary process. The largely structureless and so-called "direct democracy" of the early years was replaced by the institutionalization of new representative political institutions, a strengthening and clarification of the role of the party, a renewed emphasis on the mass organizations created during the early 1960s, and the rationalization of the administrative and planning apparatus.

The organizational principles of democratic centralism, similar to those first elaborated by Lenin and the Bolsheviks, were adopted by Cuba's revolutionary leadership as the basic guidelines for structuring participation in policymaking and policy implementation. According to these principles, input into the policymaking process was supposed to be solicited from the lower levels of all organizations as well as the population as a whole; this input was then intended to provide an important basis for the policy decisions made by the leadership at the higher levels of the system; finally, the implementation of these decisions was expected to be carried out with the participation of the lower levels of all organizations and the population in general.

As Fitzgerald argues, the introduction of this system involved much more than the establishment of a series of procedural guidelines for making and implementing decisions. In fact, it defined the distribution of decisionmaking power within the organizational structures of Cuban society. To quote Fitzgerald on this matter:

Although couched in terms of a process for making and implementing decisions optimally, the principles of democratic centralism involved much more than a set of operational procedures. They also defined a particular distribution of decision-making power. First, they stipulated that the most general or most important decisions should be made centrally, that is, by the revolutionary leadership. Second, they stipulated that the less general or less important decisions should be left to lower levels of the administrative apparatus. . . . Third, the principles of democratic centralism stipulated that, although the masses should not make decisions, they should participate in the pre-decision stage of discussion and in the post-decision stage of implementation. Mass support for decisions made at higher levels was to be obtained through limited participation. (Fitzgerald 1989:286–287)

It is important to note that this conception of democratic centralism continues to be regarded as the correct structure for decisionmaking in all organizational structures as well as in the political system (Fitzgerald 1989).

In the best of circumstances, this method of decisionmaking provides for a form of "consultative democracy" in which the members at the base of organizations are consulted on a limited range of issues before decisions are made and then later after decisions have been made with regard to how best to carry out these decisions. The main organizational mechanism for this is the production assemblies that are held in each enterprise to discuss the production plan for their enterprise. To be sure, this is not the form of self-government and self-management that the early Marxists as well as many contemporary Marxists, such as Branko Horvat and others, have advocated.

However, even though the workers do not control either production decisions or production planning in Cuba, there has been a notable increase in workers' participation in the discussion of production issues as well as in the elaboration of work center plans since the 1970s. Particularly on matters concerning the terms of their employment, the workers within each enterprise exert considerable influence on the enterprise management. This is in part due to the introduction of new forms of collective organization at the base of both the manufacturing enterprises and the state farms. Following the practices of other countries such as the Soviet Union and China, the rank-and-file workers have been organized into production brigades, called Permanent Brigades of Production in the agricultural sector and Integral Brigades of Production in the manufacturing sector (Codina Jiménez 1987:135).

These basic units of production appear to be rapidly becoming the primary organizational structure within Cuba's state enterprises and farms. One study on worker incentives in Cuba by the Cuban economist Alexis Codina Jiménez indicates that these new forms of organization have the following characteristics:

1. The workers are brought together to carry out a group job, the result of which constitutes a final product or a certain part of it (article, work, project, volume of loading and unloading, agricultural activity, etc.).

2. A brigade works on the basis of an annual plan that all the members are involved in drawing up. This plan must concur with the principle economic and production indicators and should be broken down into trimesters, and at times, months or days, according to the characteristics of the brigade's activity.
3. Each brigade is assigned the technical, material, wage, and human resources that are indispensable to the fulfillment of its productive tasks.
4. The brigade's collective task is distributed among its members according to the division and cooperation of labor that they have established.
5. A significant portion of the brigade's wage is tied to the final results of their work by which is understood the fulfillment of the planned indicators that define their activity. Wages are distributed among the members according to their participation in the collective task.
6. The brigade possesses a certain degree of operative autonomy in the execution of its task; the direction and overseeing of its achievement is provided by the brigade chief, elected by the brigade members. (Codina Jiménez 1987:135–136)

These brigades were organized to increase both the volume and quality of production as well as to reduce costs. They are also supposed to increase the skills of the workers involved and develop communist attitudes toward work.

The brigades have been formed by combining workers with the same occupation to perform a homogeneous production process or by combining workers with different occupations to perform a more complex production process involving interrelated tasks. The interests and personal characteristics of the workers are expected to be taken into account in the formation of brigades, and afterwards the brigade members are supposed to be consulted about the inclusion of new members (Codina Jiménez 1987:136).

Direction and control of the production brigades by the enterprise is largely accomplished through the planning process instead of through direct supervision. Each brigade must fulfill its part of the enterprise, plant, or department plan that corresponds to it. Moreover, payment for work is related to the output produced by each brigade as well as the complexity of its tasks, the conditions under which it works, and the established work norms. The preferred system of payment is one that is based on collective output in the form of a specified product or service that meets a certain standard of quality (Codina Jiménez 1987:136).

The brigade system provides a basis for socialist emulation because it makes possible the stimulation of competition between collective work units in the same enterprise or industry. Standards for emulation are usually based upon labor productivity, quality of production, efficient use of resources, work discipline, safety records, innovations, and so on

(Codina Jiménez 1987:136). Individual emulation within the brigades is also stimulated on the basis of demonstration of initiative and contribution to the collective's output. Prizes are awarded to brigades and individuals from the stimulation fund created by each enterprise. According to Codina Jiménez, the way this works is as follows:

> The size of each brigade's fund is calculated from the prize fund created at the enterprise level, taking into consideration each brigade's productive results and its relative weight within the company. . . . Up to 10% of the fund the brigade receives may be designated for individual prizes which are awarded to members with outstanding labor achievements directly connected to socialist emulation. Up to 5% goes to members who have completed productive tasks of special importance to the perfecting of production, introduction of new techniques or improvement in the quality of production or to workers that have maintained a flawless level of moral conduct. The remainder of the fund is distributed among all the brigade's members, taking into account each member's basic wage and performance in various areas: fulfilling or overfulfilling work norms, increasing labor productivity, saving raw material, etc. (Codina Jiménez 1987:136)

The use of material awards for emulation within a collective framework provides a mutually reinforcing combination of material and moral incentives that stimulate increased performance and productivity as well as communist principles of work and *conciencia* (consciousness).

The formation of production brigades throughout the various branches of industry and sectors of the economy was emphasized in the 1986–1990 five-year plan. It was conceived as an important means of improving the organization of production and labor productivity. Significantly, it was not presented as a means of increasing worker participation in the control and planning of production. This is unfortunate because the brigades could function as the essential building blocks of worker self-management and the democratization of decisionmaking and planning at the enterprise level. In other words, these brigades could function as the kind of semi-autonomous work units that Horvat and others argue must form the base of a self-managed enterprise (Horvat 1982:239–242). Combined within a federative structure of such groups and a "bottom-up" hierarchy of representative councils, they could control and plan the production process at the enterprise level and elect delegates to the multilevel democratic planning and coordination structure that encompassed their enterprise, their sector of the economy, and the entire country.

Apart from opportunities to participate in the decision-making process, one of the most important factors determining the distribution of power in any hierarchical organizational structure is the manner in which the individuals in the upper levels of the hierarchy are selected. If they are selected by the lower levels, then an essential condition of democratic organization is fulfilled. However, if they are instead appointed by one or a few persons at the top of the hierarchy, then the organization is essentially undemocratic. Therefore, the manner in which the directive personnel—generally referred to as "cadres" in the existing socialist societies—are selected is a critical determinant of their democratic or authoritarian character.

Mihailo Markovic's critique of the *nomenklatura* system in the Soviet Union is relevant in this regard.

> The experience of all twentieth century revolutions shows that those leaders who were responsible for the selection of cadres were able to dominate the scene, to defeat their rivals and assume dictatorial powers. The cadres policy cannot remain so important in a system of self-government where personnel cannot be simply nominated, promoted or fired but must be democratically elected. . . . There is a social need to have a survey of available talent and different kinds of competence for different functions, to record the achievements and failures of individuals in their elected public functions, to propose how the most important functions within a body of self-government should be distributed. Responsibility for cadres policy is a decisive power, and therefore it should not be in the hands of those who already have other powers—it should be separated. (quoted in Bellis 1979:43)

The selection of cadres in the Soviet Union, China, Vietnam, Cuba, and most existing socialist societies has been dominated by the party leadership, and this has guaranteed their centralized control over not only these administrative elements but the rank-and-file members below them as well.

In Cuba, the selection of the directive cadres in the state administration and state enterprises is under the control of the top leadership. Only the lowest-level cadres are appointed upon the nomination and approval of the rank and file. For example, the chiefs of production brigades are elected by the brigade members.

In recent years, emphasis has been placed on the recruitment of more women, blacks, and young people into cadre positions in the communist party. In the main report of the Third Congress of the party in 1986, Fidel made the following statement about the recruitment of party cadres:

> The mechanisms that ensure the correct selection, permanence and promotion of cadre must be improved constantly on the basis of thorough, critical, objective and systematic evaluations and with appropriate attention to development and training. . . . Women's representation, in keeping with

their participation and their important contribution to the building of socialism in our country, must be ensured, along with the existence of a growing reserve of promising young people born and tempered in the forge of the revolution. (quoted in Valdés 1989:175)

And the report also emphasized that the leadership of the party should reflect the ethnic and racial composition of the population:

In order for the Party's leadership to duly reflect the ethnic composition of our people, it must include those compatriots of proven revolutionary merit and talents who in the past have been discriminated against because of their skin color. (quoted in Valdés 1989:175)

This directive was an important admission of the continuing importance of racial discrimination in Cuba and the party's responsibility for rectifying "historical injustices" such as racism and sexism.

This admission is part of the current rectification campaign being undertaken in the party, state administration, state enterprises and mass organizations. The main intent of this campaign, however, is to confront the managerial deficiencies and increasing problems of lack of creativity and commitment among the cadres as well as the rank and file in the state organs and in the various organizational structures of the economy. This intent is shown in the following statement released in 1988 by the Political Bureau of the Party:

The leadership of the party calls upon the party and the government to resolutely confront and take concrete measures to eliminate the causes, which depend upon the quality of our management, that are responsible for carelessness and negligent attitudes and that are alien to the essence of socialism and the policies of the revolution. . . . It corresponds to the party to impart a greater degree of cohesion and dynamism in the management of production, services and administration realized by the government and the organs of People's Power, educating their cadres in the practice of criticism and the honest recognition of their errors. (quoted in Machado 1989:71)

The underlying causes behind the organizational and managerial problems that are the focus of the current rectification campaign are: (1) a cultural tradition of hierarchical and authoritarian relations that reinforces paternalistic interactions and inhibits creative decisionmaking or problem solving, except for those at the top of the hierarchy; (2) an educational system that is based on passive learning and the acquisition of knowledge rather than the development of creative thinking and independent inquiry; (3) the force of Fidel's personality which, while motivational and inspirational, reinforces the passivity and paternalism already rooted in the culture; and (4) the absence of cost consciousness among cadres and workers as a result of the virtual abandonment of cost accounting after the revolutionary triumph and the subsequent separation of considerations about production from concerns about costs. More specific managerial problems stem from:

- The low social recognition given to managerial activity;
- The fact that managers often receive inadequate training in management philosophy and practices (and none in democratic styles of management);
- Many managers are paid less than technical personnel such as engineers;
- Most managers have a great deal of responsiblity without commensurate authority;
- They spend too much time in meetings with external authorities who control and limit their power;
- They don't have the time or the encouragement to think creatively.

To these problems must be added:

- The complexity of labor legislation;
- Job categories that are too rigid and narrow;
- Lack of career development plans and opportunities for most of the workers;
- High absenteeism;
- Low productivity;
- Lack of quality consciousness;
- No incentives for night and swing shifts so few people want to work them and there is a high rate of personnel turnover;
- Many jobs are filled on the basis of seniority rather than merit;
- The personnel decision-making process is too long and bureaucratic.

Thus, at the enterprise level in Cuba, a series of vexing problems appears to undermine the effectiveness and smooth operation of production. Due to some of the deficiencies in the managerial cadres and in the work force mentioned above, there is often inadequate inventory control, poor production scheduling, inadequate health and safety regulations, and poor planning. Often the main purpose of the enterprise is not clear due to the fact that it is confronted with conflicting demands—for example, providing buses to transport local school children, building community infrastructure, providing workers for microbrigades, and making profits. Resolving these conflicting demands often means negotiating with national, provincial, and local government authorities. These negotiations take an enormous amount of time, energy, and resources. In addition, the enterprises do not have direct contact with their domestic and foreign customers and as a result they find it difficult to serve the customers adequately. The enterprises are also faced with too many regulations, procedures, and directions that they must follow; furthermore, the System for Direction and Planning of the Economy is too centralized and does not give the enterprises enough participation in the strategic decisions affecting their productivity and the quality of their production. In this regard, the enterprises often do not have input into the many changes that are made in the plans that affect them. Finally, there are often serious logistical problems and indispensable supplies do not arrive on time or in sufficient quantity.

These problems are related to and/or caused by the effects of bureaucratism in the political and major economic structures of the country. As Fitzgerald has noted:

> Bureaucratic centralism, then, arises in part from the proximate impact of systemic factors, but it also arises from socio-historical factors. The most obvious such factor in Cuba has been the multifaceted legacy of the experience of the 1960s. That decade of hypercentralized decision-making, in which workers had little voice and in which the watchword was to mobilize for production rather than to debate problems or alternatives, formed hard-to-break bureaucratic habits in many administrative personnel. As the then head of JUCEPLAN, Humberto Pérez, remarked at the end of the 1970s: "the compañeros who work in the distinct state organizations, including those who work in the Organs of People's Power, are impregnated with the old centralizing and in many ways bureaucratic habits." This remark could apply as well to the revolutionary leadership, which, although it has pushed democratic centalist principles, has itself engaged in bureaucratic centralist behavior. (Fitzgerald 1989:301)

Cuba's increasing economic difficulties and the spread of corruption in all levels of the regime have led to the present campaign of rectification, which seeks to root out the bureaucratism, organizational deficiencies, and corruption in Cuba. However, as the preceding analysis has suggested, unless the democratization begun in the 1970s is extended to the workplace and to the planning process itself, it is unlikely that Cuba's political leaders will be able to get at the roots of the organizational and ideological problems that plague the country.

Conclusion

What the Cuban case reveals is that the elimination of private property by itself does not bring about socialism. Capitalist ideas, practices, and organizational forms remain and must be eliminated in order to prevent the reproduction of bourgeois ideas and behavior. Bureaucratic and hypercentralized forms of organization are clearly not the means for achieving socialism. Only the across-the-board implantation of democratic forms of organization and planning can eliminate capitalist relations of production and prevent the bureaucratic degeneration of the transition process. In short, democratic planning in the interests of society, effective workers' control at the point of production, and a popular democratic state constitute the organizational requisites of the transition to socialism.

11
Ideology and Culture in the Transition

Marxist Views on Ideology, Culture, and Social Consciousness

In the transition to socialism, one of the main instruments of social transformation is socialist ideology (Horvat 1982:485). This ideology consists of certain fundamental human values and a body of social theory concerning how to realize these values in social life. Armed with this ideology, a revolutionary socialist movement has the intellectual means to transform both the material and the subjective or ideological domain of social life. This subjective domain consists of the values, ideals, norms, beliefs, criteria, attitudes, expectations, customs, tastes, symbols, myths, representations, and forms of knowledge possessed by the members of society. One of the most important aspects of the transition to socialism is the revolutionary transformation of this important domain (see Saul 1986).

As Erich Fromm has observed, every society "must mold the character of its members in such a way that they want to do what they have to do" (quoted in Horvat 1982:490). It follows, therefore, that the socialist transformation of society requires molding the character of its members in a fashion that is compatible with socialism. This entails the development of what Horvat calls the "associative character."

The social character compatible with socialism may be termed the *associative* character. The associative personality achieves full integration with the community—not in an unconscious, unthinking, and hence enforced way, as individuals do in the primary groups of undeveloped societies, but as a free, autonomous personality by means of a conscious choice made possible by the fundamental conditions of his or her existence. (Horvat 1982:491)

For Horvat, the way this type of socialist personality is developed under socialism is through the individual's involvement in "self-government in all fields of human activity" (Horvat 1982:491). He contrasts this type of character with the "collectivist character" formed by etatist societies. In these societies, what he calls "bureaucratic etatism" requires obedience and conformity, which give rise to "individuals that lack independence and personal dignity" and whose "personality is dissolved in the collectivity."

In place of the social alienation that characterizes the outlook of most members of capitalist societies, one of the main goals of a socialist society is to create the conditions in which human beings will develop a "social consciousness" founded on love for humanity, respect for the dignity of all human beings, critical thinking, social cooperation, social activism, and international solidarity. One of the tasks to be accomplished in the transition to socialism is the development of this type of social consciousness.

Marx and Engels on Social Consciousness and Ideology

Social consciousness is a central concept in the Marxist perspective on social reality. In the preface to *A Contribution to the Critique of Political Economy* (written in 1859), Marx stated the basic premises of his perspective on the subjective domain by using this concept of social consciousness.

In the social production of their lives, [women and] men enter into definite relations that are indispensable and independent of their will, relations of production which correspond to a definite stage of development of their material productive forces. The sum total of these relations of production constitutes the economic structure of society, the real foundation, on which rises a legal and political superstructure and to which correspond definite forms of social consciousness. The mode of production of material life conditions the social, political and intellectual life process in general. It is not the consciousness of [women and] men that determines their being, but on the contrary, their social being that determines their consciousness. At a certain stage of their development, the material productive forces of society come in conflict with the existing relations of production, or— what is but a legal expression for the same thing—with the property relations within which they have been at work hitherto. From forms of development of the productive forces these relations turn into their fetters.

Then begins an epoch of social revolution. With the change of the economic foundation the entire immense superstructure is more or less rapidly transformed. (Marx and Engels 1972:182–183)

Marx's perspective on the material basis of social consciousness has often been erroneously interpreted by Marxists as well as non-Marxists to mean that the transformation of ideas, culture, and social consciousness follows more or less automatically from the transformation of the material conditions of human beings. However, it is clear that neither Marx nor Engels thought this to be the case. In the very same passage from which the quotation above has been taken, Marx went on to say:

In considering such transformations a distinction should always be made between the material transformation of the economic conditions of production, which can be determined with the precision of natural science, and the legal, political, religious, aesthetic or philosophic—in short, ideological forms in which [women and] men become conscious of this conflict and fight it out. (Marx and Engels 1972:183)

As this last quotation indicates, Marx was well aware of the importance of the "ideological forms" in which women and men "become conscious of this conflict" (that is, the conflict or contradiction between the social productive forces and the existing social relations of production); and he contended that they "fight it out" in terms of these ideological forms.

Thus, Marx recognized that revolutionary struggle takes place on the ideological or subjective plane as well as in the economic and political spheres. Indeed, much of Marx's work was taken up with the ideological struggle to expose the class interests behind bourgeois ideas, culture, and consciousness. The tendency to view his perspective as a form of economic determinism stems in part from the fact that he and Engels were primarily concerned with revealing the hitherto unaccepted importance of the productive structures of society and the class struggle that is generated by these structures.

Engels acknowledged how their emphasis on the economic dimension gave rise to misunderstandings and distortions. In a letter written in 1893, he observed:

Otherwise only one more point is lacking, which, however, Marx and I always failed to stress enough in our writings and in regard to which we are equally guilty. That is to say, we all laid, and *were bound to lay*, the main emphasis, in the first place, on the *derivation* of political, juridical and other ideological notions, from basic economic facts. But in so doing we neglected the formal side—for the sake of the content. This has given our adversaries a welcome opportunity for misunderstandings and distortions. . . . (Marx and Engels 1972:700)

He went on to explain that he and Marx viewed the relationship between ideological and economic factors as a dialectical interaction of one upon the other, rather than a simple cause-and-effect relationship.

Hanging together with this is the fatuous notion of the ideologists that because we deny an independent historical development to the various ideological spheres which play a part in history we also deny them any *effect upon history*. The basis of this is the common undialectical conception of cause and effect as rigidly opposite poles, the total disregarding of interaction. These gentlemen often almost deliberately forget that once an historical element has been brought into the world by other, ultimately economic causes, it reacts, can react on its environment and even on the causes that have given rise to it. (Marx and Engels 1972:701)

In sum, Marx and Engels regarded the relationship between economic, political and ideological factors as a complex, dialectical interaction of one upon the other, with the economic factors being the ultimate, but by no means, only causes of historical development.

Lenin's Idea of the Need for a Cultural Revolution

Lenin and the Bolsheviks acted on the basis of this perspective and gave great importance to the ideological dimension of their revolutionary struggle against the capitalists and their allies. Thus, Lenin stressed that it was necessary to overcome the military and political resistance of the bourgeoisie, but also their "ideological resistance, which is the most deep-seated and the strongest" (Lenin 1976:628). The ideological struggle in the transition to socialism, as he saw it, required enlightening the masses, raising their class consciousness, and "cast[ing] off the old ways and habituated routines we have inherited from the old system, the private property habits that the masses are thoroughly imbued with" (Lenin 1976:624).

Because of the "backwardness" of the Soviet Union and the need to develop the social consciousness of the country's largely illiterate peasant population, Lenin was preoccupied with the need for "educational work" and a "cultural revolution" among the peasantry. For example, in 1923, he wrote the following:

Formerly we placed, and had to place, the main emphasis on the political struggle, on revolution, on winning political power, etc. Now the emphasis is changing and shifting to peaceful, organizational, "cultural" work. I should say that emphasis is shifting to educational work. (Lenin 1976:624)

Lenin further elaborated that educating the mass of the peasantry was one of the two main tasks facing the Soviet regime.

Two main tasks confront us, which constitute the epoch—to reorganize our machinery of state, which is utterly useless, and which we took over in its entirety from the preceding epoch. . . . Our second task is educational work among the peasants. And the economic object of this educational work among the peasants is to organize the latter in cooperative societies. If the whole of the peasantry had been organized in cooperatives, we would by now have been standing with both feet on the soil of socialism. But the organization of the entire peasantry in cooperative societies presupposes a standard of culture among the peasants that cannot, in fact, be achieved without a cultural revolution. (Lenin 1976:695)

He warned that the much needed cultural revolution would present "immense difficulties" of both a purely cultural as well as material nature.

Our opponents told us repeatedly that we were rash in undertaking to implant socialism in an insufficiently cultured country. But they were misled by our having started from the opposite end to that prescribed by theory (the theory of pedants of all kinds), because in our country the political and social revolution preceded the cultural revolution, that very cultural revolution that nevertheless confronts us now. This cultural revolution will not suffice to make our country a completely socialist country; but it presents immense difficulties of a purely cultural (for we are illiterate) and material character (for to be cultured we must achieve a certain development of the material means of production, must have a certain material base). (Lenin 1976:695)

He argued that the difficulties of carrying out cultural and educational work among the population stemmed from the fact that they were largely illiterate. It was for this reason, that he considered one of the most important tasks of the cultural revolution to be that of achieving universal literacy (Lenin 1976:685–686).

The Chinese Approach to Ideological and Cultural Transformation

The Chinese, Vietnamese, Cuban, and Nicaraguan revolutions have confronted similar conditions. Because of widespread illiteracy among their large rural populations, one of the first tasks involved in the cultural transformation of these societies has been to extend literacy and provide the benefits of basic education to the population as a whole—a fundamental prerequisite for overcoming the cultural and social underdevelopment of these societies.

However, it is clearly a mistake to assume that literacy and basic education alone will erase the deep-seated cultural values, norms, prejudices, and practices inherited from the prerevolutionary period. The recent developments in the Soviet Union, Eastern Europe, and China reveal that the population of these societies, even after decades of so-called socialist education, continue to hold onto prerevolutionary values and habits. For example, in the Soviet Union, there is a revival of religious and nationalist sentiments; in Poland the adherence of the population to Catholicism has remained an important aspect of not only Polish culture but its politics as well; and in China prerevolutionary cultural values and practices have resurfaced along with widespread interest in Western ideas and capitalist methods.

China provides perhaps the best case study of the tenacity of prerevolutionary culture in the face of determined efforts during the Maoist period to create a new revolutionary culture and root out the values, ideas, and practices of the past. In spite of the cultural transformations undertaken in China since 1949, including the Great Cultural Revolution carried out during the late 1960s under Mao's leadership, there is considerable evidence today that "many peasants continue to hold dear traditional values, such as sexism, localistic insularity, antipathy to the state, and traditional syncretic forms of worship and ritual" (Blecher 1989:5). Moreover, capitalist ideas and practices appear to have resurfaced and are being adopted increasingly by various sectors of the population in response to or as a result of the economic reforms that have been launched in recent years by the post-Maoist leadership.

Antonio Gramsci's theoretical contributions to Marxist thought shed light on the persistence of prerevolutionary ideas and practices in countries such as China and the Soviet Union as well as in Third World societies attempting to build socialism. This well-known Italian Marxist theorist and activist (1891–1937) developed an important theoretical perspective on the nature of ideological struggle and the relationship between politics and culture. His concept of hegemony (that is, leadership or preponderant influence) is central to understanding ideological struggle and cultural domination from a Marxist perspective. According to Gramsci:

> Ideologies are anything but arbitrary; they are real historical facts which must be combatted and their nature as instruments of domination revealed, not for reasons of morality, etc., but for reasons of political struggle: in

order to make the governed intellectually independent of the governing, in order to destroy one hegemony and create another, as a necessary moment in the revolutionizing of praxis. (Gramsci 1988:196)

Gramsci contended that the struggle to create a socialist society requires overcoming the ideological hegemony of the bourgeoisie and establishing a new proletarian or socialist ideological hegemony. For him, the political as well as ideological hegemony or leadership of the proletariat is achieved through the dominant and leading role it plays in mobilizing the majority of the population against capitalism and the bourgeois state.

Thus, he wrote that the proletariat would have to rid itself of its prejudices and win the support of the peasantry, intellectuals, and semiproletarian urban elements in order to lead a successful mass movement against the capitalist order and build a socialist society. According to Gramsci:

> The proletariat, in order to become capable as a class of governing, must strip itself of every residue of corporatism, every syndicalist prejudice and incrustation. What does this mean? That, in addition to the need to overcome the distinctions which exist between one trade and another, it is necessary—in order to win the trust and consent of the peasants and some semi-proletarian urban categories—to overcome certain prejudices and conquer certain forms of egoism which can and do subsist within the working class as such. . . . They must think as workers who are members of a class which aims to lead the peasants and intellectuals. Of a class which can win and build socialism only if it is aided and followed by the great majority of these social strata. If this is not achieved, the proletariat does not become the leading class; and these strata . . . remaining under bourgeois leadership, enable the state to resist the proletarian assault and wear it down. (Gramsci 1988:174)

Gramsci contended that the struggle for socialism required that the proletariat have a clear sense of its leadership role, that it establish and maintain class alliances with the peasantry and urban intellectuals, and that it must do this through gaining their "consent and trust." He believed that this involved establishing ideological leadership or hegemony over these social strata. According to Gramsci, the struggle for hegemony demands the establishment and maintenance of class alliances and the mobilization of popular consent. This process needs detailed ideological and political work and a "war of position" rather than a war of frontal assault (Gramsci 1988:431).

In the struggle for proletarian hegemony and socialism, Gramsci placed great importance on culture and education. His writings emphasize the need to destroy bourgeois cultural domination and build a proletarian culture.

> The proletarian revolution cannot but be a total revolution. It consists in the foundation of new modes of labor, new modes of production and distribution that are peculiar to the working class. . . . This revolution also presupposes the formation of a new set of standards, a new psychology, new ways of feeling, thinking and living that must be specific to the working class, that must be created by it, that will become "dominant" when the working class becomes dominant. . . . Together with the problem of gaining political and economic power, the proletariat must also face the problem of winning intellectual power. Just as it has thought to organize itself politically and economically, it must also think to organize itself culturally. (Gramsci 1988:70)

As the proletariat is generally quite small in most Third World countries, the importance Gramsci attributes to them in leading the rest of society may seem inapplicable to these societies. However, Amilcar Cabral, one of the most important leaders of the revolutionary struggle for national liberation in Africa, has observed that in the absence of a sizable proletariat it is still possible for a Third World revolutionary movement, which represents the exploited classes (the workers and peasants), to adopt a revolutionary proletarian consciousness and mobilize the population around the basic ideals of a socialist revolution (Cabral 1979:135–136).

In order to establish a new ideological and cultural hegemony, Gramsci contended that the proletariat (and its allies) would have to transform education:

> What the proletariat needs is an educational system that is open to all. A system in which the child is allowed to develop and mature and acquire those general features that serve to develop character. In a word, a humanistic school, as conceived by the ancients, and more recently by the Renaissance. A school which does not mortgage a child's future, a school that does not force the child's will, his intelligence and growing awareness to run along tracks to a predetermined station. A school of freedom and free initiative, not a school of slavery and mechanical precision. (Gramsci 1988:64)

He thought that the realization of communist society and the development of the socialist state would depend to a large extent on the type of schools and educational system created during the transition period. The schools would have to become "one of the most important and essential of public activities" in which people would be educated in "the social discipline necessary for the realization of communist society, with assemblies and direct participation in deliberation and the administration of the socialist state" (Gramsci 1988:69).

Gramsci's theoretical perspective was largely developed out of his concern with understanding the conditions for revolutionary struggle in Italy during the 1920s and 1930s, but it appears to be applicable to the analysis of the ideological and cultural aspects of revolutionary transformation in non-Western and Third World societies. One recent example of the application of Gramsci's theory is an excellent study by Marc Blecher on the Maoist attempt to create a new revolutionary culture in China.

According to Blecher, Mao and his followers tried to create a new ideological hegemony in China around the concept of class conflict, but this project largely failed. One of the reasons it failed was because it did not give sufficient attention to deep-seated aspects of the popular culture.

> We see in China the existence of counter-hegemonic forces throughout the period of intense Maoist efforts for a new class-based hegemony. Only one has been mentioned here: the household. But there were many others, including aspects of the "little tradition" of peasant culture, commitment to "localism," traditional economic structures having to do with marketing and production specialization, and Confucian concepts of morality and social relations. Popular culture, historically formed by and representative of pre-existing culture, was both heteroclite [deviant] and variegated. In its confrontation with a state-sponsored hegemonic project that emphasized the singular principle of class, many of its elements survived. They provided undercurrents which asserted themselves to varying degrees during the Maoist period, and whose persistence even in hibernation kept alive in popular consciousness the possibility of alternative modalities for organizing and thinking about the world. (Blecher 1989:32)

In other words, by singularly emphasizing class categories, the Maoists overlooked or did not give sufficient attention to a variety of cultural factors that contradicted the regime's attempt to create a new revolutionary culture and social consciousness.

As a result, the family and other strongholds of prerevolutionary culture undermined the regime's efforts to create a new hegemonic culture and they have continued to reproduce the old class structure at the local level. As Blecher notes:

> The fact that the household remained basically untransformed during the Maoist period eventually contributed profoundly to the demise of that [hegemonic] project. For the household provided a haven from the com-

plexities and rigors (or at least ardor) of class conflict in the Maoist period. It remained a living symbol of a very different way of organizing and thinking about the world—part of a counter-hegemony. No wonder, then, that one of the first acts associated with the renunciation of the Maoist class-based hegemonic project was the rise of the system of household contract production in the countryside. (Blecher 1989:28)

Blecher contends that the Maoist project also failed because it was carried out in a confusing and extremist fashion, which bewildered and alienated many ordinary Chinese. According to him, the post-Maoist leadership in China has attempted to legitimize itself by criticizing and distancing itself from the Maoist class-based hegemonic project. Moreover, China's new leaders appear to be promoting their own "market-based hegemonic project" that is compatible with many of the prerevolutionary ideas and practices that have survived at the family and village levels (Blecher 1989:29–30).

Blecher's analysis, based on Gramsci's conceptual framework of ideological and cultural hegemony, reveals how difficult it is to transform the social consciousness of a largely peasant population that is steeped in traditional cultural values as well as petty capitalist ideas. Blecher's analysis confirms an earlier observation by Paul Sweezy on the dangers of China "slipping back" into its former modes of thought and practice.

Despite all its initial advantages, China has never been free of the danger of slipping back into the old forms and relations which for centuries had molded Chinese human nature. The old "ensemble of social relations" continued and still continues to exist in the minds and consciousness of hundreds of millions of Chinese. As Marx expressed it in *The Eighteenth Brumaire*, "The tradition of all the dead generations weighs like a nightmare on the brain of the living." To overcome this ineluctable fact—not to nationalize property or build heavy industry or raise material living standards, important though all these things are—is the central problem of the transition to socialism. (Sweezy 1980:53)

For Sweezy, as for Gramsci and Blecher, the central problem of transition involves overcoming the prerevolutionary social relations that continue to exist in the consciousness of the general population.

What the Chinese case illustrates with regard to the question of ideological and cultural transformation during the transition to socialism is that this type of transformation cannot succeed if the state tries to impose a new socialist cultural hegemony on the population instead of painstakingly mobilizing the consent of the people around new values and a new outlook on the world around them. Thus, Blecher concludes:

Things could well have turned out differently. Maoism could probably have survived if it had been willing to take a much more measured, protracted, flexible and creative approach to its hegemonic project. . . . The Chinese case suggests that the possession of even immense state power does not necessarily signal an end point in the hegemonic struggle. Nor does it even permit a shortcut in that struggle. In fact it produced the dialectical opposite: in China the attainment by the Communist Party of overwhelming power appears to have led to its overweening exercise, which in turn produced early and unnecessary setbacks. The Chinese case, then, reaffirms Gramsci's great insight that a new hegemony cannot be imposed on civil society, but rather must grow organically from within it in the course of struggle for it. (Blecher 1989:33)

As Blecher indicates, Gramsci's perspective on this question was that a new socialist hegemony cannot be constructed through imposition; rather it has to be created through carefully and effectively mobilizing the consent of the popular classes around the new ideas, values and norms of social conduct associated with socialism.

Cuba's Approach to the Creation of *Conciencia Comunista*

Cuba offers another excellent case study of a revolutionary regime's continuing efforts to create a new ideological hegemony and social consciousness through various forms of ideological and cultural transformation. Cuba's leaders have sought to create a new revolutionary culture through developing a new kind of person, often referred to as either "the new socialist man" or the "twenty-first-century man." Richard Fagen has argued that the "radicalism of the Cuban leaders is nowhere more in evidence than in their determination to create a new society through transforming the common man into a revolutionary man," defined by Cuba's leaders as "a man devoid of *egoism* [selfishness], guided by *conciencia* [consciousness], who puts service to society above service to self . . ." (Fagen 1989:57).

The development of a new culture began in Cuba with the nationwide literacy campaign carried out in 1961. It was the first major national mobilization campaign undertaken by the revolutionary regime. This campaign was especially focused on the rural areas, where the highest incidence of illiteracy existed. Throughout the 1960s and into the mid–1970s, it was followed by a continuing adult-education program aimed at raising the minimum education of the adult population to a sixth-grade level (Leiner 1989:446–447).

Raising the educational level of the population was considered to be essential to the creation of a new revolutionary culture and a fundamental prerequisite for overcoming the cultural and social underdevelopment of Cuban society. Literacy and popular education (carried out in a non-traditional manner) were viewed as important means to liberate the population from the material and ideological conditions that had reproduced their exploitation and oppression prior to the revolution. And because education was viewed as emancipating, it was designed and carried out in forms that are quite different from conventional forms of public education. Generally speaking, popular forms of education have been developed in Cuba that seek to raise the level of social and political consciousness of the people as well as provide them with useful skills and knowledge. In this sense, education is far more "political" in content and seeks to encourage the participants to take an active role in social affairs (MacEwan 1981:74–79).

One of the best examples of Cuba's revolutionary approach to education is the school in the countryside (*escuela en el campo*). It also reflects the importance that the regime has given to developing the rural areas and to the ruralism that is an important feature of the regime's revolutionary ideology (Fagen 1989:53–54). Each *escuela en el campo* is a secondary school (either junior or senior high school) with its own dormitories, dining hall, recreational facilities, and school farm (Leiner 1989:450–451). They are boarding schools for between 500 and 600 students (with an equal number of boys and girls), and transportation is provided to take the students to their homes and back again every weekend. The students spend half of each school day attending classes and the other half working on the school farm.

The curriculum of these rural secondary schools is based upon the kind of work/study focus that is consistent with socialist values. According to Fidel Castro, this type of school "unites fundamental ideas from two great thinkers: Marx and Martí, [who] both conceived of a school tied to work, a center where youth are educated for life" (quoted in Leiner 1989:451). These schools, of which there are hundreds, scattered across the countryside, represent a major investment of public resources and educate nearly half of all secondary students in the country. Along with other major investments in education—in higher education as well as in primary and vocational/technical education—these schools have made Cuba one of the leading Third World nations in educational development. However, as the Cubans are beginning to recognize, their educational system does have certain shortcomings that must be overcome, particularly the continued use of traditional teaching techniques and an overemphasis on testing (Leiner 1989:454–455). The latter, for example, encourages cheating and rote learning in place of creative forms of learning and critical inquiry.

The development of a socialist consciousness is pursued in a variety of other contexts outside of education. In the workplace, the mass organizations, the neighborhood activities, and the mass media, there has been a continuous emphasis on *conciencia* or *conciencia comunista* (communist consciousness) and the need to act in accordance with the communist value of service to the collectivity and personal improvement for the benefit of society rather than self-aggrandizement. As Richard Fagen noted:

> Whether in educational programs, the work of the mass organizations, the operation of the Communist Party, or the controversy over moral versus material incentives . . . a massive, societywide, and continuing effort at human transformation dominates the revolutionary tapestry, tying together its disparate elements, tonalities, and textures. (Fagen 1989:57)

The national rectification campaign launched by the party in 1986 seeks to renew emphasis on the development of a higher form of social consciousness among the population. It gives preeminence to the subjective factor in the transition to socialism and seeks to revive the revolutionary morale of the population. As Fidel Castro said in 1987:

> We are rectifying all those things—and there are many—that strayed from the revolutionary spirit, from revolutionary work, revolutionary virtue, revolutionary effort, revolutionary responsibility; all those things that strayed from the spirit of solidarity among people. (quoted in Tablada 1989:20)

The renewed emphasis on raising the revolutionary consciousness of the population stems from the leadership's assessment that in recent years there has been a tendency to place too much faith in economic measures and to forget about the importance of subjective factors. Moreover, according to Fidel, "we have achieved our best results working with the pride and honor of people, with their consciousness, and . . . the same can be said for party members and cadres of the mass organizations" (quoted in Tablada 1989:20).

One of the most interesting and positive aspects of the regime's current critical analysis and efforts at revolutionary renewal is the official recognition that not only has an incipient form of class stratification begun to take place in Cuban society but that official measures must be taken to address this as well as other forms of social equality. For example, Fidel has criticized the emergence of a layer of administrators in the state enterprises who have taken on petty bourgeois traits and has acknowledged that there is continuing gender and racial inequality in Cuba. He has stated publicly that this requires a concerted effort on the part of the party and mass organizations to promote women, blacks, and mestizos (people with a mixed Indian and Hispanic ancestry) and to ensure that the membership of these organizations represents the population as a whole (Angotti 1988:540–543; Tablada 1989:22–29).

This policy represents a departure from the past practice of refusing to pursue an open policy of "positive discrimination" aimed at giving special attention to blacks and women, following the initial measures taken to abolish officially all forms of discrimination in Cuba. This also reflects a break in the egalitarian facade that has been presented by the regime, wherein the continuing racial, gender, and class differences in contemporary Cuban society have been minimized (Casal 1989a; Fagen 1989:56–57). The recent measures strengthen the regime's resolve on both the racial and gender equality questions. However, it remains to be seen whether this will lead to a continuing and concerted effort to attack the various forms of racism and sexism that exist in Cuba. Racist ideas and language as well as various manifestations of sexism continue to contradict the revolutionary regime's egalitarian ideals and mar its claims that Cuba is an egalitarian society.

The lingering influence of racist and sexist ideology in Cuban society can be attributed to the historical legacy of centuries of slavery and the paternalistic nature of prerevolutionary society. However, it also appears to stem from a failure on the part of the regime to give sufficient importance to the elimination of these contradictions. This failure is characteristic of the brand of Marxism practiced by the revolutionary vanguard and of the type of ideological hegemony the regime has sought to maintain in Cuba.

As noted by Fagen, the ideology of the Cuban revolution has been distinguished by its voluntarism, egalitarianism, and ruralism, as well as the relative absence of Marxist class analysis.

> [Cuba's] leaders believe that social, cultural, organizational, and ethnic schisms are in some basic sense "unnatural," the product of an imperfect past and a still imperfect revolutionary experience. . . . Thus, the egalitarianism and ruralism . . . blur class lines without ever coming to grips theoretically with the "class problem." (Fagen 1989:56)

Moreover, the emphasis placed on creating national unity around a new national identity devoid of racial and class distinctions has further contributed to the regime's reluctance to acknowledge openly the continuing racial, gender, and class differences that exist in Cuba. Yet, without this acknowledgement and decisive measures to confront these differences, these contradictions continue to reproduce themselves and undermine the regime's ideology.

The importance given to maintaining national unity, especially in the face of U.S. imperialism and three decades of continuing hostility, has made the regime also reluctant to tolerate internal political dissent and criticism. One of the most noted examples of this intolerance was the Padilla case in 1971, which generated a great deal of criticism from foreign intellectuals normally sympathetic to the Cuban regime. In this instance, the well-known Cuban poet Heberto Padilla was arrested and then pressured to make a public confession of self-criticism in which he accused himself and many of his colleagues of vanity and egoism (Casal 1989b:510). Padilla was accused by the regime of having encouraged foreign intellectuals to criticize Cuba and for thinking he was above the revolution. In more recent years, a greater degree of criticism in art and literature has been tolerated, but the regime still does not permit unbridled criticism or open political dissent (see Black 1988). Fidel's statement in 1961 about the rights of writers and artists still holds for Cuba today: "Within the revolution, everything; against the revolution, nothing" (Black 1988:382).

Complete freedom of expression and freedom of the press do not exist in Cuba. It is not clear whether this is purely the product of the regime's fears that the U.S. government and the Cuban exiles will take advantage of these freedoms to sow treasonous dissent against the revolution or if it derives from a more fundamental opposition to greater political freedom. George Black describes the regime's views on this question:

Anyone hoping for signals of an opening to dissenters in Castro's July 26 [1988] speech would have been disappointed. "We must safeguard the ideological purity of the revolution," he declared. "Cuba will never adopt the methods, styles and philosophies or idiosyncrasies of capitalism." One-party rule was a greater need than ever, and no one should harbor illusions of creating "pocket-size parties to organize counter-revolutionaries, the pro-Yankees, the bourgeoisie. . . . We have no need of capitalist formulas. They are complete garbage." The reason was as straightforward, and as depressingly vindicated by history, as it had always been: "We must never forget where we are located. We are not in the Black Sea, but in the Caribbean Sea. Not ninety miles from Odessa but ninety miles from Miami." (Black 1988:377)

Yet the pressures for a great degree of political openness or *apertura* have been mounting in recent years, especially as a result of the changes taking place in the Soviet Union and Eastern Europe.

In 1989, Cubanologist Saul Landau argued that the time has now come for this kind of *apertura*.

> Today Cubans are educated, healthy and politicized: they are also ready for a political debate, whose results cannot be preordained by a single great man. Few Cubans I spoke with in 1987 and 1988 favored creating multiple political parties. Most of the Party members who offered their views wanted to keep the system on course and apply rectification, just as Fidel favored. But others wanted a Communist Party open to the diversity of viewpoints that exists in the general population, and caucuses that could advocate positions and organize both within and outside the Party. Some mentioned their desire to cut the implicit link between dissent and treason. . . . Instead of insisting on ritualistic displays of unity that mask people's thoughts and feelings, the Party could foster diversity, allow for independent newsletters, encourage discussion of (U.S.-operated) Radio Martí broadcasts, and even open debate with exiles. Fidel has often paraphrased Antonio Gramsci: Revolutionaries should not fear the truth, for the truth is always revolutionary. (Landau 1989:48)

However, it is not clear that the regime's ideological hegemony will undergo a Cuban version of *glasnost* in the near future. Unlike either post-Maoist China or the contemporary Soviet Union, the Cuban regime is not confronted at present with an ideological crisis (Black 1988:382).

The Ideological Struggle in Revolutionary Nicaragua and Chile

Turning to Nicaragua, we see that during the decade it was in power the Sandinista regime failed to consolidate the ideological hegemony attained initially by the revolutionary forces in their successful struggle to overthrow the Somoza dictatorship. Nicaragua's revolutionary leaders were aware of the immense difficulties that they had to overcome in order to transform the ideological and cultural dimension of their social reality. This was revealed in the following statement by Comandante Bayardo Arce, one of the nine members of the collective leadership of the Sandinista Front: "Revolutionaries can with relative ease take control of the economic or political power of a society. However, it is far more difficult, and it can take years, for them to take over the ideological power of that society" (Arce 1982:19). Unfortunately, the Sandinistas failed to win the ideological struggle and they never really gained control over the economy for the reasons previously mentioned. They were confronted with a difficult ideological struggle over issues of religion, ethnicity, race, language, and territorial identity. These issues were seized upon by the United States and the domestic enemies of the revolution as part of their efforts to undermine the legitimacy of the revolutionary regime and turn important sectors of the population against it.

The intensity of the ideological struggle in Nicaragua increased dramatically during the decade following the formation of the revolutionary regime in 1979. Both the bourgeois internal political opposition to the regime and the conservative hierarchy of the Catholic Church in Nicaragua waged an intense ideological war aimed at discrediting the Sandinista regime and assisting the cause of the counterrevolutionary forces backed by the United States.

The hierarchy of the Catholic Church in Nicaragua was probably the most effective voice of the bourgeois opposition within Nicaragua as well as an important source of moral support for the counterrevolutionary movement. Prior to the revolution, most of the Catholic and Protestant clergy in Nicaragua had helped to legitimize the political and ideological domination of the population by the conservative bourgeois oligarchy and the Somoza dictatorship. As opposition to the Somoza dictatorship increased and the revolutionary movement gained popular support, the Catholic Church was split between the many lay Catholics and priests who joined the struggle against the dictatorship and those who supported the church hierarchy and sought to prevent the FSLN from taking power (Serra 1985:159–161).

Following the establishment of the Sandinista regime, the Church hierarchy quickly moved to support the bourgeois opposition. It clearly recognized that it had considerable ideological power and repeatedly used this power to try to undermine popular support for the new regime. Among the many tactics used by the church hierarchy were the following:

- The transfer out of the country of priests who sympathized with the revolution;
- The creation of a host of community level organizations aimed at broadening its social base and developing antigovernment attitudes among the population;
- The appearance at meetings of the bourgeoisie's organizations and opposition parties of key members of the reactionary clergy;
- The diffusion of antigovernment propaganda through pastoral letters, sermons, its radio programs, and the opposition newspaper *La Prensa* (Serra 1985:162).

The Sandinista regime counted among its top officials a number of progressive Catholic clergymen, for example, Father Miguel D'Escoto was foreign minister; Father Ernesto Cardenal was minister of culture; and Father Fernando Cardenal was coordinator of the National Literacy Crusade and minister of education. The regime also stressed its respect for freedom of religion and attempted to broaden its support among the more progressive elements within the Catholic Church and other religious groups in the country (Serra 1985:164–171). However, it was never able to isolate or neutralize the ideological opposition of the hierarchy of the Catholic Church. This was more than a thorn in its side; the church constituted an important internal front of the counter-revolution on the ideological battlefield.

Because of the Sandinista strategy of national unity and the important role played by "revolutionary Christians" in the movement, the regime was forced to act with considerable constraint in the face of the unrelenting attempts of the Catholic Church and certain Protestant religious groups to discredit the regime and mobilize public opposition to its policies, such as the unification of the educational system (which affected the curriculum of church-run private schools as well as the public schools) and the introduction of compulsory military service (Serra 1985). In a sense, religion was a weak flank of the Sandinista regime that was skillfully exploited by the bourgeoisie and the counterrevolutionary movement.

Another weak flank of the regime was its failure to incorporate the indigenous and non-Hispanic peoples of the Atlantic Coast region of Nicaragua into the revolutionary process. The Sandinistas' attempts to create a genuine national state for the first time in Nicaraguan history required the effective integration of all regions of the country into a unified national political community governed by a strong central government in Managua. The initial lack of understanding shown by the revolutionary regime toward the particular conditions and interests of the various ethnic and racial groups on the Atlantic Coast created distrust and hostility, especially among the Miskitos, the largest group in the region (Ortiz 1987). This situation provided fertile soil for the U.S. government and its counterrevolutionary allies, who organized and armed two indigenous forces (largely drawn from the Miskitos) to fight the Sandinista government in the Atlantic Coast region.

The Sandinistas, recognizing the threat posed by the disaffection of many of the Atlantic Coast inhabitants, attempted to recuperate their lost ground. They initiated discussions, involving the entire Atlantic Coast population, on the issue of regional autonomy within the Nicaraguan state. A ceasefire was arranged with the armed indigenous forces, and special provisions were included in the new national constitution to guarantee the indigenous communities special rights and local self-determination (Ortiz 1987). However, their troubled relationship with the Atlantic Coast region undercut the Sandinistas' moral superiority and provided the counterrevolution and the U.S. government with both a propaganda and military lever to use against the revolutionary regime.

The Sandinistas' difficulties in incorporating the minority ethnic and racial communities of the Atlantic Coast into the new social order provide further evidence of the importance of cultural and ideological factors in the struggle to create a revolutionary society. Unless the importance of these factors is taken adequately into account by the revolutionary forces, they can become a major obstacle to the successful transformation of the social order and prevent the revolutionaries from consolidating their ideological hegemony. The same can be said of the problems presented by the incorporation of religious communities into the revolutionary process. In the Nicaraguan case, both of these sources of internal contradiction were utilized by the bourgeois-led counterrevolution and its allies to wage an intense ideological struggle against the revolutionary regime.

These problems have confronted national liberation movements in other parts of the Third World. The writings of Amilcar Cabral, one of Africa's most famous revolutionary leaders, bear directly on this question. Cabral skillfully applied Marxist analysis to the particular conditions faced by liberation movements in colonial Africa. His analysis deals with the cultural diversity of the colonized peoples and the need to create national unity through respecting this diversity. For example, he observes:

> For culture to play the important role that falls to it in the framework of development of the liberation movement, the movement must be able to conserve the positive cultural values of every well-defined social group, of every category, and to achieve the *confluence* of these values into the stream of struggle, giving them a new dimension—a *national dimension.* Faced with such a necessity, the liberation struggle is, above all, a struggle as much for the conservation and survival of the cultural values of the people as for the harmonizing and development of these values within a national framework. . . . If broad strata of the population become aware of these aims and this is shown in determination in the face of all the difficulties and all the sacrifices, it is a great political and moral victory. (Cabral 1979:147)

Cabral's analysis led him to conclude that no matter how complex the cultural diversity of the population might be, it is necessary for a liberation movement to distinguish the essential progressive elements within this cultural diversity and forge the liberation struggle around the progressive aspects of the diverse cultural identities and aspirations of the people.

However, the Sandinista regime not only faced a complex situation in terms of the cultural diversity of the Nicaraguan population, it also was confronted with problems because of the complexity of its revolutionary project. This project combined the pursuit of national unity, the reconstruction and development of the country, the establishment of a mixed economy, the institutionalization of representative democracy and political pluralism, the defense of national sovereignty, the pursuit of an anti-imperialist and non-aligned foreign policy, the creation of a unified national state, and the implementation of policies aimed at achieving some degree of redistribution of national income in favor of the impoverished majority of the population. It can be argued that different aspects of this revolutionary project contradicted each other in both principle and practice. For example, the regime's attempt to achieve national unity by avoiding an open class struggle with the bourgeoisie undercut its efforts to achieve most of the other aspects of the revolutionary project.

The complexity and contradictory elements of the Sandinista project made it difficult for the regime to consolidate its ideological hegemony and proceed with the transformation of Nicaraguan society. This fact is revealed in an excellent study by Fred Judson on the revolutionary ideology of the Sandinistas. Judson shows that some of the Sandinista leaders recognized this problem. For example, he notes that Comandante Tomás Borge, one of the original founders of the FSLN and minister of the interior in the revolutionary regime, was aware that their "complicated project" was not as "clearly defined" as the Cuban project and, therefore, tended to "confuse the masses." To quote from Judson's study:

> The revolutionary process since 1979 is as much the source of, and problem for, revolutionary morale as was the struggle before. Tomás Borge summed up this paradox when he said that "Ours is an entangled and complicated project. . . . Political pluralism, the mixed economy, the general outlines of the revolution tend to confuse the masses. There is not, nor can there be, as clearly defined an ideological project as that which existed in Cuba." . . . This complexity produces space in which the enemies of the revolution can exercise influence on the masses, according to Borge. (Judson 1987:36)

The complexity and contradictions of the Sandinista revolutionary project appear to have made it difficult for them to succeed on the various fronts—political, economic and ideological—where they were confronted by the bourgeois opposition, the counter-revolutionary forces and the U.S. government.

To a degree, the Chilean situation appears to have been similar. The Popular Unity government of Salvador Allende tried to achieve too many things at once and lacked ideological clarity (Oppenheim 1989:179). It sought to increase the incomes of the working class and the peasantry while attempting to introduce major structural reforms in the economy.

Moreover, it did not prepare its supporters psychologically for a difficult struggle involving considerable sacrifice. The differences within the Popular Unity coalition over strategy and priorities as well as the open ideological debate between the different leftist factions within the coalition hindered the regime's implementation of its project, alienated the politically important middle sectors of Chilean society, and gave the bourgeois opposition an excellent opportunity to discredit the legitimacy of the regime and the feasibility of its project for the transformation of Chilean society (Oppenheim 1989:179).

Furthermore, as Bitar has argued, the open debate within the coalition over the concept of "dictatorship of the proletariat" confused the public and seemed to contradict the Popular Unity's professed commitment to a democratic and legal transition to socialism. As Bitar indicates:

> The concept of the dictatorship of the proletariat confused the political situation in as much as it was not clear in what way this dictatorship was consistent with the institutional road [to socialism] and pluralism. If at the theoretical level it was possible to juxtapose the dictatorship of the proletariat—as the exercise of power by that class—to the dictatorship of the bourgeoisie, in the common understanding of the term it appeared to be juxtaposed to democracy. Here then the UP provided an advantageous ideological position to the opposition, who argued that democracy, in the hands of the left, was a tactical expedient that in subsequent stages would be replaced by "totalitarian" forms of government. (Bitar 1979:322)

Because of these kinds of mistakes, the Popular Unity forces were unable to consolidate their ideological hegemony and the bourgeois media and political parties were able to undermine support for the regime and its policies (Oppenheim 1989:167).

Conclusion

Every case of revolutionary transition examined above demonstrates that the ideological struggle to replace bourgeois capitalist with revolutionary socialist ideas is a crucial aspect of the transition to socialism. Moreover, it is clear that this struggle must confront a variety of cultural, religious, intellectual, and political contradictions. These contradictions cannot be overcome by relying on purely economic or political measures; they must be confronted on the ideological battlefield and resolved in this domain as well as in the other spheres of social existence. Thus, it is not enough to transform the material conditions of underdevelopment; the subjective conditions must also be transformed, and in their place must be developed a new revolutionary culture and a new revolutionary social consciousness.

All attempts to create a new socialist woman and man based upon the development of a new socialist consciousness and a revolutionary new socialist culture have fallen short of the expectations of the early Marxists as well as of the ideas of people such Gramsci and Guevara. This does not mean that this ideal of Marxism and socialism is impractical or ill founded. The domain of ideology and culture is clearly difficult to transform in a short period of time, and revolutionary leaders have not given it as much attention and priority as they have given to the transformation of the political and economic domains.

Propaganda and indoctrination are not the most effective means of ideological and cultural transformation. Gramsci's thoughts on the creation of a new ideological hegemony, realized through the mobilization of popular consent around the ideals of socialism and through popular forms of education based upon creative and active learning, suggest more appropriate means of ideological and cultural transformation. Guevara's ideas on moral stimulation and collective incentives are also appropriate as well as contemporary conceptions of empowerment offered by radical feminists. Part of the problem also stems from the failure to create more effective forms of democratic self-management in the workplace and democratic self-government at the community level in the existing socialist societies because these institutions could serve as the practical "schools" for learning basic values and norms of socialist democracy as well as for the development of the kind of "associative personality" described by Horvat.

Cuba, more than any other existing socialist society, seems to offer the most insight into this important question. Important elements for the foundation of a socialist culture have been introduced there, but other elements are missing or contradicted by practices that reproduce nonsocialist values and patterns of behavior. Future socialist transformations will undoubtedly give more attention to this domain and avoid many of the errors of the existing socialist societies.

12

The Emancipation of Women

Marx, Engels, and Lenin on the Emancipation of Women

In *Socialism: Utopian and Scientific*, Engels credited Charles Fourier, the great French utopian socialist, with being the "first to declare that in any given society the degree of woman's emancipation is the natural measure of the general emancipation" (Marx and Engels 1972:406). This statement as well as others in the writings of Marx and Engels is evidence that they regarded the emancipation of women as a fundamental goal of socialism and a criterion by which social progress could be measured.

In *The Origin of the Family, Private Property and the State*, Engels set forth what later became the basic premises of the orthodox Marxist-Leninist view of women's emancipation. In essence, he argued that the liberation of women from their subordination and oppression in capitalist society depends upon (1) women taking part in socially productive work rather than being confined to housework, (2) the family being abolished as an economic unit, and (3) the socialization of domestic work through the establishment of public child care facilities, laundries, kitchens, and so on (Marx and Engels 1972:510–516).

At all events, the position of the men thus undergoes considerable change. But that of the women, of *all* women, also undergoes important alteration. With the passage of the means of production into common property, the individual family ceases to be the economic unit of society. Private housekeeping is transformed into a social industry. The care and education of the children become a public matter. . . . Here we see that the emancipation of women and their equality with men are impossible and must remain so as long as women are excluded from socially productive work and restricted to housework, which is private. The emancipation of women becomes possible only when women are enabled to take part in production on a large, social scale, and when domestic duties require their attention only to a minor degree. (Marx and Engels 1972:511, 579)

Following their seizure of power in Russia this perspective was adopted by Lenin and the Bolshevik party as the basis for the new Soviet regime's policies toward women.

The Bolsheviks removed all the preexisting legal barriers to women's emancipation by enacting laws granting full equality to women in marriage and divorce ("free union"), inheritance, custody of children, education, political rights, and so on. They also established a women's department, called the *Zhenotdel*, within the party to attend to women's issues. However, Lenin and many of the Bolsheviks recognized that these were only the first steps to be taken in the liberation of women from their historical oppression and subordination. Thus, Lenin and the revolutionary leadership, on various occasions, made it clear that other measures would have to be undertaken in order to bring about genuine equality between women and men. For example, in his essay *Women and Society*, Lenin wrote:

You all know that even with the fullest equality, women are still in an actual position of inferiority because all housework is thrust upon them. Most of this housework is highly unproductive, most barbarous and most arduous, and it is performed by women. (*The Woman Question* 1973:52)

Not only did Lenin recognize that women had to be liberated from housework and permitted to gain economic independence from men through their equal participation in the labor force, he also acknowledged that men would have to change their behavior toward women and share the tasks of domestic life.

This is shown by his statement during his famous conversations on the woman question with Clara Zetkin, one of the founders of the communist party of Germany:

So few men—even among the proletariat—realize how much effort and trouble they could save women, even quite do away with, if they were to lend a hand in "woman's work." But no, that is contrary to the "right and dignity" of a man. The home life of the woman is a daily sacrifice to a thousand unimportant trivialities. The old master right of the man still lives in secret. . . . Our Communist work among the women, our political work, embraces a great deal of educational work among men.

We must root out the old "master" idea to its last and smallest root, in the party and among the masses. (Zetkin 1973:93)

Throughout the 1920s, the Bolshevik regime maintained a genuine commitment to ending the inequality of women in Soviet society, but this commitment was undermined by widespread popular resistance (particularly among the peasantry), massive social dislocation, severe shortages in housing and child care, and the grinding poverty suffered by most of the population (Goldman 1989). In the 1930s, under Stalin's leadership, the regime retreated from its earlier stance on women's liberation. The *Zhenotdel* was abolished, and new laws were introduced that made divorce more difficult, prohibited abortion, and emphasized more traditional family values.

The Position of Women in the Soviet Union and Eastern Europe

Although the position of women in the Soviet Union today has progressed considerably beyond the low point reached in the 1930s under Stalin, women's issues are still subordinated to other issues, and full equality between women and men has not been achieved. The present situation in the Soviet Union is summarized in the following quote from a recent analysis of the woman question in contemporary Soviet society:

Despite the Soviet regime's consistent theoretical support for the equality of the sexes, evidence suggests that in each period of Soviet history the formulation of women's issues has been relative to other policy priorities. It is the CPSU [Communist Party of the Soviet Union] that draws up policy and defines the relevance of women to policy priorities and the significance of policy for women. . . . In keeping with this, there are no women's organizations outside the party or official trade unions to speak for women's independent interests. These are thought to be unnecessary since the CPSU works for everyone. Separate women's institutions, runs the official line, would therefore be divisive and serve to pander to the mistaken views of bourgeois feminism. (Buckley 1989:276)

According to this study, women's roles and the nuclear family are viewed in conservative terms, there are few women in key decision-making posts, sexuality is rarely discussed in critical terms, and the emergence of unofficial women's organizations has met with official disapproval.

The status of women in the Soviet Union and other socialist countries has been severely criticized by contemporary radical feminists (see Molyneux 1982 and 1986; Eisenstein 1989). The feminists fault the orthodox Marxist-Leninist approach to women's liberation for overemphasizing the importance of integrating women into public employment and for failing to focus attention on the need to equalize *all* the relations between men and women in the existing socialist societies. Feminist critics also argue that these societies have failed to carry out the kind of ideological struggle and consciousness raising that is needed to revolutionize gender relations. They attribute this failure to the "phallocratic" perspective inherent in Marxism (Eisenstein 1989), the erroneous orthodox Marxist-Leninist view that women's oppression will eventually disappear as a result of economic transformations, and to the emphasis placed on conventional notions of motherhood and family stability by the male-dominated regimes in these countries.

Moreover, radical feminists point out that the majority of women who are employed in the socialist countries are, like women in capitalist societies, concentrated in gender-specific occupations, which tend to be paid less than those held primarily by men (Molyneux 1982:88–89). They also note that the underrepresentation of women in key decision-making positions is similar to that in capitalist societies.

For example, Hungary appears to have been one of the most progressive East European regimes in providing state support for women. Abortion was legalized in 1956, day care was provided for nearly 90 percent of preschool-age children, and a generous maternity leave policy was established in 1967 (Lampland 1989:312–313). However, the study showed that female members of the work force were generally paid less than their male counterparts despite legislation aimed at redressing this problem. Women were also encouraged to go into fields of study and training that prepared them for work performed almost exclusively by women, and they held few positions of importance in the country's governmental and political hierarchies.

Some of the feminist critics acknowledge that in Eastern Europe there have been some efforts to reduce gender typing in employment and to increase the opportunities for women in areas where they are underrepresented, but they point out that the sexual division of labor has not been radically transformed and there has been no significant equalization of labor in the home (Molyneux 1982; Eisenstein 1989). Finally, they contend that women's interests can only be advanced in these countries if they are represented by independent women's organizations.

Women's Liberation in China and Vietnam

The existing socialist regimes in China, Vietnam, and Cuba reveal many of the same shortcomings of the orthodox Marxist-Leninist approach to women's liberation found in the Soviet Union and Eastern Europe.

In addition, they also show the kind of structural conditions often found in the Third World that obstruct full equality between women and men. For example, the Chinese communist party holds to the orthodox line that the emancipation of women requires their participation in production and public life. However, the massive participation of women in the work force and laws recognizing the equality of women and men have not put an end to the inferior status women have held traditionally in Chinese society (Davin 1989).

Within the Chinese peasant family women still have an inferior status, and preference is given to sons over daughters. This sex discrimination can be attributed to the persistence of the patrilineal structure of the peasant family and traditional gender relations. Moreover, the economic reforms that have led to the dissolution of both the communes and collective farming have restored the family economy in Chinese agriculture and appear to have weakened the drive to improve the position of women in rural society (Davin 1989:356–357). In the urban sectors of the economy women are generally better off, but very little progress seems to have been achieved in increasing the participation of women in decision-making positions or in reducing their concentration in low-paying jobs.

During the Cultural Revolution, conventional gender relations were temporarily disrupted by the active participation of women in the campaign to root out bourgeois tendencies and official corruption (Young 1989). A major effort was made to incorporate women, especially young women, into political activity, and they were encouraged to place their political responsibilities above their obligations to family and home. Furthermore, gender neutrality was extolled and women were expected to be "genderless" in their appearance and public behavior.

However, the emphasis on class and class struggle during the Cultural Revolution made it difficult for women to raise gender issues because these were already suspect from an orthodox Marxist-Leninist perspective as manifestations of bourgeois feminism (Young 1989:235). As a result, the official Women's Federation was disbanded and women's issues were ignored during this period.

In the years since the Cultural Revolution, the reforms undertaken by the regime in the post-Mao era have repudiated the policies and ideas associated with this chaotic period. The "Iron Girl Brigades" of the Cultural Revolution as well as the genderless style of dress and behavior that women were encouraged to adopt are now the subject of officially sanctioned criticism and derision. In contrast, the "modernizing" reforms have placed a great deal of importance on restoring women's place in Chinese society and extolling their distinctive virtues. This has promoted certain gender stereotypes rather than women's liberation (Davin 1989).

In Vietnam, as in China, the economic reforms undertaken during the 1980s have encouraged the development of the role of the family in production, particularly in agriculture. However, due to the disastrous effects of the country's long war for national liberation and the continued mobilization of many men in the military, the work force in agriculture is predominantly female (C. White 1989).

Thus, the recent reforms have tended to benefit rural women as they are the effective heads of the majority of the family units that are now able to farm on a subcontract basis for the state and sell their surplus at free market prices. Consequently, in contrast to the present situation in China, the restoration of family production has *not* reinforced the patriarchal patterns of traditional rural Vietnamese society.

On the other hand, since there is no male labor power in many families, rural women must do everything. In the words of Christine Pelzer White, a feminist social scientist who has studied the condition of women in contemporary Vietnam, the present circumstances of postwar economic crisis and impoverishment have made "the Leninist route to women's emancipation by drawing women into productive labor seem a cruel joke, a formula for total exhaustion rather than liberation" (C. White 1989:175). Moreover, very few women hold positions of importance in the administrative and political structures of the country.

The Status of Women in Cuba and Nicaragua

Turning now to Latin America and the Caribbean, we note that although considerable progress has been made in improving the status of women in revolutionary Cuba and Nicaragua, equality between women and men has not been achieved. For example, when the revolutionary regime in Cuba was established in 1959, only some 15 percent of Cuban women were involved in work outside the home (MacEwan 1981:80–81). During the 1960s, the revolutionary government sought to integrate women into the work force, and the official Federation of Cuban Women made an effort to encourage women to enter the labor force as well as participate in public affairs. This situation reflected the orthodox Marxist-Leninist position as expressed by Fidel Castro:

> The whole question of women's liberation, of full equality of rights for women and the integration of women into society is to a great extent determined by their incorporation into production. This is because the more women are incorporated into work . . . so will the way to their liberation become easier and more clearly defined. (Castro 1974:3)

However, the results of the regime's efforts to incorporate women into production were quite poor during the first decade of the revolution. In 1973, only 24 percent of Cuban women were involved in the labor force, and in the rural areas the situation was worse (MacEwan 1981:81). In recent years, the figures have improved (in 1984, women constituted 37 percent of the workforce), but the regime's efforts to integrate women into the work force and promote equality between women and men have been hindered by traditional patriarchal attitudes of *machismo*, the "double shift" that most working women must endure (that is, a full workday plus housework and child care), men's resistance to helping with housework and child care—what they regard as "domestication"—and also by unfavorable economic conditions that have obstructed the movement of women into the work force (Nazzari 1989).

The difficulty experienced during the first decade and a half of the revolution in recruiting and retaining women in the work force as well as the low participation of women in local government and community affairs led the revolutionary regime to reexamine its efforts to involve women in production and public life. Out of this reexamination came the enactment of the new Family Code in 1975. The most controversial aspect of this new law was the section requiring the equal division of housework and child care between husband and wife in order to guarantee the full equality of both partners in the socialist institution of marriage (Azicri 1989:468).

The introduction of the new Family Code represented a new approach focused on the individual rather than the social level (Nazzari 1989:118). Unlike the earlier approach, which entailed the costly provision of child care facilities, public laundries, dining halls, and so on, in order to facilitate the incorporation of women into production and civic affairs, this one is far less costly because it requires a change within the family unit, particularly in the behavior of men.

The first solution attempted, socializing child care and housework, tried to move women toward equality by transferring their family duties to social institutions without disturbing men's lives or roles. Cuban economists calculated that for every three women who joined the workforce, a fourth must be employed in institutions supplying supportive services to facilitate their incorporation. The great cost of this solution meant that it had to compete with other investment needs in the national budget. . . . The Family Code, on the other hand, provided a solution to the Woman Question that did not need to come out of the national budget. . . . It did, nevertheless, require a change in individual men's lives, and men resisted. (Nazzari 1989:118)

This change in approach to the emancipation of women was followed in 1977 by a new policy requiring parents to pay part of the cost of what had previously been free child care. This is further evidence of the fact that the regime's efforts to encourage women to enter the workforce, constrained by economic considerations, had shifted away from the provision of social services to a more ideological approach.

Cuba's limited material resources and the high cost of providing socialized domestic services would appear to be important factors that have prevented the regime from providing the level of domestic services required to attract a larger number of women into the workforce and free all working women from the infamous "double shift." Moreover, the regime has so far failed to do much about the stubborn resistance of most men to assuming an equal share of house work and child care (Nazzari 1989: 122). As a result, despite the regime's announced commitment to full equality for women, its efforts have been inadequate.

Another way of looking at this problem is to see it in terms of the choices that the regime has made between competing interests. Looked at in this way, it is possible to argue that Cuba's leaders chose in the 1980s to invest the country's scarce resources in accordance with priorities that downgraded the importance of facilitating the entry of women into the work force and alleviating their domestic burdens. Fidel has, in fact, admitted this. In a 1987 provincial meeting of the communist party, he told the delegates:

> Those who advocated reactionary ideas within the revolution argued that building a day-care center was a social expense. Social expenses were no good, investing in production was good; as if those who work in the factories were male and female mules and not human beings, not men and women with their problems, especially women with their problems. . . . (quoted in Tablada 1989:27)

However, since the rectification campaign has been in effect, the microbrigades have been building day-care centers in increasing numbers throughout the country (Tablada 1989:27).

The leadership has also publicly called upon all the mass organizations and the party to promote more women to important positions. In a report to the February 1986 session of the Communist Party Congress, Fidel stated that the correction of "historical injustices" such as gender and racial inequality could not be left to chance:

> To really establish total equality takes more than simply declaring it law. It has to be promoted in the mass organizations, in youth organizations, in the party. And that's why we said in the report that we should reflect

the ethnic composition of our society, that we cannot leave the promotion of women, blacks and mestizos to chance. It has to be the work of the party. We have to straighten out what history has twisted. (quoted in Tablada 1989:29)

In recent years, as the Cuban regime has focused more attention on the equalization of the relations between men and women, it has increased the number of women in higher education to over 40 percent of the total and guaranteed women full membership rights in the new agricultural cooperatives (Deere 1986:135–136).

In contrast to the Cuban case, the Nicaraguan revolution began during the period of the "new feminism," and women played an important role in the revolutionary struggle. Some 30 percent of the combatants in the armed FSLN units were women, and women constituted a large proportion of the membership of the popular organizations that emerged to oppose the Somoza dictatorship (Molyneux 1986:287; Wells 1983:109). In El Salvador, there appears to be an even larger percentage of women combatants involved in the FMLN forces. This is a significant phenomenon in countries that continue to be characterized by overtly sexist traditions.

The Sandinistas adopted a somewhat different approach to the emancipation of women than that of previous revolutionary movements with orthodox Marxist-Leninist views on this subject. For example, the Sandinistas did not consider feminism to be a "diversion" that would undermine the unity of the revolutionary forces, which has been the orthodox position in the past (Molyneux 1986:287). Also, the independent, but pro-Sandinista women's organization AMNLAE did not subscribe to the orthodox approach that women's emancipation is achieved primarily through integration into the work force (Ruchwarger 1987:188–189). AMNLAE also emphasized the need to develop new relations between men and women and to combat the patriarchal patterns of behavior characterizing Nicaraguan society. One of its slogans was "no revolution without women's emancipation; no emancipation without revolution" (Molyneux 1986:288).

On the other hand, the Sandinista regime was limited by the conservative influence that the Catholic Church exercises over the population and by the small base of popular support that exists for feminism within the country (Molyneux 1986:294). In fact, there is considerable hostility among the population to the ideas of women's emancipation, and *machista* sexist attitudes are prevalent among women as well as men. Among other things, this helps to explain why the pro-Sandinista unions were reluctant to discuss women's demands (Ruchwarger 1987:216).

In spite of these difficulties, important steps were taken by the revolutionary regime to improve the position of women in Nicaraguan society. New anti-sexist laws were introduced that put an end to the discrimination against women in questions of marriage, divorce, parental support, child custody, adoption, and family relations. In addition, child-care facilities were established all over the country to assist working women, and the government's literacy and health campaigns benefited women in some ways more than they did men. Women were incorporated in significant numbers into the Sandinista mass organizations, the militia (where they represented 50 percent of the members) and in the FSLN itself, in which they constituted approximately one-quarter of the membership and one-third of the leadership by the mid-1980s (Molyneux 1986:297; Ruchwarger 1987:189–217).

Economic scarcity, the U.S.-backed counterrevolutionary war, and the national mobilization for defense appear to have taken their toll on the revolutionary regime's commitment to women's emancipation, which, like many other ideals of the Sandinista revolution, was subordinated to the struggle for survival (Molyneux 1986:299–300). In this respect, Nicaragua offers another example of the tendency in contemporary revolutions to subordinate women's issues to other revolutionary goals. This subordination has led radical feminists to the conclusion that women's interests must be effectively represented in the key decision-making centers of the revolutionary regime by their own independent organizations in order to ensure that the elimination of gender inequality is equated with other revolutionary policies.

Conclusion

The historical evidence indicates that Marxism must be refocused to encompass the feminist perspective, and socialist regimes must take the appropriate steps to create the ideological context and material conditions for the genuine emancipation of women and the elimination of gender inequality in all its forms. This conclusion has been forcefully stated by Zillah Eisenstein:

Refocusing the Marxist method (as well as its content) via feminism necessitates a reordering of priorities, particularly the question of consciousness in relation to the conditions of society. Questions of consciousness become a part of the discussion of the social reality. Reality itself comes to encompass the relations of class and sex and race. The relations between the private (personal) and public (political) become a major focus having particular consequence for the relations defining sexuality, heterosexuality, and homosexuality. Along with this comes a focus on the importance of ideology. . . . This new way of viewing things—that society's ideas and people's consciousness are part of the objective social reality and that they operate out of the relations of sex, class, and race—is a product of the feminist assault on the inadequacies of the left, both in theory and practice. (Eisenstein 1989:41-42)

A refocused Marxist perspective that encompasses the relations of capitalist patriarchy involves utilizing the Marxist method of class analysis while at the same time moving beyond class analysis. Eisenstein makes it clear that "class analysis is necessary to our understanding" of capitalist patriarchy "but it is not sufficient. . . ." Feminist theory must also be employed to comprehend and transform relations of sex, race, and class.

13
Lessons and Prospects for Socialism in Latin America

The Continuing Relevance of Marxism

The preceding chapters have demonstrated how Marxist thought on the transition to socialism can be applied to the analysis and interpretation of contemporary revolutionary transformations, including those that have taken place in Latin America and the Caribbean. A number of generalizations can be derived from the comparative analysis of the cases examined in this book. In this final chapter, these generalizations or "lessons" about the transition to socialism are summarized and applied to the contemporary Latin American and Caribbean context.

The first of these lessons concerns the applicability of the basic theoretical framework provided by Marxism. Although classical Marxist theory did not address the problems of constructing socialism in Latin America and the Caribbean, the evidence presented in the preceding pages suggests that it provides an invaluable framework for understanding the attempts that have been made in this region to bring about a transition to socialism. It also provides an important perspective for understanding the fate of the revolutionary regimes that were established in Nicaragua and Grenada at the beginning of the 1980s. The applicability of Marxism to these cases is due in part to the fact that the thought and practice of leftist leaders in the countries concerned have been greatly influenced by Marxist thought. It is also due to the fact that the basic concepts developed by Marx and Engels on the transition to socialism are applicable to a much wider range of historical conditions than either Marx or Engels could have imagined.

This does not mean that classical or contemporary Marxist theory should be applied in a dogmatic fashion to the reality of the contemporary societies of Latin America and the Caribbean. In fact, in the strictest sense of the term, Marxist thought cannot be "applied" to any society because it was never meant to be imposed on reality as a fixed framework. Marxism is not an abstract theory that can be applied to all situations; rather it provides a holistic conceptual and analytical framework for analyzing a contemporary society in terms of that society's specific historical conditions. Once a society has been subjected to this kind of analysis, Marxism also provides the basis for developing a strategy of creative action aimed at bringing about a socialist transformation of this society.

During the early years of the Soviet Union, Lenin and the Bolsheviks largely rejected the mechanistic and dogmatic application of Marxist thought to their reality. In fact, their relative success in adapting Marxism to their social reality seems to have stemmed from the "elastic relationship" that existed between their use of Marxist theory and their revolutionary practice (Cerroni 1973:110). Like the leaders of the Russian Revolution, the leaders of the Chinese, Cuban, Vietnamese, Nicaraguan, and Salvadoran revolutions also appear to have used Marxist thought in a flexible manner, although not always successfully.

What these cases reveal is that when Marxist thought is combined with an adequate understanding of the experiences of other countries that have already made an attempt to construct socialism, it can be an invaluable weapon in the arsenal of revolutionaries seeking to construct a socialist order in their particular historical context. On the other hand, there is also a great deal of evidence that this body of thought has been misapplied in either an inflexible dogmatic manner or in an opportunistic distorted form. In fact, during the course of the last century, dogmatism and opportunism among so-called socialist regimes have done more to discredit Marxism and the ideal of socialism that it advances than the efforts of the enemies of these regimes.

The Latin American and Caribbean experience confirms the proposition that there are no universal models for Marxist revolutionaries to follow in constructing socialism. The founders of Marxism created a conceptual framework for critically analyzing and interpreting the complex, changing reality of *each* capitalist society. They had no intention of producing a static, theoretical model that could be applied to all societies under all historical circumstances.

The Marxist concept of the transition from capitalism to socialism entails the following:

1. The destruction of the pre-existing capitalist state;

2. The establishment of a revolutionary regime that functions as a genuine democracy for the popular classes and as a class "dictatorship" against those who seek to overthrow the new regime;
3. The expropriation of large forms of private property in industry, commerce, and agriculture;
4. Economic planning that ensures the harmonious development of the forces of production and the satisfaction of all basic needs;
5. The socialization of the major means and the relations of production;
6. Democratic workers control of production;
7. A continuing struggle against bourgeois ideology, sexism, racism, and classism;
8. The development of a new socialist consciousness and culture.

The Latin American and Caribbean experience tends to verify that these basic transformations are necessary for a successful transition to socialism.

Cuba's Vice President Carlos Rafael Rodríguez has stated that the "variety of contemporary roads to socialism . . . reflects the enormous influence of socialism on the social life of our times" (C. Rodríguez 1978:14). Moreover, it is is important to heed Rodríguez's warning that if this rich variety of experience is reduced to a single model that others are supposed to follow, there is a very high risk of closing off the discovery of new roads to socialism in the future. Therefore, one of the lessons that arises from an analysis of the rich history of socialist revolutions is that the success of any attempt to carry out a transition to socialism depends upon the extent to which Marxist thought and the lessons of previous socialist experiences are adapted to the reality of the society in transition. This adaption entails a dialectical process in which Marxist thought and the knowledge of past socialist experiences influence, and in turn are influenced by, each new attempt to construct socialism.

The process of adapting Marxist thought and the lessons from past attempts at socialist transformation to a specific reality involves the modification of both these sources of knowledge. They must be adjusted in accordance with the necessities and specific conditions faced by the social forces propelling the transition. This process includes updating Marxist thought and the lessons from past experience so that both are enriched by the knowledge that results from new efforts to realize socialism.

This brings us to a consideration of the present period of historical development and the validity of Marxism as an intellectual instrument for developing a democratic socialist project in contemporary Latin America and the Caribbean. The task involves the application of the lessons that can be derived from previous experiences as well as a critical analysis of the contemporary perspectives and politics of leftist movements and parties in the region.

The Crisis of Marxism and the Left in Latin America

Perhaps the most appropriate place to start is with the recognition that Marxism and the Left are presently in a state of crisis and change. Widespread evidence of this situation exists throughout Latin America and the Caribbean (Chilcote 1990:3–13; Munck 1990:114–115). It stems in part from the defeat and brutal repression suffered by the Left as a result of the military seizures of state power in various Latin American countries during the 1960s and 1970s—beginning with Brazil in 1964 and then followed by Chile, Uruguay, Bolivia, and Argentina during the 1970s. In these countries the Left was dismembered and almost eliminated by the military as the latter carried out its ruthless project of political repression and popular demobilization. This period of military rule, especially in the Southern Cone, can be referred to as the holocaust of the Latin American Left.

The current crisis of Marxism and the Left in Latin America can also be traced to the failure of the revolutionary armed movements established in many parts of the region during the sixties and seventies. These revolutionary movements were for the most part precipitous, and they failed to mobilize sufficient popular support. As a result, they were either eliminated or disbanded. Many Leftists suffered demoralization and disillusionment as a result of the failure of these movements. They also were discouraged by the factionalism, dogmatism, and opportunism that were endemic in the Left during the 1960s and 1970s.

During the 1980s, a series of unexpected developments that for most leftists were difficult to explain caused confusion and uncertainty in the Left: the collapse of the self-styled "workers' states" in Eastern Europe, fundamental changes in the orientation of the Soviet and Chinese regimes, the failure of the Grenadian revolution, the brutalization and derailment of the Nicaraguan revolution at the hands of the United States and its Nicaraguan allies, and finally the political democratization of the formerly militarized states of the Southern Cone and Brazil. These developments brought about what can perhaps best be described as a "sea change" in the international as well as the regional political environment (Gautier 1989).

In this new historical context, most leftist intellectuals and the leadership of leftist organizations sought to revise their ideological and political positions, explain the current conjuncture as best as they could, and devise new strategies for mobilizing popular support and gaining political legitimacy. There has been a tendency on the part of some Latin American and Caribbean leftists to avoid taking responsibility for their past errors and to blame their defeats and setbacks upon the military, U.S. imperialism, and other leftist parties (Barros 1987:66). In addition to absolving themselves of any responsibility for past failures, many leftists have distanced themselves from their former positions and adopted new perspectives that are more compatible with the course of current developments. The hard lessons learned during the last two decades are now often expounded without reference to the fact that they generally contradict many of the former positions held by the Left.

Throughout the region, the Left's attempts to renew itself have been largely focused on the question of political democracy. Thus, "democracy" has replaced "revolution" as the central concept in the political vocabulary of the Left. This change holds for armed revolutionary movements such as the FMLN/FDR in El Salvador as well as for the political parties of the Left in the Southern Cone, Brazil, the Andean states, and the Caribbean. This focus on democracy appears to stem from four factors:

- The Left's participation in the struggles waged in defense of human rights under repressive military regimes;
- Their involvement in the process of limited political democratization that has accompanied the transition from military to civilian rule during recent years;
- The recognition on the part of some leftists that the lack of importance given to democracy in the past—both in their programs and in the internal organization of their parties—was to some degree responsible for many of their past errors and failures;
- The influence of the discussions on democracy and the process of political democratization that took place in the Soviet Union and Eastern Europe during the late 1980s (Barros 1987:65–66; Lawner 1989:2–4).

In the early 1990s, the differences among the leftists in Latin America and the Caribbean have more to do with their positions vis-à-vis the question of democracy than they do with almost anything else. For example, Roberto Barros has identified three distinct positions on democracy and socialism found among the Left in Latin America and the Caribbean (Barros 1987:67). The first position or tendency emphasizes the contradictions between democracy and capitalism and sees the struggle for democratic forms of government as a tactic to be used by the working class in a more or less orthodox Marxist-Leninist revolutionary strategy for arriving at socialism. This approach is found among those who still hold onto the objectives and strategies developed by the revolutionary Left in the 1960s and 1970s. The communist party of Chile has held this kind of position in recent years. Other parties representative of this line are to be found in the Unified Left (*Izquierda Unida*) coalition in Peru (Salcedo 1989).

The second position is held by those who try to avoid using the terms "revolution," "Marxism," "socialist transition," and in some cases even "socialism." They argue that the Left should give priority to the consolidation of democratic institutions and the development of a democratic political culture to sustain these institutions. They have turned their backs on Marxism and have adopted a new political vocabulary that excludes "class" and "class struggle" as well as the terms mentioned above. Their "post-Marxism" emphasizes the political and ideological domains and gives little attention to the influence of the economic and social spheres on these domains (Vasconi 1990:26–27). One of the best examples of this tendency is the Movement Toward Socialism (*Movimiento al Socialismo* or MAS) in Venezuela, which refuses even to identify itself with the rest of the Left in that country (Ellner 1989:148). Another example is the moderate Núñez faction of the now divided Chilean Socialist Party. To distinguish itself from the more "traditional" Almeyda faction, which in 1988 took the name of the Left Socialist Party, the Núñez faction adopted the label of the Party for Democracy—thus dropping the term "socialist" from its name (Garretón 1989b:37).

This tendency among repentent leftists can be criticized for its abstract approach to political democracy and its failure to give importance to the influence which the particular context and popular demands can have on the development of democratic institutions. On this point, Barros states:

> By de-contextualizing democracy, these predominantly political and institutional perspectives on democratization run the risk of ignoring how objective institutions and strategic interactions intertwine to produce very different types of democracy, including variants that are not able to satisfy popular democratic demands or lead to a greater democratization. (Barros 1987:74)

Given this deficiency in the perspective of those who adhere to the "democracy without socialism" position, they run the risk of playing into the hands of the centrist political parties and expending their energies on the consolidation of political regimes that are dominated by the interests of the bourgeoisie.

This tendency among the leftists also contributes to what James Petras has characterized as the revival of neoliberalism (Petras 1988). He is critical of what he sees as an attempt on the part of neoliberal politicians and intellectuals to gain ideological hegemony in the recent period following the transition from military to civilian rule in Latin America. The contradictions inherent in the present process of democratization and the democratic positions of the ex-leftists turned neoliberals are revealed in the following quote from Petras's critique:

> What neoliberals describe as the "democratization process" has the dual character of reconsolidating authoritarian state power—both the military institution and accumulation model—while conceding political space for individual expression and limited social mobilization. The contradictory nature of this conjunctional process creates the basis for deepening the alienation of those majoritarian social movements which conceived of democratization as a process in which regime change would be accompanied by profound change in the state apparatus and the accumulation model. The delusions and self-deceptions of these ex-leftists turned neoliberal and their adaptation to the needs of capital leads directly to an attack on the class content and program of labor unions and left parties. (Petras 1988:10)

As Petras notes, the "delusions and self-deceptions" among the Left, or former Left, have led them to support a "democracy built on the twin pillars of the terrorist state and supply-side economics." They also disassociate themselves from the emerging class-based struggles of the working class and peasantry, who, as Petras observes, "do not read the texts about classless democracy but feel the painful class effects of their policies" (Petras 1988:11). This situation is evident in Chile, where the "renovated" Left supports the government of President Patricio Aylwin, whose economic policies are fundamentally the same as those of the preceding military regime (Hojman 1990).

The third position seeks to bring about a renewal of the Left through a "secularization" of Marxism and the pursuit of a radical democratic project that will lead to democratic socialism. It seeks to overcome the rigid dogmatism and pseudoreligious nature of Marxism-Leninism, the disunity and debilitating fragmentation of the Left, the confusion and disillusionment of many of its supporters, and the tired discourse of the "old Left" about the heroic working class.

In contrast to the other two positions mentioned above, this leftist tendency is concerned with reorganizing the Left around a common project of radical democratization. Perhaps the best example of this tendency is Brazil's Workers' Party (*Partido Trabalhista* or PT), which won thirty-five mayoral positions in the November 1988 municipal elections and fielded a very strong candidate who won 47 percent of the popular vote in the November 1989 presidential elections (Hinchberger

1990). In the English-speaking Caribbean, efforts have been made by the Committee for Labor Solidarity (CLS) to organize a workers' party along similar lines in Trinidad (Abdulah 1989).

According to the proponents of groups such as the PT and the CLS, the Left must commit itself to a radical democratic project that is based on the experiences, popular culture and concrete struggles of the lower classes. And it must provide a radical democratic alternative to the limited democratic and hierarchical institutions of contemporary society. To quote Barros again:

> The immediate task, then, is the development of alternative forms of culture, organization and struggle that undermine hierarchical norms and institutions and, as a result, contribute to the formation of popular subjects endowed with the autonomy and will to participate actively in public life. In line with this, the Gramscian themes of "moral and intellectual reform," the "critique of common sense," "hegemony," and the construction of a "national popular will" provide the raw material for the elaboration of a radical democratic alternative to limited democracy. Here democracy, understood as the active praxis of the lower classes, emerges as something inseparable from both the self-development of the historical popular subjects and from socialism, which is conceived of as the expansion and deeping of democratic control over social existence. (Barros 1987:78)

The virtue of this third position is that it makes a serious effort to articulate democracy with socialism, at least at the level of theory and ideology. It also tends to rely upon Gramsci's contributions to Marxism and thus emphasizes the ideological and cultural dimensions of revolutionary struggle as well as the more explicitly political and economic dimensions. Moreover, unlike the other two tendencies, it stresses the importance of developing local and intermediate forms of participation— something that we have already seen is a critically important counterweight to the alienating effects of both bureaucratism and purely formal democratic institutions. Holders of this approach appear to have learned the lessons on these questions that can be drawn from the previous experiences of the Left in Latin America and the Caribbean.

This third tendency calls for the development, *prior* to the transition to socialism, of the organizational and ideological forms appropriate to a future democratic socialist society. This development is understood as an inherently democratic process. Indeed, the entire process leading up to and throughout the transition to socialism is conceptualized as a process of radical (unlimited) democratization. However, the process is not considered to be irreversible and is dependent upon the support of the majority of the population as expressed through democratic political processes (Garretón 1989b:25–26).

The problem with this position, however, is that it has not produced a clear concept of *how* to realize the kind of radical democratic project it proposes. That is to say, the exponents of this perspective have not produced a concrete strategy indicating how the major limitations of this project can be overcome. As a result, it is not clear what the future prospects are for the realization of this kind of radical democratization nor how such a project can be translated into a successful transition to socialism. Finally, perhaps the most critical shortcoming of this tendency is that it does not give enough importance to the lessons that can be learned from past unsuccessful attempts to promote radical democratization.

The Prospects for a Radical Democratic Project

The popular mobilizations in favor of the return to civilian rule as well as the political accomplishments of the new social movements and grass-roots organizations that were established in the 1970s and early 1980s do not in themselves offer much evidence in favor of a radical democratization project. As Ronald Chilcote notes in his analysis of this question, bourgeois democracy constrains these forms of popular political expression.

> In the transition from dictatorship, political instability and economic crisis usually characterize the period of democratic opening. Popular movements emerge; for example, Brazil during the late 1970s and early 1980s was marked by labor-organized strikes and thousands of neighborhood groups and ecclesiastic base communities that mobilized millions of supporters. The importance of these movements diminished, however, as the political parties organized. The problem here relates to the limitations of bourgeois democracy, the constraints on direct forms of participation and the need, perceived by compromised politicians and intellectuals, of ensuring political stability through the parliamentary system. (Chilcote 1990:16)

In fact, the political history of countries such as Brazil, Chile, and Uruguay provides stark evidence of the failure of previous attempts at radical political democratization, which ended in repression and defeat for the Left. These attempts were terminated by the military dictatorships preceding the current neoliberal civilian regimes.

Chile provides a significant case of the tragic results that can befall a radical democratization project in Latin America (Bitar 1979; Garretón 1989a; and Smirnow 1979). Starting in the 1930s, Chile underwent a process of increasing political democratization, which involved the expansion of popular participation and highly politicized struggles for social democratization (that is, demands for the extension of social welfare benefits to the lower classes). During the 1960s, this process became more radical. There were mass mobilizations and the establishment of a large number of grass-roots organizations that predated the popular social movements of the 1980s.

In this context, the centrist Christian Democratic regime of President Eduardo Frei came to power and introduced a number of moderate reforms. These reforms failed to contain the popular mobilizations and the increasing demands for greater political, social, and economic democratization. In this context, the two main parties of the Chilean Left, the socialists and the communists, formed the UP electoral alliance with several smaller center-Left elements. In 1970, this leftist coalition succeeded in winning the presidential elections and placing their candidate—Senator Salvador Allende—in the presidency. In essence, the coalition's program was a project for a radical (but peaceful) democratization and transition to socialism in Chile.

The UP coalition's faltering attempts to implement their project further polarized the political system and gave rise to a bloody military coup backed by the bourgeois right-wing parties as well as the petty bourgeois Christian Democratic Party (Bitar 1979; Garretón 1989a; and Smirnow 1979). This coup brought to an end the democratization process in Chile and ushered in a period of harsh political repression and military dictatorship. The Chilean people and the Chilean Left have been trying to recover from this tragic period of military dictatorship, which has only recently come to an end with the election of a civilian regime (led by President Patricio Aylwin, who, it should be noted, was one of the members of the Christian Democratic Party who originally supported the military coup in 1973).

Elsewhere, I have examined some of the reasons why this attempt to bring about a democratic transition to socialism failed. The leftist forces did not gain complete control over the state, especially the armed forces. They did not move quickly enough to expropriate the economic power base of the large capitalists and so they never gained control over the main levers of the economy. They also failed to establish ideological hegemony. In fact, the ideological and political splits within the Left coalition and the propaganda efforts of the bourgeoisie undermined the credibility of the regime and turned the critical middle sectors against the UP and its project. As a result, the UP government's democratic socialist project did not have the support of a majority of the population (Garretón 1989b:15–16).

The economic policies of the UP government gave rise to crippling inflation and consumer goods shortages that also alienated the middle sectors. Finally, the Allende government did not provide arms to its working class and peasant supporters to defend their expropriated factories, newly acquired lands, and the leftist government itself against the inevitable intervention of the military, which predictably terminated the radical democratization process before it moved too far in the direction of socialism.

Even if one accepts the argument that it was the errors of the UP coalition that gave rise to the military's coup d'etat, this experience still suggests that a radical democratization project is quite dangerous because it is likely to provoke a military takeover that leads to the violent repression of the radical democratic forces. In this and other respects, Latin America and the Caribbean are not like Eastern Europe. The ruling elites and the armed forces in this region will not acquiese peacefully when confronted with popular mobilizations and rising demands for fundamental changes in the system.

Nicaragua provides another, more recent, example of how difficult it is to move in the direction of socialism through a democratic route and within the context of an economy that is basically capitalist. The Sandinistas thought they could develop a mixed economy, democratize the political system, and achieve national unity—while remaining in control of the process. However, they were mistaken. The Nicaraguan bourgeoisie, backed by the United States and the hierarchy of the Catholic Church, used its control over the productive process to undermine the economic project and popular support of the revolutionary regime. It sabotaged the economy, prevented the Sandinistas from gaining ideological hegemony, and succeeded in using the electoral process established by the revolutionary regime to defeat the Sandinistas at the polls.

Eleven years after coming to power, the Sandinistas lost the national elections in February 1990 to a bourgeois-led coalition of parties. This loss was partly because the Sandinistas' project to create a mixed economy failed miserably, partly because the population was exhausted by the war of attrition that the United States waged against the country, and partly because the Sandinistas tried to use a bourgeois form of representative democracy to legitimize their regime.

Instead of establishing a revolutionary popular form of democracy, the Sandinista regime chose to install a Western European style parliamentary democracy based upon territorial and proportional representation. By choosing this form of government, they discarded the opportunity to establish a radical democratic political system, based upon bottom-up forms of self-government and self-management that would have given the workers and peasants not only direct control over the revolutionary process but ownership and management of the means of production. Like so many revolutionaries before them, the Sandinistas did not give the people control over the revolutionary process. Under the stress of the U.S. blockade and the war of attrition waged by the U.S. backed counterrevolutionary forces, the Sandinistas instituted austerity measures and were forced to suspend their more progressive social and economic policies.

By 1990, they had lost the confidence and the trust of the majority of the Nicaraguan people (Vilas 1990). This explains their electoral defeat by a heterodox political coalition composed of right-wing, centrist, and leftist political parties, who won the elections not so much because they mobilized popular support on their behalf but because they took advantage of popular discontent and disillusionment with the Sandinistas' revolutionary project.

The revolutionary movement in El Salvador, while always more leftist than the Sandinistas, began to follow their footsteps during 1990 and 1991. After launching at the end of 1989 the most significant offensive in the history of the armed struggle in El Salvador, the FMLN/FDR shortly thereafter initiated negotiations with the right-wing National Republican Alliance (ARENA) government to end the armed confict, demilitarize the country, and accept the FMLN/FDR as a legitimate political force in Salvadoran politics (Gonzalez 1989).

The first indications of this reorientation of the revolutionary movement were revealed in a widely publicized article by Comandante Joaquín Villalobos in early 1989. In this important document, Villalobos stated that the revolutionary movement's aim was peace, development, and the creation of real democracy. There was no mention of a socialist revolution in this document. According to Villalobos:

> Revolutionary movements do not have to subject themselves to any predetermined scheme nor succumb to the pressure of a war. In these new circumstances, revolutionary movements are determined to maintain peace and achieve development as quickly as possible. Also under the new circumstances, movements are permitted to become more flexible and open. We do not view this evolution as a concession but rather as a purer expression of the democratic nature of revolutionary changes. For revolutions are essentially democratic. They can and should be defended not only by a solid correlation of forces but also by a flexible democratic program representative of broad sectors, tendencies, and realities, both internal and external. The aim is to create real democracy for the entire people in the economic and political arenas. (Villalobos 1989:112)

The new circumstances that Villalobos referred to were those having to do with the new international correlation of forces resulting from the changes in Eastern Europe and the Soviet Union as well as the important changes taking place in the region—particularly the so-called peace process undertaken by the political leaders of the five Central American countries (including Nicaragua).

Although Villalobos's statement was issued before the electoral defeat of the Sandinistas in Nicaragua, it clearly anticipates the fact that one of the outcomes of the Central American peace process, supported by the Sandinistas, would be the isolation of the armed struggle in El Salvador (Vilas 1990:18). Undeniably, a political resolution of the armed conflict in El Salvador means an end to the terrible loss of life and the massive displacement of the civilian population caused by the country's decade-long civil war. However, in a country dominated by a right-wing regime and a military establishment with perhaps the bloodiest record of torture, terror, and repression in Latin America, it is hard to imagine that the FMLN/FDR could seriously believe they could operate freely within El Salvador's pseudodemocratic political process. The slaughter of the leftist guerrillas in Colombia after laying down their arms and accepting a political amnesty is ample evidence of what can happen to revolutionaries when they give up the armed struggle and try to become a legal political force in a political system governed by a regime that has a record of brutal repression (Gonzalez 1989:110).

Moreover, the 1989 elections in El Salvador were a clear sign of what the Left can expect if they replace armed struggle with electoral politics. The slate of candidates belonging to the Democratic Convergence (*Convergencia Democrática*), which was organized at great risk by some of the leaders of the revolutionary movement's civilian wing, received only 4 percent of the votes cast instead of the 15 percent that they anticipated they would win in their first effort to contest elections (Gonzalez 1989:111). To make matters worse, the civilian members of the revolutionary movement blamed their poor showing in the elections on their armed brethren in the FMLN, which had belatedly called for a boycott of the elections because the government had failed to agree to a ceasefire and to postpone the contest for several months so that the FMLN would have enough time to organize an adequate electoral campaign.

The conciliatory orientation of the FMLN, as well as their moves toward electoral democracy, does not auger well for the possibility of a future transition to socialism in El Salvador in the 1990s. Due to changes in the regional and international context, the revolutionary movement appears to have decided to adopt the goals of peace and democracy instead of socialism. However, the class struggle in El Salvador, which has a sizable working class and a large impoverished semiproletarianized peasantry, cannot be resolved by that country's pseudodemocratic and repressive political system. This class struggle has been engendered by one of the most retrograde bourgeois oligarchies in Latin America. The only reason the political representatives of this class reluctantly accepted the introduction of a limited form of political democracy in El Salvador is because of the pressures applied by the United States government during the Reagan administration, which had to clean up the image of the regime in order to obtain the approval of the U.S. Congress for continued U.S. military and economic aid. The political propensity of the country's ruling class is such that it has preferred in the past to rely upon death squads and military repression to control the popular classes rather than rigged elections and false promises of minor reforms.

The Prospects for Democratic Socialism

Cuba is the only country in the Western Hemisphere that currently has a regime committed to socialism. The contradictions and limitations of Cuba's socialist regime have been discussed at length in this book. In view of the changes that have taken place in Eastern Europe and the Soviet Union as well as Cuba's dependence upon Soviet economic assistance and its special trading relations with the Soviet Union and Eastern Europe, it must now reorient its economic relations and policies to accommodate the new world situation. The current rectification campaign in Cuba does not address all the changes that must be made in both the political system and the economy in order to adapt the country to the changing world context and the need for greater democracy in all spheres of Cuban society. If the regime embarks upon a more democratic socialist course of development, Cuba could once again become the standard bearer for progressive forces throughout Latin America and the Caribbean. If it does not, it runs the risk of isolation, degeneration, and a capitalist restoration similar to that taking place in Eastern Europe.

The prospects for democratic socialism may be better in other parts of Latin America and the Caribbean. However, there are many obstacles and dangers. Peru offers a highly instructive case of what can happen to the Left in a partially democratized political system with a repressive military establishment and a social order characterized by extreme social inequality and chronic economic crisis. Between 1980 and 1990, the numerous leftist political parties and organizations in Peru were confronted with the choice of either participating in that country's newly democratized political system or taking up arms to bring about the revolutionary overthrow of the system.

The Peruvian case is important also because all three positions on political democracy mentioned above have been manifested by the leftist parties and organizations. In addition, perspectives thought to be obsolete in other parts of the region concerning the viability of revolutionary armed struggle are also very much a part of the Peruvian ideological and political spectrum. Thus, in a sense the entire range of positions held by the Left over the last two to three decades is present in contemporary Peru.

The prospects for a transition to socialism in Peru through peaceful democratic means appear to be quite poor due to the repressive nature of the regime, the divisions within the Left, and the nature of the revolutionary armed movements that have become increasingly active in various parts of the country. By 1991, the most important of the revolutionary movements in Peru, the atavistic Maoist Communist Party of Peru—*Sendero Luminoso* (Shining Path)—controlled large zones in the Andean mountain regions of southern and central Peru as well as in the Amazon jungle valleys. Morover, it was also developing bases of support in the poorest sections of Lima, the country's capital and largest city (Balbi 1989). In addition to *Sendero Luminoso,* Peru has another leftist guerrilla movement called the Revolutionary Movement of Túpac Amaru (*Movimiento Revolucionario Túpac Amaru* or MRTA). The MRTA does not have as much support among the peasant population as *Sendero Luminoso* and is based primarily in Peru's jungle valleys. However, it has also extended its operations to the urban areas (Bourque and Warren 1989:12–13).

Peru also has a large number of legal leftist parties that are involved in the country's parliamentary politics. In fact, most of these parties formed a coalition in the 1980s that won considerable electoral support. But in August 1989, after nine years of uneasy unity, the parties in this electoral coalition, called the United Left (*La Izquierda Unida* or IU), split into two antagonistic factions (Salcedo 1989). The four most moderate leftist parties in the IU split away and formed their own coalition called Socialist Accord (*Acuerdo Socialista* or ASI), and the seven remaining parties kept the name of the original coalition. The *Sendero Luminoso* guerrilla movement, which is totally opposed to working within the existing political system, regards all of these groups as "bourgeois reformists" and has carried out attacks on their leaders and members. In contrast to the "bourgeois parliamentarianism" of the IU and ASI parties, the members of *Sendero Luminoso* see themselves engaged in what they regard as a "protracted people's war" against Peru's "semi-feudal" and "semi-colonial order."

The moderate leftist parties in the ASI coalition have attempted to bring about social change in Peru through democratic means, and they have defended the country's limited democratic system. Their project is to create a more democratic political system and a mixed economy and to defend the existing political order from the attempts on the part of *Sendero Luminoso* and others to destabilize it and provoke an open civil war. Although some of the parties in this moderate leftist coalition still claim they are Marxist-Leninists, they speak of a renovated Marxism-Leninism that encompasses the goals held by democratic socialists—that is, the achievement of socialism through democratic means.

The IU parties represent a broader spectrum of political positions than the ASI. This coalition is dominated by three of the largest leftist parties in Peru—the Unified Mariateguist Party (*Partido Unificado Mariateguista* or PUM), the Union of the Revolutionary Left (*Izquierda Revolucionaria* or UNIR) and the the Worker Peasant Student Popular Front (*Frente Obrero Campesino Estudiantil Popular* or FOCEP). They hold more radical views than the moderates in the ASI and seek the revolutionary transformation of Peruvian society. They regard democracy as only one means of struggle to arrive at socialism. These parties, particularly the Maoist UNIR, have not ruled out armed struggle.

The remaining parties within the IU are more moderate (Salcedo 1989). For example, the MAS is a Christian socialist party that seeks to create a socialist society based upon popular direct democracy. It does not accept armed struggle and seeks to defend the existing democratic system. In this respect it is closer to the parties in the ASI but has chosen to stay in the IU coalition. Another moderate leftist party in the IU coalition is the Peruvian Communist Party (Partido Comunista Peruano or PCP), which has the largest following of any of the parties in the IU coalition. Although the younger radicals within this formerly pro-Soviet party support all forms of struggle, the leadership of the party advocates a democratic route to socialism. It is closely tied to the labor movement and well represented in the Peruvian parliament. Generally speaking, it is the pivotal party in the IU coalition.

The original IU coalition was formed in opposition to the conservative regime of Fernando Belaúnde Terry, to which the military transferred power in 1980. It managed to stay together during this regime and during most of the reformist administration of Alan García, who followed Belaúnde. As it gained electoral strength and the elections of 1990 approached, everyone began to predict the IU coalition would have a good chance of victory. However, the prospect of moving from opposition to the possible formation of a government made the Left's differences over goals and strategy much more important than before, and it split the coalition.

Moreover, the *Sendero Luminoso* insurgency gained ground and increased its attacks against the IU and ASI parties (Balbi 1989). It also provoked the military and police into indiscriminately attacking leftists. Because of this situation, the more radical elements within the IU coalition began to argue that the Left had to take up arms to defend itself against the regime as well as against *Sendero Luminoso*. This issue also split the coalition.

The difficulties in the Latin American context of staying within the boundaries of a limited bourgeois democratic regime while still struggling for socialism are brought out clearly by the plight of the Left in contemporary Peru. Even if armed revolutionary movements did not exist in Peru, the real differences between the various tendencies on the Left constitute a major obstacle to the formation of the kind of cohesive coalition that would be capable of winning elections, forming a viable government with a coherent program, and working together on the successful realization of a project that would lead to democratic socialism.

Therefore, the Peruvian case brings into sharp focus the dilemma that leftist parties and movements in Latin America must confront if they seek to arrive at socialism through peaceful democratic means. They can pursue a strategy of gathering strength and democratic legitimacy by participating as a coalition in the electoral process and by building an increasingly larger popular base of support through linkages with local grass roots organizations, the unions, and the more progressive elements of the petty bourgeois middle sectors. However, if this strategy succeeds, they run the risk of precipitating a military coup and breaking into antagonistic moderate and radical wings when faced with the challenges and choices of governing the country (this is what occurred in Chile during the UP government). Or, and the Peruvian case illustrates this danger, the democratic forces of the Left can be undermined by a revolutionary armed movement such as *Sendero Luminoso* that succeeds in polarizing and militarizing the political process. And, of course, there is always the prospect of U.S. economic aggression, subversion, and/or military intervention to back up indigenous forces intent on preserving the status quo in the event a radical democratic regime gains power long enough to initiate significant transformations in the social order.

Thus, the Peruvian case reveals quite clearly, to paraphrase Oskar Lange, that the struggle for socialism is not for the timid! In order to overcome the obstacles standing in the way of a democratic socialist project in the present historical conjuncture, experience indicates that the unity of the Left is indispensable. Only if they are united can they hope to mobilize the popular classes not just for electoral victories but for the defense of democracy against the forces of the Right, who have revealed in the past that they will resort to undemocratic means to prevent progressive forces from winning elections and implementing socialist policies if they are elected to office.

The historical experience reveals that the struggle for socialism must be one in which democracy is both an important end as well as an important means. Every case examined in this book indicates that this is an important lesson that the Left must act upon in the future. However, political democracy cannot and should not be placed above all other ends and means. What the Marxist perspective shows is that democracy is not above classes and the class struggle. This fact is what many of the "renovated" socialists, who have abandoned class analysis, refuse to recognize. In their efforts to renovate socialism and apply it to the present historical conjuncture, they have thrown the proverbial baby out with the bath water.

Marxist theory and practice reveals that the genuine democratization of societies requires much more than transformations in their political and ideological structures. Major social and economic changes must accompany these political and ideological transformations. This point is well stated in the following passage taken from a recent essay written by Tomás Vasconi on the prospects for democracy and socialism in South America.

> Marxism allows us to think of democracy not simply as a cultural-ideological or political-institutional state, but as an integral process which involves the social base as well: the productive forces and their development and the social relations of production. As a consequence, we begin to think of *integral democracy* as *socialism*—as a mode of production and as "intellectual and moral reform"—as a historical project of constructing a new civilization. (Vasconi 1990:34)

Tomás Vasconi, who is an Argentine Marxist scholar resident in Cuba, has presented the classical Marxist perspective on the question of democratization quite clearly, namely that the struggle for political democracy must go hand in hand with the struggle for economic and social democracy. If the organized Left and other progressive forces choose to struggle solely for political democracy within the constraints imposed by the existing social order, they give a decisive advantage to their bourgeois opponents who are able to use their control over the economic and social structures of the prevailing capitalist system to preserve the status quo and manipulate the existing political processes to their benefit.

In this regard, it is important to note what one of Brazil's most outstanding Marxist intellectuals, Francisco Weffort, has sought to reiterate to the Left in his country: namely, that democracy and revolution have gone hand-in-hand throughout modern history. He also points out that what distinguishes modern revolutions is not violence, but the predominance of the structures of direct democracy over representative democracy. Thus, he states:

What distinguishes a revolution is not violence, rather it is the predominance of the mechanisms of direct democracy over the mechanisms of representation. In the Russian Revolution the decisive moment was when the locus of events passed from the Duma (or parliament) to the Soviets, that is to say the workers' councils. In the French Revolution the pressure of the "clubs" and especially the masses of Paris on the assembly are examples of the same phenomenon. In a democracy the armed forces are "the people in arms" in the sense that they are obedient to institutions that represent the people. In a revolution, the militias are "the people in arms" without the mediation of a representative system. There are many other examples. (Weffort 1989:12)

What is important to emphasize here is that revolutions are inherently motivated by the most fundamental democratic ideals and that what has been most revolutionary about contemporary revolutions has been the emergence in their midst of direct forms of democracy.

However, both direct and representative democratic structures must be combined in a new revolutionary society in order to prevent a bureaucratic and authoritarian degeneration of the revolutionary project. Thus, Weffort argues that "popular councils, enterprise councils, etc., have to coexist with parties and parliaments" (Weffort 1989:14). The lessons of past attempts to bring about revolutionary change and to construct socialist societies clearly support this argument.

Weffort's analysis is focused on Brazil, but he has identified what needs to be done in order to create a genuinely democratic society under prevailing conditions in Latin America. As the following quote indicates, Weffort argues that political democracy in Brazil requires major economic and social changes as well as a radical democratization of the country's psuedodemocratic political system.

To create a democracy in a society such as ours, supposes without a doubt the re-establishment of direct elections at all levels, the re-establishment of the full prerogatives of the Congress, the independence of the judiciary, the annulment of the National Security Law, the suppression of the laws that impede the full exercise of union freedom and autonomy, as well as the freedom to organize political parties, and the dismantling of the organs of the so-called "security community." . . . It also supposes drastic alterations in the functioning of the economy in order to attend to the demands of the people. How can democracy function in a country where more than 30 million people vegetate in a condition of absolute misery? It cannot stop there. It is obvious that democracy should contribute to the elimination of the extreme social inequalities that keep the majority of the people from exercising their citizenship. In this sense the realization of an agrarian reform is an urgent democratic task. (Weffort 1989:16–17)

As Weffort indicates in the case of Brazil, a genuine process of democratization in the Latin American context requires: the elimination of laws that limit the freedom of the unions and the formation of political parties; the dismantlement of the repressive security apparatus inherited from the previous period of repressive military rule; the implementation of economic policies that attend to the demands of the people, especially the rural and urban poor; and the urgent implementation of an agrarian reform program.

In essence, Weffort argues that the accomplishment of these democratizing tasks requires a socialist revolution. This is because capitalism in the 1990s is not able to solve any of the major problems of the region or attend to the demands of the popular classes. Since the mid 1980s, Latin America and the Caribbean have undergone a severe economic crisis. Real per capita income and employment have fallen throughout most of the countries of the region, and the countries have accumulated enormous foreign debts. As a result, poverty and social deprivation suffered by the popular classes has increased over the decade as real spending on education, health, and housing has declined. Under these conditions, the proponents of capitalism have little evidence that they can show the popular classes to convince them that the present system serves their interests.

To these conditions must be added the end of both the Cold War and the democratization of the so-called socialist regimes in Eastern Europe. These momentous changes in the international context have given the Latin American Left the opportunity to shed the stigma of being linked with "totalitarianism" and the accusations that they were the local instruments of Soviet-Cuban expansionism (Casteñeda 1990). Now that it is in a position to get rid of these "handicaps," the Left has the chance to gain widespread popular support for a new democratic socialist project that addresses the needs of the popular classes and offers viable policy alternatives to the neoliberal economic and social policies of the prevailing procapitalist regimes.

In other words, in the present historical conjuncture, a viable democratic socialist project is needed both to guarantee the increased democratization of the Latin American and Caribbean societies as well as to fulfill the basic needs of the majority of their populations. As the Chilean leftist scholar, Manuel Antonio Garretón, has so ably put it, a socialist project is needed for the following reasons.

First, socialism furthers the perfection of political democracy and the extension of democratic principles to other areas of society. Second, socialism creates the material and social conditions—those same conditions which capitalism in our countries negates in practice—in which political democracy can flourish. Third, although not in an exclusive way, it gives democracy a social subject: labor and the popular classes. Fourth, . . . socialism introduces another element which is both utopian and practical: a permanent questioning which leads to the reduction and overcoming of forms of domination in all social arenas. Thus, socialism constitutes an ethical appeal of enormous symbolic force, which drives the ongoing transformation of society. (Garretón 1989b:35)

As Garretón notes, both socialism and democracy are needed to combat the long-standing social, economic and political ills that plague the peoples of the region.

However, socialism cannot be presented to the people as an abstract or a distant future goal (Weffort 1989:17). It has to be presented as a concrete program of action that is put into practice on a daily basis by creating alternative centers of popular power that form the foundations of the future democratic socialist regime prior to the establishment of this regime. If this is not done, the Left inadvertently conveys the idea that the existing capitalist order is the only realistic alternative for the present. This false idea reinforces the ideological hegemony of the bourgeoisie and undermines the appeal of socialism. Thus, the Left must organize the popular classes around a revolutionary democratic socialist project that creates alternative centers of popular power at the grassroots level and in the workplace while it mobilizes sufficient popular support to take power at the national level. It may do this either through nonviolent actions and elections or through a revolutionary seizure of power, or both—depending on the actions of the repressive forces at the command of the dominant classes.

In view of the increasing evidence that the existing neoliberal democratic regimes are as incapable of dealing with the major economic and social problems of their societies as the preceding military regimes, and that the social inequalities and conditions of the popular classes are growing worse, it is not unreasonable to assume that the prospects during the 1990s will greatly improve for the Left in Latin America and the Caribbean.

The coupling of democracy with socialism is a logical solution to the continuing social and economic problems of peripheral capitalism. Thus, a democratic socialist project offers a focal point around which the leftist parties and other progressive forces in Latin America and the Caribbean can unify and mobilize widespread popular support for the long-postponed social and economic reforms.

The Need for a Renovated Marxism

A renovated Marxism can provide both the analytical and normative framework for a revolutionary democratic struggle in this region of the world. In order to fulfill this function, it must be employed in a manner that addresses the interests of both the old and new elements of the working class. Moreover, it must be used to unite the interests of all the popular classes, the feminist movement, other new social movements, and racial as well as ethnic communities that have been historically oppressed and deprived of their identity. In other words, Marxism in Latin America and the Caribbean has to be purged of sectarianism and dogmatism and refocused to give priority to the goals of feminism, cultural pluralism, and the struggle for racial equality, in order for it to provide the intellectual framework and moral basis for a successful democratic socialist movement.

The experience accumulated during the twentieth century as a result of attempted revolutionary transformations and socialist transitions offers a series of lessons that any future socialist project in Latin America and the Caribbean must take into account if it hopes to succeed. One of the most important of these lessons is that without a popular democratic state, a revolutionary regime will succumb to bureaucratic statism, class inequalities, and popular disaffection. Equally as important is the lesson that unless all forms of large capital are rapidly expropriated by a new socialist regime, the bourgeoisie and the United States will use their economic power to sabotage the economy and effectively undermine the new regime. Past experience also indicates that unless coherent financial policies and price mechanisms are instituted to control commodity relations and monetary transactions, the result will be hyperinflation, serious disruptions in the distribution of goods, black marketeering, and the possible total collapse of the economy.

One of the most important lessons is that the socialization of peasant-based agriculture has to be based on land redistribution, the gradual cooperativization of the peasant producers, and the regulation of the commodity market in agricultural products rather than collective farms and state requisitioning of agricultural products. Furthermore, the accumulated experience of past efforts to construct socialist societies indicates that the expansion of the forces of production should be based upon the voluntary and creative participation of the producers rather than forced schemes of accumulation that are politically undesirable and tend to achieve poor economic results. A socialist strategy of development must replace the overemphasis on agroexports that characterizes the present system with a strategy of development that leads to self-sufficiency in the production of basic food products, diversification of the economy, and diversification of the sources of external assistance and trade.

Moreover, a new system of material and moral incentives must be rapidly developed to stimulate and reward collective forms of work and a new socialist work ethic; otherwise, the work force will continue to respond only to capitalist material incentives. Past experience suggests that effective forms of worker participation in planning and decision-making must be established in order to end the alienation of the work force from the work process and to prevent capitalist relations of production from reproducing themselves at the point of production.

Another major lesson arising from past experience is that effective social planning and the genuine socialization of the relations of production require the establishment of self-managed units of production within a federative structure that is coordinated by new forms of democratic planning and decisionmaking. The development of these new democratic relations of production will require extensive preparation and a social learning process in which workers, managers, the general citizenry, and public officials develop organizational, decisionmaking, and planning skills based upon genuine democratic values and procedures.

Finally, a critical analysis of past experience reveals the need to establish gender and racial equality as well as cultural pluralism, freedom of thought, and liberty of expression in all spheres of social life. This requires the creation of a new ideological hegemony that, instead of being imposed on the people, is based on the mobilization of their acceptance of the new values and ideals. Otherwise, patriarchal, racist, classist, and other exploitative and dehumanizing forms of social relations will reproduce themselves in the ideological and cultural domains and in the political and economic spheres. The preceding critical analysis of the historical experience of existing socialist regimes indicates quite clearly that gender and racial equality as well as freedom of thought and expression have not been given sufficient priority under these regimes. A future democratic socialist project, therefore, must give priority to the realization of these forms of equality and freedom.

Conclusion

The prospects for socialism in Latin America and the Caribbean depend upon the development of a new democratic socialist project. Marxism, which has played an important role in shaping past socialist projects in the region, will be needed to formulate and realize this new project. The progressive forces in this important part of the world cannot afford to discard this powerful body of knowledge and experience, which is the product of more than a century of rich theoretical and international development. It does not explain everything or provide answers to all problems. Nevertheless, it is needed to establish an equitable and just social order in Latin America and the Caribbean.

The uneven and inequitable nature of capitalist development in this region, the great gap between the affluent upper classes and the impoverished lower classes, the reactionary political role played by the military as the guardians of the status quo, and the interventionist and hegemonic policies of the United States—all preclude the expansion and deepening of democracy under the existing neoliberal regimes. Therefore, a popular democratic socialist movement, guided by a renovated Marxism and offering a concrete program of major social and economic reforms, is needed to expand and deepen the democratization of the Latin American and Caribbean societies.

Previous experience has shown that in order to be successful, a movement of this sort will need to mobilize the support of the lower classes as well as significant sectors of the middle class. Once this has been achieved, this popular movement, which most likely will be a coalition or front of parties and movements, will have to gain political power through either electoral means, a popular insurrection (which could take the form of mass nonviolent action) or both. Once in power, it will have to immediately replace the existing armed forces and state apparatus with a federative (bottom-up) democratic state composed of both direct and representative democratic structures; it will also have to rapidly expropriate the productive property of the large and medium producers; and proceed rapidly with the socialization of the major means of production through the establishment of self-managed enterprises and farms and democratic planning and coordinative structures. Other important social, ideological, and cultural transformations will have to be undertaken simultaneously with these measures in order to eliminate gender, racial, and cultural inequality and create a new social order based upon genuine social equality and cultural pluralism.

There are many obstacles and pitfalls lying in wait for such a course of development. Previous attempts to construct socialism and to introduce radical democratic reforms in Latin America and the Caribbean have included many mistakes and encountered fierce resistance from the forces who support the status quo. However, a critical undertanding of these past attempts can provide the intellectual basis for developing a successful strategy for overcoming many of these obstacles and avoiding many of the mistakes of the past. Moreover, democratic socialism will increasingly become a more appealing alternative for the progressive forces in Latin America and the Caribbean when the shock of the changes in Eastern Europe and the Soviet Union has worn off, and when the market reforms in these countries, like the neoliberal policies of the democratic regimes in Latin America, fail to improve the living standards of the majority of the population. This alternative course of socialist development offers a much more democratic and materially rewarding future for the great majority of the Latin American and Caribbean peoples than the present system of dependent capitalist development and limited political democracy.

Many different schools of thought and practice stem from the Marxist tradition. It is my contention and hope that the best aspects of this tradition will serve as the intellectual and moral foundations for the construction in the twenty-first century of genuinely democratic socialist societies—that is to say, societies that are more humane, just, productive, democratic, respectful of the natural environment, and peaceful than all previous social systems created by humanity.

I firmly believe that the promise of achieving this kind of social order is at the center of Marxist thought. This is one of the reasons Marxist ideas have been an important element in most of the social revolutions and movements for progressive social change that have occurred during this century. In spite of the setbacks, obstacles, errors, betrayals, distortions, and failures that have kept the promise of democratic socialism contained in Marxism from being fulfilled, I believe that the classical Marxist ideal of achieving a genuinely democratic social order can be realized in the years to come. However, I also believe this can only take place if the best aspects of Marxism are combined with a critical understanding of the lessons to be learned from the social revolutions of this century. Only on this basis will it be possible to develop a new praxis for socialist transformation that is thoroughly democratic, undogmatic, and adaptable to the specific conditions of each society that undertakes the transition to socialism.

References

Abdulah, David. 1989. "Toward a Party of the Workers," *Against the Current*, Vol. 4, No. 1 (March-April):30–33.

Amin, Samir. 1980. *Class and Nation, Historically and in the Current Crisis*. New York: Monthly Review Press.

——. 1981. *The Future of Maoism*. New York: Monthly Review Press.

——. 1985. "The Prospects for Socialism," in Milos Nicolic (ed.), *Socialism on the Threshold of the Twenty-first Century*, 16–28. London: Verso.

Angotti, Thomas. 1988. "The Cuban Revolution: A New Turn," *Nature, Society and Thought*, Vol. 1, No. 4:527–549.

Arce, Bayardo. 1982. "El dificil terreno de la lucha: el ideologico," in *Hacia una politica cultural de la revolucion popular sandinista*. Managua: Ministerio de Cultura.

Avineri, Shlomo. 1971. *The Social and Political Thought of Karl Marx*. Cambridge: Cambridge University Press.

Azicri, Max. 1989. "Women's Development Through Revolutionary Mobilization," in Philip Brenner, William LeoGrande, Donna Rich, and Daniel Siegel (eds.), *The Cuba Reader: The Making of a Revolutionary Society*, 457–470. New York: Grove Press.

Aziz, Sartaj. 1976. *Rural Development: Learning from China*. New Dehli: Asia Publishing House.

Babu, Abdul Mohamed. 1981. *African Socialism or Socialist Africa?* London: Zed Press.

Balbi, Carmen. 1989. "Sendero Minados," *Quehacer*, No. 61 (October-November):48–57.

Barros, Robert. 1987. "Izquierda y democracia: debates recientes en América Latina," *Cuadernos Políticos* (Mexico) (October-December):65–81.

Bartra, Roger. 1982. *El reto de la izquierda*. Mexico City: Grijalbo.

Beaucage, Pierre. 1975. "Modos de producción articulados o lucha de clases?" *Historia y sociedad*, No. 5 (Spring):37–58.

217

Bellis, Paul. 1979. *Marxism and the U.S.S.R.* Atlantic Highlands, New Jersey: Humanities Press.

Benjamin, Medea, Joseph Collins, and Michael Scott. 1984. *No Free Lunch: Food and Revolution in Cuba Today*. San Francisco: Institute for Food and Development Policy.

Bernardo, Robert. 1971. *The Theory of Moral Incentives in Cuba*. University, Alabama: University of Alabama Press.

Bettelheim, Charles. 1976. *Class Struggles in the USSR: First Period, 1917-1923*. New York: Monthly Review Press.

――――. 1978. *The Transition to Socialist Economy*. Brighton, England: Harvester Press.

Bitar, Sergio. 1979. *Transición, socialismo y democracia: la experiencia chilena*. Mexico City: Siglo XXI.

Black, George. 1988. "Cuba: The Revolution: Towards Victory Always, But When?" *The Nation*, October 24, 1988:373-385.

Blecher, Marc. 1989. "China's Struggle for a New Hegemony," *Socialist Review*, Issue 89/2:5-35.

Bollinger, William. 1985. "Learn from Others, Think for Ourselves: Central American Revolutionary Strategy in the 1980's," *Review of African Political Economy*, No. 32 (April 1985):56-63.

Boorstein, Edward. 1968. *The Economic Transformation of Cuba*. New York: Monthly Review Press.

Bourque, Susan, and Kay Warren. 1989. "Democracy without Peace: The Cultural Politics of Terror in Peru," *Latin American Research Review*, Vol. 24, No. 1:7-34.

Brezhnev, Leonid. 1981. "Report to the 26th Party Congress," *Current Digest of the Soviet Press*, Vol. 33, No. 8 (March 25).

Brinton, Maurice. 1975. *The Bolsheviks and Workers Control, 1917 to 1921*. Montreal: Black Rose Books.

Brus, Wlodzimierz. 1975. *Socialist Ownership and Political Systems*. London: Routledge & Kegan Paul.

Brutents, Karen. 1983. *The Newly Free Countries in the Seventies*. Moscow: Progress Publishers.

Buckley, Mary. 1989. "The Woman Question in the Contemporary Soviet Union," in Sonia Kuks, Rayna Rapp, and Marilyn Young (eds.), *Promissory Notes: Women in the Transition to Socialism*, 251-182. New York: Monthly Review Press.

Bukharin, Nicolai. 1971. *Economics of the Transition Period*. New York: Bergman.

――――. 1982. *Selected Writings on the State and the Transition to Socialism*. Armonk: M. E. Sharpe.

Cabral, Amilcar. 1979. *Unity and Struggle: Speeches and Writings of Amilcar Cabral*. New York: Monthly Review Press.

Casal, Lourdes. 1989a. "Race Relations in Contemporary Cuba," in Philip Brenner, William LeoGrande, Donna Rich, and Daniel Siegel (eds.), *The Cuba Reader: The Making of a Revolutionary Society*, 471-486. New York: Grove Press.

Casal, Lourdes. 1989b. "Cultural Policy and Writers in Cuba," in Philip Brenner, William LeoGrande, Donna Rich, and Daniel Siegel (eds.), *The Cuba Reader: The Making of a Revolutionary Soceity,* 506–513. New York: Grove Press.

Castaños, Alfonso. 1977. *Tiene el socialismo su prehistoria?* Barcelona: Editorial Blume.

Casteñeda, Jorge. 1990. "Latin America and the End of the Cold War," *World Policy Journal,* Vol. 7, No. 3:469–492.

Castro, Fidel. 1974. *Granma Weekly Review* (Havana, Cuba), December 15.

_____. 1989. Speech of October 1, 1989, in *Granma Weekly Review,* October 15.

Center for Cuban Studies. 1976. "Resolution on the Economic Management and Planning System," *Center for Cuban Studies Newsletter,* Vol. 3, No. 2 (March–June):17–22.

Cerroni, Umberto. 1973. *Teoría política y socialismo.* Mexico City: Ediciónes Era.

Chan, Anita. 1990. "China's Long Winter," *Monthly Review,* Vol. 41, No. 8 (January):1–14.

Chan, Anita, Stanley Rosen, and Jonathan Unger. 1985. *On Socialist Democracy and the Chinese Legal System: The Li Yizhe Debates.* Armonk, New York: M. E. Sharpe.

Chilcote, Ronald. 1990. "Post-Marxism: The Retreat from Class in Latin America," *Latin American Perspectives,* Issue 65 (Spring):3–24.

Codina Jiménez, Alexis. 1987. "Worker Incentives in Cuba," *World Development,* Vol. 15, No. 1:127–138.

Collins, Joseph. 1986. *Nicaragua: What Difference Could a Revolution Make?* New York: Grove Press.

Comisso, Ellen. 1979. *Workers' Control Under Plan and Market: Implications of Yugoslav Self-Management.* New Haven: Yale University Press.

Connor, James E. 1968. *Lenin on Politics and Revolution.* New York: Pegasus.

Conroy, Michael. 1985a. "Economic Legacy and Policies: Performance and Critique," in Thomas Walker (ed.), *Nicaragua: The First Five Years,* 214–244. New York: Praeger.

_____. 1985b. "External Dependence, External Assistance, and Economic Aggression Against Nicaragua," *Latin American Perspectives,* Issue 45 (Spring):39–68.

Coraggio, José Luis. 1986. "Economics and Politics in the Transition to Socialism: Reflections on the Nicaraguan Experience," in Richard Fagen, Carmen Deere, and José Luis Coraggio (eds.), *Transition and Development: Problems of Third World Socialism,* 143–170. New York: Monthly Review Press.

Davin, Delia. 1989. "Of Dogma, Dicta and Washing Machines: Women in the People's Republic of China," in Sonia Kuks, Rayna Rapp, and Marilyn Young (eds.), *Promissory Notes: Women in the Transition to Socialism,* 354–358. New York: Monthly Review Press.

Deane, Hugh. 1989. "Mao's Rural Policies Revisited," *Monthly Review,* Vol. 40, No. 10 (March):1–9.

Deere, Carmen Diana. 1986. "Agrarian Reform, Peasant and Rural Production, and the Organization of Production in the Transition to Socialism," in Richard

Fagen, Carmen Deere, and José Luis Coraggio (eds.), *Transition and Development: Problems of Third World Socialism*, 97–142. New York: Monthly Review Press.

Dos Santos, Theotonio. 1985. "Socialism: Ideal and Historical Practice," in Milos Nicolic (ed.), *Socialism on the Threshold of the Twenty-first Century*, 180–195. London: Verso.

Duggett, Michael. 1975. "Marx on Peasants," *The Journal of Peasant Studies*, No. 2 (January):159–181.

Edelman, Marc. 1985. "Lifelines: Nicaragua and the Socialist Countries," *NACLA Report on the Americas*, Vol. 19, No. 3 (May/June):33–56.

————. 1987. "Supportive Pragmatism: The USSR and Revolutionaries," *NACLA Report on the Americas*, Vol. 21, No. 1 (January/February):19–40.

Eisenstein, Zillah. 1989. "Reflections on a Politics of Difference," in Sonia Kuks, Rayna Rapp, and Marilyn Young (eds.), *Promissory Notes: Women in the Transition to Socialism*, 333–387. New York: Monthly Review Press.

Ellner, Steve. 1989. "The Latin American Left Since Allende: Perspectives and New Directions," *Latin American Research Review*, Vol. 24, No. 2:143–167.

Envío. 1989. "Nicaragua's Economic Crisis," Vol. 8 (May):18–30.

Escoto, René, and Freddy Amador. 1991. "El contexto macroeconómico de la reforma agraria," *Revista de economía agrícola*, No. 1 (Febrero):10–28.

Esteva, Gustavo. 1978. "Y si los campesinos existen?" *Comercio exterior* (Mexico City), No. 28 (June):699–732.

Fagen, Richard. 1989. "Continuities in Cuban Revolutionary Politics," in Philip Brenner, William LeoGrande, Donna Rich, and Daniel Siegel (eds.), *The Cuba Reader: The Making of a Revolutionary Society*, 51–62. New York: Grove Press.

FitzGerald, E.V.K. 1982. "The Economics of the Revolution," in Thomas W. Walker (ed.), *Nicaragua in Revolution*, 203–221. New York: Praeger.

————. 1984. "The Problem of Balance in the Peripheral Socialist Economy: A Conceptual Note," *World Development*, Vol. 13, No. 1:5–14.

————. 1986. "Notes on the Analysis of the Small Underdeveloped Economy in Transition," in Richard Fagen, Carmen Deere, and José Luis Coraggio (eds.), *Transition and Development: Problems of Third World Socialism*, 28–53. New York: Monthly Review Press.

Fitzgerald, Frank. 1989. "The Reform of the Cuban Economy, 1976–86," *Journal of Latin American Studies*, No. 21:283–310.

Friedland, William. 1982. *Revolutionary Theory*. Totowa, New Jersey: Allanheld, Osmun.

Fuller, Linda. 1987. "Power at the Workplace: The Resolution of Worker-Management Conflict in Cuba," *World Development*, Vol 15., No. 1:139–152.

Garretón, Manuel. 1989a. "Popular Mobilization and the Military Regime in Chile: The Complexities of the Invisible Transition," in Susan Eckstein (ed.), *Power and Popular Protest*, 259–277. Berkeley: University of California Press.

————. 1989b. "The Ideas of Socialist Renovation in Chile," *Rethinking Marxism*, Vol. 2, No. 2:8–37.

Gautier, Emilio. 1989. "Por un marxismo vivo," *Cuadernos* (Santiago, Chile), No. 8 (June):23–25.

Gianotten, Vera, Ton de Wit, and Rodrigo Montoya. 1987. *Nicaragua: cuestión agraria y participación campesina.* Lima: Centro de Estudios y Promoción del Desarrollo.

Goldman, Wendy. 1989. "Women, the Family and the New Revolutionary Order in the Soviet Union," in Sonia Kuks, Rayna Rapp, and Marilyn Young (eds.), *Promissory Notes: Women in the Transition to Socialism*, 59–81. New York: Monthly Review Press.

Gonzalez, Mike. 1989. "The Future of the Central American Revolution," *International Socialism*, No. 45 (Winter):105–112.

Gramsci, Antonio. 1988. *Selected Writings.* London: Lawrence and Wishart.

Griffith-Jones, Stephany. 1981. *The Role of Finance in the Transition to Socialism.* London: Frances Pinter.

Guevara, Che. 1987. *Che Guevara and the Cuban Revolution.* New York: Pathfinder Press.

Harnecker, Marta. 1975. *Los conceptos elementales del materialismo histórico*, Mexico City: Siglo XXI.

_____. 1979. *Cuba: Dictatorship or Democracy?* Westport: Lawrence Hill.

_____. 1986. *Reflexiónes acerca del problema de la transición al socialismo.* Managua: Nueva Nicaragua.

Harding, Neil. 1984. *The State in Socialist Society.* London: The Macmillan Press.

Harris, Richard. 1978. "Marxism and the Agrarian Question in Latin America," *Latin American Perspectives*, Issue 19 (Fall):2–26.

_____. 1987. "The Revolutionary Transformation of Nicaragua," *Latin American Perspectives*, Issue 52 (Winter):3–18.

Harris, Richard, and Carlos Vilas. 1985. *Nicaragua: A Revolution Under Siege.* London: ZED Books.

Harrison, James. 1989. *The Endless War: Vietnam's Struggle for Independence.* New York: Columbia University Press.

Heine, Jorge (ed.). 1990. *A Revolution Aborted: The Lessons of Grenada.* Pittsburgh: University of Pittsburgh Press.

Hinchberger, William. 1990. "Lula: We Can Take Power," *NACLA Report on the Americas*, Vol. 24, No. 1 (June):4–7.

Hinton, William. 1989. "A Response to Hug Deane," *Monthly Review*, Vol. 40, No. 10 (March):10–36.

Hojman, David. 1990. "Chile after Pinochet: Aylwin's Christian Democrat Economic Policies for the 1990s," *Bulletin of Latin American Research*, Vol. 9, No. 1:25–47.

Horvat, Branko. 1982. *The Political Economy of Socialism.* New York: M. E. Sharpe.

Huberman, Leo, and Paul Sweezy. 1971. "The Peaceful Transition from Socialism to Capitalism," *Monthly Review*, Vol. 22, No. 8, (January):1–18.

Iturraspe, Francisco (ed.). 1986. *Participación, cogestión y autogestión en America Latina.* San José, Costa Rica: Nueva Sociedad.

Judson, Fred. 1987. "Sandinista Revolutionary Morale," *Latin American Perspectives.* Issue 52 (Winter):19–42.

Karl, Terry. 1975. "Work Incentives in Cuba," *Latin American Perspectives*, Issue 7:21–41.

Kay, Cristobal. 1978. "Agrarian Reform and the Class Struggle in Chile," *Latin American Perspectives*, Vol. 5, No. 3 (Summer):117–140.

Lampland, Martha. 1989. "Biographies of Liberation: Testimonials to Labor in Socialist Hungary," in Sonia Kruks, Rayna Rapp, and Marilyn Young (eds.), *Promissory Notes: Women in the Transition to Socialism*, 306–325. New York: Monthly Review Press.

Landau, Saul, 1989. "After Castro," *Mother Jones*, Vol. 14, No. 6 (July-August):20–27, 46–48.

Lange, Oskar. 1971. "On the Policy of Transition," *Monthly Review*, Vol. 22 (January 1971):38–44.

Lawner, Miguel. 1989. "Ideal y teoría socialista: crisis de los proyectos historicos," *Cuadernos*, No. 8 (June):2–4.

Leiken, Robert. 1987. "The Salvadoran Left," in Marvin Gettleman et al. (eds.), *El Salvador: Central America in the New Cold War*, 187–200. New York: Grove Press.

Leiner, Marvin. 1989. "Cuba's Schools: 25 Years Later," in Philip Brenner, William LeoGrande, Donna Rich, and Daniel Siegel (eds.), *The Cuba Reader: The Making of a Revolutionary Society*, 445–456. New York: Grove Press.

Lenin, V. I. 1937. *Selected Works*. London: Martin Lawrence.

_____. 1976. *Selected Works*. New York: International Publishers.

LeoGrande, William. 1989. "Mass Political Participation in Socialist Cuba," in Philip Brenner, William LeoGrande, Donna Rich, and Daniel Siegel (eds.), *The Cuba Reader: The Making of a Revolutionary Society*, 186–199. New York: Grove Press.

Lewis, Gordon K. 1987. *Grenada: The Jewel Despoiled*. Baltimore: Johns Hopkins University Press.

Liss, Sheldon. 1984. *Marxist Thought in Latin America*. Berkeley: University of California.

Lockett, Martin. 1983. "Organizational Democracy and Politics in China," in C. Crouch and F. Heller (eds.), *Organizational Democracy and Political Processes*, 591–635. New York: John Wiley & Sons.

Lowy, Michael. 1986. "Mass Organization, Party, and State: Democracy in the Transition to Socialism," in Richard Fagen, Carmen Deere, and José Luis Coraggio (eds.), *Transition and Development: Problems of Third World Socialism*, 264–279. New York: Monthly Review Press.

Lutjens, Sheryl. 1992. "Democracy and Socialist Cuba," in Sandor Halebsky and John Kirk (eds.), *Cuba in Transition: Crisis and Transformation*. Boulder, Colorado: Westview Press.

Luxemburg, Rosa. 1971. *Selected Political Writings*. New York: Monthly Review Press.

_____. 1972. *The Russian Revolution*. Ann Arbor: University of Michigan Press.

MacEwan, Arthur. 1981. *Revolution and Economic Development in Cuba*. London: Macmillan.

Machado, Dario. 1989. "Para un estudio del fenómeno del burocratismo en Cuba," *Cuba socialista*, Año 9, No. 6 (November-December):53–74.

Mackinnon, Catharine. 1989. *Toward a Feminist Theory of the State*. Cambridge: Harvard University Press.

Mandel, Ernest. 1968. *Marxist Economic Theory*, Vol. 2. New York: Monthly Review Press.

_____. 1978. "On the Nature of the Soviet State," *New Left Review*, No. 108 (March-April):212–242.

Manley, Michael. 1982. *Jamaica: Struggle in the Periphery*. London: Writers and Readers.

Mao Tse Tung. 1971. *Selected Readings from the Works of Mao Tse Tung*. Beijing: Foreign Languages Press.

Mars, Perry. 1984. "Destabilization and Socialist Orientation in the English-speaking Caribbean," *Latin American Perspectives*, Issue 42 (Summer):83–110.

Marx, Karl. 1967. *Capital*, Vol. 1. New York: International Publishers.

Marx, Karl, and Frederick Engels. 1972. *Selected Works*. New York: International Publishers.

Matthews, Robert. 1986. "Sowing Dragon's Teeth: The U.S. War Against Nicaragua," *NACLA Report on the Americas*, Vol. 20, No. 4 (July-August 1986):13–38.

Meisner, Robert. 1977. *Mao's China: A History of the People's Republic*. New York: Free Press.

Michels, Robert. 1962. *Political Parties: A Sociological Study of the Oligarchical Tendencies of Modern Democracy*. New York: Macmillan.

Mistral, Carlos. 1974. *Chile: del triumfo popular al golpe fascista*. Mexico City: Ediciónes Era.

Mitrany, David. 1951. *Marx Against the Peasant*. London: Werdenfeld and Nicholson.

Molyneux, Maxine. 1982. "Socialist Societies: Progress Toward Women's Emancipation," *Monthly Review*, Vol. 34, No. 3 (July-August):56–100.

_____. 1986. "Mobilization Without Emancipation? Women's Interests, State and Revolution," in Richard Fagen, Carmen Deere, and José Luis Coraggio (eds.), *Transition and Development: Problems of Third World Socialism*, 280–302. New York: Monthly Review Press.

Munck, Ronaldo. 1990. "Farewell to Socialism? A Comment on Recent Debates," *Latin American Perspectives*, Issue 65 (Spring):113–121.

Narkiewicz, Olga. 1970. *The Making of the Soviet State Apparatus*. Manchester: University of Manchester Press.

Nazzari, Muriel. 1989. "The 'Woman Question' in Cuba: An Analysis of Material Constraints on Its Resolution," in Sonia Kruks, Rayna Rapp, and Marilyn Young (eds.), *Promissory Notes: Women in the Transition to Socialism*, 201–214. New York: Monthly Review Press.

Ngo Vinh Long. 1988. "Some Aspects of Cooperativization in the Mekong Delta," in David Marr and Christine White (eds.), *Postwar Vietnam: Dilemmas in Socialist Development*, 163–176. Ithaca: Southeast Asia Program, Cornell University.

Nicolic, Milos (ed.). 1985. *Socialism on the Threshold of the Twenty-first Century*. London: Verso.

Nove, Alec. 1983. *The Economics of Feasible Socialism*. Boston: George Allen & Unwin.

Núñez Soto, Orlando. 1986. "Ideology and Revolutionary Politics in Transitional Societies," in Richard Fagen, Carmen Deere, and José Luis Coraggio (eds.), *Transition and Development: Problems of Third World Socialism*, 231–248. New York: Monthly Review Press.

Nuti, D. M. 1979. "The Contradictions of Socialist Economies: A Marxist Interpretation," in R. Miliband and J. Saville (eds.), *The Socialist Register 1979*, 34–49. London: Merlin.

Oppenheim, Lois. 1989. "The Chilean Road to Socialism Revisted," *Latin American Research Review*, Vol. 24, No. 1:155–183.

Ortiz, Roxanne Dunbar. 1987. "Indigenous Rights and Regional Autonomy in Revolutionary Nicaragua," *Latin American Perspectives*, Issue 52 (Winter):43–66.

Palacios, Alvaro. 1989. "Los años 80 y el marxismo en Chile," *Cuadernos del instituto de ciencias*, No. 8 (Junio):25–30.

Paré, Luisa. 1977. *El proletariado agrícola en México*. Mexico City: Siglo XXI.

Perez-Stable, Marifeli. 1987. "Castro Takes the Economy in Hand," *The Nation*, September 26:298–300.

Petras, James. 1988. "State, Regime and the Democratization Muddle," *LASA Forum*, Vol. 18, No. 4 (Winter):9–12.

Pierre-Charles, Gerard. 1976. *Genesis de la revolución cubana*. Mexico City: Siglo XXI.

Pryor, Frederic. 1986. *Revolutionary Grenada: A Study in Political Economy*. New York: Praeger.

Rizzi, Bruno. 1980. *La burocratización del mundo*. Barcelona: Ediciónes Peninsula.

Rodríguez, Carlos Rafael. 1978. *Cuba en el transito al socialismo (1959–1963)*. Mexico City: Siglo XXI.

Rodríguez, Gonzalo. 1980. *El proceso de industrialización de la economía cubana*. Havana: Editorial de Ciencias Sociales.

Rossanda, Rossana, et al. 1976. *Teoría marxista del partido politico*, No. 38 in series Cuadernos de Pasado y Presente. Mexico City: Siglo XXI.

Ruchwarger, Gary. 1987. *People in Power: Forging a Grassroots Democracy in Nicaragua*. Boston: Bergin & Garvey.

Salcedo, José. 1989. "Izquierda unida: el drama recién comienza?" *Quehacer*, No. 57 (February-March):26–40.

Sanchez Vazquez, Adolfo. 1985. "The Idea of Socialism Re-examined," in Milos Nikolic (ed.), *Socialism on the Threshold of the Twenty-first Century*, 266–282. London: Verso.

Saul, John. 1984. "The Role of Ideology in the Transition to Socialism," in Richard Fagen, Carmen Deere, and José Luis Coraggio, *Transition and Development: Problems of Third World Socialism*, 212–230. New York: Monthly Review Press.

Schram, Stuart. 1970. *The Political Thought of Mao Tse Tung*. New York: Praeger.

Serra, Luis. 1985. "Ideology, Religion and Class Struggle in the Nicaraguan Revolution," in Richard Harris and Carlos Vilas (eds.), *Nicaragua: A Revolution under Siege*, 151–174. London: Zed Books.

Smirnow, Gabriel. 1979. *The Revolution Disarmed: Chile 1970–1973*. New York: Monthly Review Press.

Smith, Richard. 1989. "Neither Market Nor Socialism," *Against the Current*, Vol. 4, No. 4 (September-October):30-35.

Spoor, Max. 1988. "State Finance in the Socialist Republic of Vietnam," in David Marr and Christine White (eds.), *Postwar Vietnam: Dilemmas in Socialist Development*, 111-132. Ithaca: Southeast Asia Program, Cornell University.

Stahler-Sholk, Richard. 1985. "External Constraints," in Thomas Walker (ed.), *Nicaragua: The First Five Years*, 245-264. New York: Praeger.

Stallings, Barbara. 1986. "External Finance and the Transition to Socialism in Small Peripheral Societies," in Richard Fagen, Carmen Deere, and José Luis Coraggio, *Transition and Development: Problems of Third World Socialism*, 54-78. New York: Monthly Review Press.

Stephens, John. 1986. *The Transition from Capitalism to Socialism*. Urbana: University of Illinois.

Sweezy, Paul. 1980. *Post-Revolutionary Society*. New York: Monthly Review Press.

Tablada, Carlos. 1989. *Che Guevara: Economics and Politics in the Transition to Socialism*. New York: Pathfinder.

Taslim, Mohammad Ali. 1984. "The Evolution of Market Socialism in Yugoslavia: A Critical View," *The Insurgent Sociologist*, Vol. 12, No. 1-2 (Winter-Spring):39-56.

Thomas, Clive. 1974. *Dependence and Transformation: The Economics of the Transition to Socialism*. New York: Monthly Review Press.

———. 1978. "The Non-Capitalist Path as Theory and Practice of Decolonization and Socialist Transformation," *Latin American Perspectives*, Vol. 5, No. 2 (Spring):11-19.

Trotsky, Leon. 1972. *The Revolution Betrayed*. New York: Pathfinder.

Tyson, Laura. 1980. *The Yugoslav Economic System and Its Performance in the 1970s*. Berkeley: University of California Press.

United States Senate. 1976. *Hearings Before the Select Committee to Study Government Operations with Respect to Intelligence Activities and Covert Action in Chile*. Washington, D.C.: Government Printing Office.

Vajda, Mihaly. 1981. *The State and Socialism*. London: Allison and Busby.

Valdés, Nelson. 1989. "The Changing Face of Cuba's Communist Party," in Philip Brenner, William LeoGrande, Donna Rich, and Daniel Siegel (eds.), *The Cuba Reader*, 172-176. New York: Grove Press.

Van Atta, Donald. 1989. Theorists and Agrarian Perestroika," *Soviet Economy*, Vol. 5., No. 1:70-99.

Vasconi, Tomás. 1990. "Democracy and Socialism in Latin America," *Latin American Perspectives*, Vol. 17, No. 2 (Spring):25-38.

Vergara, Ricardo. 1988. "Transito democrático al socialismo," *Socialismo y participación*, No. 42 (June):79-90.

Vilas, Carlos. 1985. "The Workers' Movement in the Sandinista Revolution," in Richard Harris and Carlos Vilas (eds.), *Nicaragua: A Revolution Under Siege*, 120-150. London: ZED Books.

———. 1986. *The Sandinista Revolution: National Liberation and Social Transformation in Central America*. New York: Monthly Review Press.

———. 1990. "Nicaragua: What Went Wrong?" *NACLA Report on the Americas*, Vol. 24, No. 1 (June):10-18.

Villalobos, Joaquín. 1989. "A Democratic Revolution for El Salvador," *Foreign Policy*, No. 74 (Spring):103–122.

Vuskovic, Pedro. 1985. "The Crisis of Capitalist Development and the Perspectives for Socialism in Latin America," in Milos Nicolic (ed.), *Socialism on the Threshold of the Twenty-first Century*, 282–293. London: Verso.

Waters, Mary-Alice. 1970. *Rosa Luxemburg Speaks*. New York: Pathfinder Press.

Weber, Max. 1966. *The Theory of Social and Economic Organization*. New York: Free Press.

Weffort, Francisco. 1989. "Democracia y revolución," *Cuadernos politicos* (January–April):5–18.

Wells, Carol. 1983. "Women's Participation in the Central American Revolutions," *Latin American Perspectives*, Issue 36 (Winter):109–113.

Wheelock, Jaime. 1983. *El gran desafio*. Managua: Nueva Nicaragua.

White, Christine. 1989. "Vietnam: War, Socialism and the Politics of Gender Relations," in Sonia Kruks, Rayna Rapp, and Marilyn Young (eds.), *Promissory Notes: Women in the Transition to Socialism*, 172–192. New York: Monthly Review Press.

White, Gordon. 1983. "Socialist Planning and Industrial Management: Chinese Economic Reforms in the Post-Mao Era," *Development and Change*, Vol. 14:483–514.

White, Gordon, Robin Murray, and Christine White (eds.). 1983. *Revolutionary Socialist Development in the Third World*. Brighton, England: Harvester Press.

The Woman Question: Selected Writings from Marx, Engels, Lenin and Stalin. 1973. New York: International Publishers.

Young, Marilyn. 1989. "Chicken Little in China: Women after the Cultural Revolution," in Sonia Kuks, Rayna Rapp, and Marilyn Youngs (eds.), *Promissory Notes: Women in the Transition to Socialism*, 233–250. New York: Monthly Review Press.

Zetkin, Clara. 1973. "Lenin on the Woman Question," in *The Woman Question: Selected Writings from Marx, Engels, Lenin and Stalin*. New York: International Publishers.

About the Book and Author

At a time when the validity of Marxism is being questioned because of the collapse of the Communist regimes in Eastern Europe, Richard Harris examines the relevance of Marxism and socialism for Latin America and the Caribbean. Dr. Harris discusses recent revolutionary regimes and attempts at socialist transformation in the region in terms of Marxist theory, comparing them with the historical experiences of the Soviet Union, China, Yugoslavia, and Vietnam.

The author argues that Marxist theory offers a framework for understanding recent revolutionary transformations as well as the contradictions and limitations of existing democratic regimes in the region. Particular attention is given to revolutionary Cuba, the Allende administration in Chile, the Popular Revolutionary Government in Grenada, the Sandinista regime in Nicaragua, and contemporary leftist parties and movements throughout Latin America. He contends that democratization and the solution of the region's economic and social problems require a democratic socialist project.

Richard L. Harris is a coordinating editor of *Latin American Perspectives* and has served on the faculties of Harvard University, the University of California, and universities and research institutes in Argentina, Chile, Mexico, and Nicaragua. He has authored several books and numerous articles on politics and economic development in Africa, Asia, and Latin America.

Index